Letters to Lydia:
'beloved Persis'

Barbara Eaton

Fact and Fiction:
the 19th-century love affair between Henry Martyn,
a chaplain of the East India Company,
and his 'beloved Persis' in Cornwall, Lydia Grenfell,
based on their letters and diaries

Hypatia
Publications

© Barbara Eaton 2005

The right of Barbara Eaton to be identified
as the Author of the Work has been asserted by her
in accordance with the Copyright, Designs and Patents Act 1988.

First Published in 2005
by Hypatia Publications Ltd
Hypatia Trust, UK Charity No.1060663
Trevelyan House, 16 Chapel Street, Penzance, TR18 4AW
www.hypatia-trust.org.uk e-mail: info@hypatia-trust.org.uk

1 3 5 7 9 8 6 4 2

Cataloguing in Publication Data is available from the British Library.

ISBN: 1-872229-54-9

Designed by Tim Eaton and set in Garamond Premier Pro

Printed by Cromwell Press, Trowbridge.

for Tim

Contents

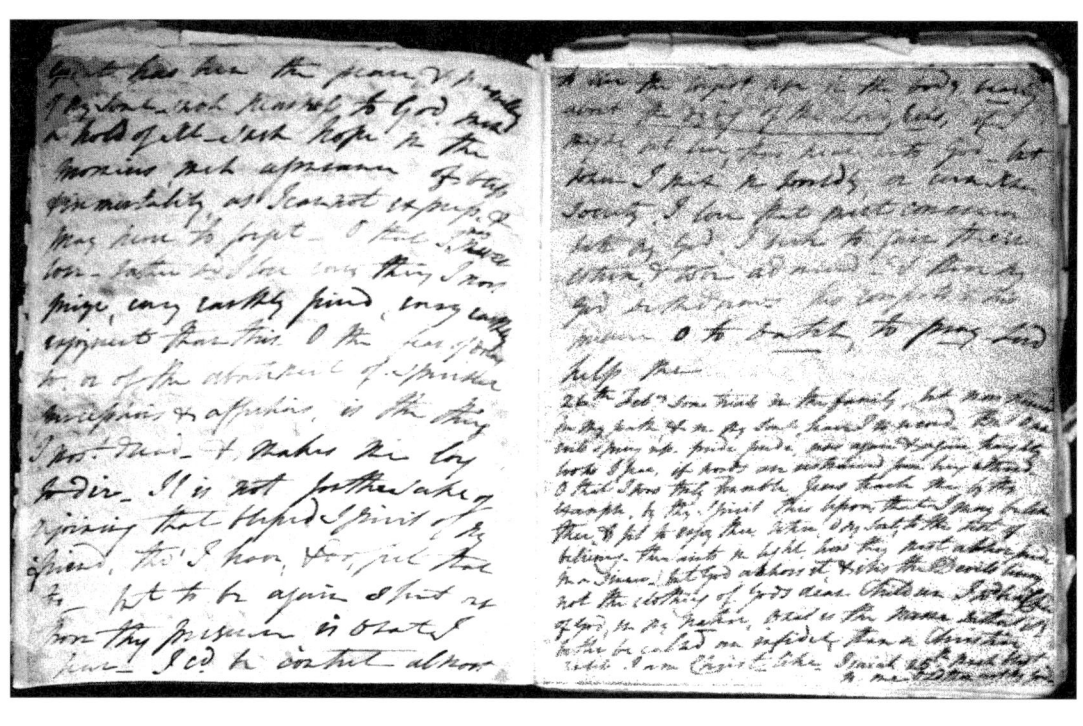

Lydia's Diary
February 1813

Introduction

The life of the missionary Henry Martyn (1781– 1812) has been well documented and his name is still revered in the context of his religious vocation and his translation of the New Testament into Arabic, Urdu and Farsi (Persian). Yet one area of his life has been neglected: his love affair with Lydia Grenfell (1775 – 1829) which has merited little more than a passing reference. Lydia was portrayed in an unflattering light both in biographies of Henry and in a 19th-century work of fiction.

Lydia kept a diary[1] which she started probably one or two years prior to 1801. These pages, which would have included her religious conversion in 1800, have either been lost or destroyed. It now starts somewhat abruptly on October 19th, 1801, her 26th birthday: *This day enter my 27th year. In reviewing that which is last past, I find great cause to be humbled before the Lord, who hath followed me from my youth up until now with mercies; but oh, how multiplied my provocations!* The Diary continues until June 18th, 1826, three years before her death, although there are only eight entries made in 1825 and seven in 1826. It has been suggested by Henry Martyn Jeffery, who edited the Diary, that it ends in 1826 *by reason of her mental affliction.*

When Lydia wrote her Diary she had no thought of it ever being published for in it she poured out her most private feelings. The Diary was discovered on the death of a niece of Lydia's, Mrs. Charlotte Rogers (neé Willyams), in 1888, when it was passed to Lydia's grand nephew, John

---

[1] Now in the Courtney Library of the Royal Institution of Cornwall Museum, Truro.

Barclay of Falmouth, who remembered seeing her when he was a child. He produced a bound manuscript copy of her original Diary which he painstakingly transcribed by hand and added notes. It is written on single sides of 4to paper and is about 1,150 sides in length.[2] Because of her connection with Henry Martyn he passed it to Henry Martyn Jeffery, who was the grand nephew of Henry Martyn, for editing. *Extracts from the Religious Diary of Miss L. Grenfell, of Marazion, Cornwall* [3] was published in 1890. Sadly Barclay, who had been closely involved with the edition, did not live to see it published, dying suddenly in October 1889. In his Introduction Jeffery explains the basis for his selection: *from the great bulk of these daily records (1), all references to her "dear friend" during life, and "the beloved Martyn" after death; and (2), such other extracts as shall generally elucidate her life and conversation.* These edited extracts reveal much about her and her family and the growing Methodist movement in Cornwall at the beginning of the 19th century and its effect on her. They also reflect the choices which were open to a woman from her background at the beginning of the 19th century but far more poignantly they reveal from 1804, once she has started noting Henry's presence in her Diary, her innermost feelings about her tormented struggle between her growing love for Henry and her continuing obsessive sense of remorse over her broken engagement to a Mr. Samuel John, compounded by her feeling of vicarious responsibility for his happiness as well as the demands of filial duty. Sadly all the letters she wrote to Henry have been lost but 17 of the letters which Henry wrote to Lydia from July 27th, 1805 until his last letter just before he left Tabriz in Persia on August 28th, 1812 were given by Lydia to John Sargent, Henry's biographer and close friend from Cambridge days. Sargent knew and admired Lydia. He paid this tribute to her when writing of Martyn: *He had conceived a deeply fixed attachment for one, of whom less ought not, and more cannot be said, than that she was worthy of him.*

The Diary is extremely pious in tone and is about 1,000 pages in length including hymns and sermons in her spidery longhand and the occasional

---

[2] Also in the Courtney Library.

[3] Also in the Courtney Library. Presented by J.H. Barclay, son of John Barclay of Falmouth, on June 26th, 1922; letter from him to this effect to Royal Institution of Cornwall in Courtney Library. MS bound transcript of Lydia Grenfell's Diary by John Barclay also in the Courtney Library.

note of personal expenditure. The thin paper, ranging from 8vo to smaller sheets, is stitched together by hand into a series of booklets which vary in length; the shortest booklet which covers October till December 12th, 1810 is 16 sides, while the period from October 1801 until April 1805 is the largest booklet with 264 sides. The writing is flowing copperplate, closely spaced with occasional sections written sideways across the page. The hand reflects to some extent her state of mind as in 1813, when she receives tumultuous news of Henry, the writing is much larger, filling the pages, and less well formed. By the last booklet, 52 sides written between January 1823 and June 1826, the writing has become markedly more of a scrawl. Each year on her birthday, October 19th, she would choose a religious motto to begin her next year — for 1808: *Choose for my motto this year "They shall be my people, and I will be their God."*

She records in 1801 on October 28th: *On this day for the first time with my dear mother's leave, I went to Meeting.* However, her mother who was to play such a decisive role later, did not approve of Lydia's embracing Methodism nor of her attendance at the Wesleyan Meeting House at Marazion. Perhaps it was the warmth and personal nature of Methodist worship which attracted Lydia thus fulfilling some psychological need which Anglicanism failed to meet. Whether she fully discerned the difference between Methodism and Evangelicalism is debateable: Martyn clearly did. Throughout the Diary it remains one of Lydia's dearest wishes to convert her mother:

> *January 13th, 1805: Conversed with my dear mother on our fallen state, the sinfulness of our hearts, and our need of Christ. I was enabled to speak faithfully on the dangerous state we were all in, who trusted in anything but Jesus Christ, and to tell her plainly she was trusting in herself and in her works, and not in Christ, who if the Bible was true, was the only way to God. The Lord gave me many portions of His word, and O that they may fasten on her memory, though for the present she seemed to laugh at all I said, yet she was not angry; this is a mercy, and must encourage me to seize every opportunity of renewing this subject. O how great would be the happiness of being instrumental to her*

conversion! Lord, by any means, O effect Thy purpose of mercy to her soul.

Sadly for Lydia, as numerous subsequent entries reveal, she remained unsuccessful. The centrality of her faith to her life and the continuing disapproval at home is shown when later that same year the chapel was threatened with closure and she reports her distress on March 12th: *Heard today that the Lord was about to deprive me of the gospel at Marazion: O what a loss! ... and there are moments when I am cast down at the idea of having no House of God to go to on the Sabbath, and the contention my not going will occasion at home.* However, her mother appears to mellow in her attitude towards Lydia's faith. In 1808 Lydia records: *The Lord seems doing a wonder in inclining my dear mother to give us a place of His worship.* It is recorded in the Quarter Sessions held at Truro on April 11th, 1809 <u>Protestant Meeting House.</u> *House in Marazion belonging to Miss Lydia Grenfell, and opposite her own house, registered as meeting house for protestant dissenters.*

Over the years she charts her increasing commitment to the Methodist revival and its effects on her: her growing isolation within her family; her torment over her relationship with Henry Martyn, as well as references to her friends and family. She comments on their ambitions and dissensions from which she kept aloof, yet cannot disguise her opinions about them when it comes to religious matters. One of her older sisters, Phillis, did not approve of Lydia's new found faith: *Felt great heat today in conversing with poor Phillis, whose hatred of the people of God grieves me. She demands my prayers on this account. Lord stir me up to pray for her.* She also met opposition from her friends in the tight-knit community and records on May 24th, 1802: *I have been to no church today. Lord meet me here if it be Thy blessed will. Went to Meeting for the first time with the consent of my friends.*

During her life Lydia suffered recurrently from some kind of mental affliction. She refers to this in her Diary at the end of 1801 when she thanks her Lord for her better mental health: *O how thankful should I be for the calm I have enjoyed in my mind. No violent tumults there now. Bless the Lord for ever, O my soul! forget not His benefits.* She has found comfort in her faith and increasingly there is a synergy between her faith and her mental state. On

March 21st, 1802: *At meeting the service was interrupted by the appearance of a poor maniac, and my soul filled with fears and alarm. O may I be thankful to God for the restored use of my reason, and pity and pray for all under this heaviest of all afflictions. Lord Jesus be with me this night, keep me from terrors of every kind.* Jeffery refers to it in his Introduction: *It is painful to be told that this gifted and highly favoured lady was placed for a year under care for mental derangement; but she recovered, and retained her faculties to the close of her life.* Jeffery does not state when this mental affliction started but it may have been caused by the traumatic breaking off of her engagement in 1800 to Samuel John to which she makes several references. Jeffery refers to her state of mind: *It remains for me to speak of the preservation and state of the pages of the* Diary. *It begins abruptly on October 19, 1801, but I should infer that the previous entries for one or two years have been lost, since the writer was usually methodical and formal analysing the motives of her actions, and she set great store on her* Diary *as a religious discipline, and besides, her religious life began in the preceding year. It may well be that we have the latest records of her thoughts on June 18, 1826, by reason of her mental affliction.* This would suggest that she became mentally ill in 1826 and may have been affected similarly in 1800 and intermittently thereafter which might account for some pages of her Diary having been removed either by Lydia, or by someone else after her death. There is a note attached to the Diary: 1826 – 29: *During the interval or part of it she was in retirement, <u>under care</u> about 1827 – 1828.* There are many references in her Diary to mental anguish and feelings of melancholia. George, the youngest of the Grenfell sons, whom Lydia refers to as *my dearest George* and to whom of her four brothers she was the closest, also appears to have suffered similarly. In an entry for 1823 she refers to *my dearest George afflicted mentally.* As the love affair progresses her mental anguish is reflected in her entries and she becomes increasingly more and more obsessed with her faith and her torment about her relationship with Henry as well as expressing guilt over breaking off the former engagement.

So dramatic and tragic was the course of their love affair that Harriet Parr, a successful novelist, based her hugely successful love story for young girls on it. It is called *Her Title of Honour*, published in 1871 and Parr uses entries in Lydia's Diary and the 17 letters which Henry wrote to her as her primary sources. Parr was writing fiction but the fact remains that the limited opportunities open to a woman in education and marriage in Lydia's time, and the effects these would have on two lives, are so tragically apparent from the poignantly moving letters which Henry wrote to Lydia and from the entries in her Diary.

Henry also kept journals and wrote many letters to friends and family in which references to the woman he loved so passionately appear. Henry's letters, journals and account of his final journey to Persia and stay in Shiraz were not necessarily intended for publication either. However, *A Memoir of the Rev. Henry Martyn BD,* written by John Sargent, then Rector of Lavington, in which Lydia is referred to as L–, had been published in 1819, during her lifetime. She refers to the publication in her Diary with some anxiety in case her identity is revealed. All 17 letters were not published until 1862, more than 30 years after Lydia's death, when they were added to the appendix of the tenth edition. In the Preface to this edition the following explanation appears*: During Miss G's lifetime, or while her death was yet recent, there would have been manifest impropriety in giving publicity to such a correspondence; but when both parties, and all their connexions, had long since descended to the tomb, it was felt that all ground for the continuance of this privacy was taken away; and accordingly, in the large edition of all Mr Martyn's Journals and Letters, published in the year 1837, these letters for the first time appeared. It now seems desirable, for the complete filling up of Mr M's portraiture, to add these letters to the present volume.* Jeffery in his Introductory Preface to *Extracts from the Religious Diary of Miss L. Grenfell* comments: *These sixteen letters have been valued as well for their tenderness and delicacy in Christian courtship as for the submission of the writer's strongest feelings to duty and to a Higher Power.* The first of the 17 letters is not included as the register and tone are much more formal. John Sargent died in 1833 but Samuel Wilberforce — third son of William Wilberforce, and later Bishop of Oxford and then of Winchester, who had married John Sargent's daughter, Emily, in 1828 — edited the 1837 edition of Martyn's letters. Jeffery edited and published a further set of letters in 1883. The *Journals, Letters* and *Narrative* (his narrative of his time in Persia) are a valuable record of Henry Martyn's evangelical faith which is exemplified by his life and work in India and Persia but they also reveal much about his relationship with the woman he loved so deeply, Lydia Grenfell, whom he intended to make his wife.

Strict codes of etiquette governed letter writing in the early 19th century ensuring that the social rules of propriety were observed. For two people in love but not bound by a formal engagement communicating by letter openly was not approved but for two people in love who became separated by such a vast distance it was the only means of communication. So it often fell to friends or relations to act as go-betweens. Henry was a keen letter writer. From reading his correspondence — with Lydia's sister, Emma Hitchins, who acted as advisor and confidant to both Henry and Lydia; her husband the Reverend Thomas Martyn Hitchins and his father, the Reverend Malachy Hitchins; Charles Simeon, his religious mentor; Daniel Corrie, from Cambridge days who was in India with him; John Sargent, his close friend, who would write his first biography; and, most importantly, the 17 surviving letters which he wrote to Lydia — we can follow the tragic love story as it unfolds and its effect on Lydia and himself. Later it is Lydia who expresses her concern at the propriety of continuing their correspondence when she feels she has encouraged him, albeit unwittingly. It is Lydia who bows to the social pressure exerted by her family and breaks off the correspondence. After repeated requests by Henry through intermediaries to re-establish it she agrees on her own new terms, to which Henry delightedly agrees.

However, Lydia was destined to remain in Cornwall, unlike Henry, close to her familiar but somewhat constricted life of family, friends and chapel. The Diary reveals Lydia to be an intelligent and articulate woman who was deeply religious and courageous in her espousal of her faith, bearing in mind that her mother was opposed to it. Lydia expresses all her frustrations with her life and upbraids herself constantly for her own shortcomings in her Diary. The real tragedy is that this love affair starts when Henry is on a farewell visit to Cornwall in 1804 prior to making preparations for his new life in India, and flowers in 1805 when his ship is unexpectedly delayed at Falmouth en route to India not so very far from Marazion where Lydia lived. Time was against them and the lack of propriety in the perceived brevity of the courtship was one reason why there was strong opposition from her family, especially her mother.

Part One — Fact

The Old Chapel at Marazion

E C Boule published by J P Vibert 1832

Chapter 1 — Marazion, Cornwall

At daybreak on July 17th, 1805, just three months before the Battle of Trafalgar, *Union*, an EastIndiaman, part of a fleet under the command of Captain Byng, set sail from Portsmouth. *Union's* destination was India and on board was a young Cornishman of 24 who had recently been appointed a chaplain of the East India Company in Bengal. He had said his final farewells to friends, family and loved ones and, although apprehensive of what lay ahead, was filled with evangelical zeal to save the souls of the unconverted in that far off sub-continent. The young man's name was Henry Martyn. But much to Henry's surprise and delight, two days later, the fleet put into Falmouth harbour, a few miles from Truro where he had been born and brought up. It remained there for almost three weeks while Byng awaited further instructions. This unexpected delay was to have far-reaching consequences for Henry.

As a child Henry had played at the vicarage at St. Hilary, about 20 miles west of Falmouth where his father's first cousin, the Reverend Malachy Hitchins, was vicar.[4] Not only did Henry and his brother and two sisters play with their second cousins, but they also met the Grenfell family who lived at Marazion, a small fishing village, surrounded by mines, with a cobbled causeway linking it to St Michael's Mount, from whose sheltered port tin had been exported to the Mediterranean since the Iron Age. Later the

---

[4] Reverend Malachy Hitchins, a High Churchman, performed the office of a Computer to the Astronomer Royal, was employed as the Comparer and was resident for some time at The Royal Observatory.

Benedictine Monastery on the Mount became a place for pilgrimage. Marazion — Marghas byghan, 'little market' in Cornish — was in Hitchens's parish and lay just two miles away along narrow winding lanes from the inland hamlet of St. Hilary. The hamlet lies close to what then would have been mining and fishing communities where Methodism flourished.

Several wealthy families who had made their money as merchants, naval captains and mining adventurers lived a pleasant and comfortable life in the tight-knit village of Marazion where the Grenfells lived. They were a prosperous and well connected family living in a substantial house — *consisting of three parlours, kitchen, back kitchen, drawing-room, with bed chambers, &c. a large courtlage, wherein is a pump, with excellent water; a dairy, wine-cellar, poultry court; two walled gardens, adjoining to the courtlage, one stocked with fruit-trees, now in full bearing, and a terrace walk in the garden, most pleasantly situated; two of the parlours, in front, and the drawing-room, as also the terrace, commanding a most delightful view of St. Michael's Mount, and Mount's-Bay*[5] — a leased property with fine views over Mount's Bay, on the corner of Chapel Street and Fore Street, the main street which hugs the rugged and wind-swept coast. Opposite the Grenfells' house stood the Chapel of Ease of the neighbouring St. Hilary which Lydia, the youngest of the Grenfell daughters, would desert for the Wesleyan chapel tucked away in a side lane. Although it is possible that it was in the Grenfells' house that John Wesley preached in 1789 when on a tour of Cornwall — *Calling at Marazion, on my way to Penzance, where I had promised to preach once more, the house was filled in a few minutes, so I could not refrain from preaching a short sermon, and God was there in truth.*[6] — it seems unlikely as Mr. and Mrs. Grenfell clearly did not approve of the activities of the Methodists in 1799. In a letter to her son, Pendarves, written on April 6th Mrs. Grenfell's sister-in-law, Catherine Tremenheere, writes: *Mrs Reade has fallen in with the Methodists! And is in a fair way to losing that respect that has hitherto been shown to her. She has acted a wrong part towards the Grenfell family for which she will never be forgiven by them. She has undertaken to carry*

---

[5] *Sherborne Mercury,* Monday, July 20th, 1801.

[6] see page 85 in *The Charter Town of Marazion*; © Marazion Town Trust 1995.

about a petition for Mrs W. (unsanctioned by any of her family) and taken the smallest donations from people particularly amongst the Methodists. Your Uncle and Aunt Grenfell are both in a violent rage with her, in fact he is like a madman about it ... and others of the Sect who took pleasure in hurting the pride of the Grenfells.[7]

Anglicans saw Methodists as challenging the social order of squire, magistrate and cleric so it is hardly surprising that Mrs. Grenfell disliked them, particularly in Penzance where her uncle 'Doctor Borlase (1694 – 1776) who, in his capacity as a magistrate led the opposition to the Wesleys during their early visits (1743 – 1747).'[8]

Pascoe Grenfell, 1729 – 1810, Lydia's father, appears to have spent much of his time away from home and by the end of the century his marriage was no longer a happy one. He was Commissary — or agent — to the States of Holland and like his sons was involved in the copper and tin trades. Davies Giddy describes him: *He was a man of various abilities but of such inordinate vanity and conceit ...*[9] It would seem from his will drawn up in 1802 he was not an overly generous man: he left 1/– (5p) to his wife and each of his eight children *while under trouble and sorrow of mind occasioned by the ill treatment of my wife, for which may God forgive my wife, as I do, and my children ...*[10] His wife, Mary, whom he married in 1758, was born in 1734. She was a Tremenheere, a well-known family of solicitors of Penzance and was a niece of Dr. William Borlase, Rector of Ludgvan and Vicar of St. Just, a well-known and eminent Cornish antiquary and historian. Mrs. Grenfell appears to have been much aware of her social standing in the local community and a woman of strong will when it came to getting her own way. It was she who was later to stand in the way of Lydia and Henry's future happiness.

There were four surviving sons — Pascoe, William, John and George — and four surviving daughters of the marriage — Mary, Phillis, Emma and

---

[7] *Tremenheere Papers:* Morrab Library, Penzance.

[8] John Pearce: *The Wesleys in Cornwall,* 1964.

[9] *Davies Giddy's Diary* (DG /14) November 24th, 1789: CRO; Truro.

[10] Quoted in *Henry Martyn's Dulcinea:* Penny Watts-Russell: *The Cornish Banner;* Nov. 2002. As are all other references here to the *Tremenheere Papers.*

Lydia: Lydia was born on October 19th, 1775 when her mother would have been 41. She was baptised a month later on November 19th at St. Hilary (her name is transcribed in the register as Lydia Grenvile).

Life was comfortable for Lydia growing up in Marazion and nearby Penzance: there were Assemblies and balls for her to enjoy as well as the Ladies' Book Club (established in 1770). Lydia's aunt, Catherine Tremenheere, writing to her favourite son, Henry Pendarves Tremenheere[11] in 1793 when all four Grenfell girls were single, describes a social scene of some provincial sophistication: *Our Assemblies goes very well and has never had less than 16 or 18 couples of dancers with three or four card tables.* She describes the setting with some pride: *The room was very prettily lighted with three handsome chandeliers and eight girandoles* (a branched support for candles or lights). In 1796 on November 3rd Mr. Grenfell threw a ball for Phillis, who would have been in her late twenties and would marry the following year, and Lydia, who would have just turned 21. However, just four years later Lydia would have turned her back on the gaiety of such social events and would have broken off her engagement to a Penzance solicitor, Samuel John. Instead she gave her heart to the growing Methodist movement.

Lydia's mother appears not to have fully approved of Lydia's engagement to Samuel John in June 1800. There was jealousy on her part that Lydia was to live with his mother. Henry Pendarves Tremenheere, when writing to his mother, Catherine, in April 1799, refers to Mrs. Grenfell's going on a tour to visit all her children and mentions that she will possibly stay permanently in London (in fact to Farnham near Taplow, close to Pascoe, her eldest son) before commenting: *but there is one motive which will have great weight with her and that is to keep S John and Liddy at a distance from each other, as Liddy is to live with his mother, and I am satisfied there is still some jealousy on that score in the family: though he makes the town of Penzance think he is paying his addresses to Liddy Reade, but those who know the character of the Johns think*

---

[11] Henry Pendarves Tremenheere (1774 – 1841): *The Tremenheeres;* S.G. Tremenheere. Pendarves embarked on a distinguished naval career at 13. Sailed regularly out to India. Made captain in 1804. Wrecked on his ship *Asia* in 1809 on a sandbank in the Hooghli off Calcutta. Cleared of any blame and given command of a new *Asia*. Retired in 1817 a wealthy man. Invested his fortune in land in Cornwall.

that is nothing but a blind. Although Catherine's son found Samuel John charming and good company, as no doubt Lydia did, his comments as to this trait of duplicity will prove all too true in financial matters later.

In 1805, when Henry arrives so unexpectedly, she was 29, five years older than Henry, and still unmarried. In 1799 one of her older sisters, Emma, had married one of Henry's cousins, the Reverend Thomas Martyn Hitchins, the second son of the Reverend Malachy Hitchins, so she and Henry were related through marriage. More importantly, her mother was by then 71 and her father 77. Her older sisters had all married and left home but Lydia continued living at home with her parents as a dutiful if somewhat rebellious young woman when it came to religion.

As an unmarried daughter, still in her wealthy parents' home, Lydia had restricted opportunities. Parental opinion and approval needed to be sought on major decisions affecting her life and contemporary ideas on propriety were to be observed. When it came to the question of marriage for someone of Lydia's social background there was the economic and social necessity of a young woman making 'a good marriage' — a fact which Jane Austen, born in the same year as Lydia, emphasises at the opening of her novel *Pride and Prejudice*. There was also the strong concept of filial duty which meant that someone in Lydia's situation was often governed by her parents' over-riding wishes for their unmarried daughter to remain at home as an insurance for them in their old age. The role of the daughter would be that of companion, housekeeper and, if need be, nurse to her parents in their declining days. She would remain economically dependent on her father and her autonomy would be restricted. Her interests would revolve round friends and family, writing letters — which could occupy much time — embroidery, reading and gentle walks. If she were religious then her leisure time could also encompass good works: tending to the sick, visiting the poor, teaching in a school set up to educate poor children, and keeping a religious diary in which she would record her journey in search of salvation.

In her Diary Lydia is not only critical of others who do not live by her faith but also highly self-critical. She constantly berates herself for vanity. She writes on January 22nd, 1802:

Mrs Grenfell

(Lydia's mother)
1734 - 1826

Pascoe Grenfell

(Lydia's father)
1728 – 1810

I see myself as very vain and affected in company, and never feel so dissatisfied with myself, as after having conversed with strangers. Self — I know self is all; I seek to be praised, even when I speak of the Lord's dealing with me, of His mercy. Pride, that sin creeps in. O Lord, destroy it!

She spends much time in self-analysis as this entry reveals for October 19th, 1806:

My birthday. One-and-thirty years have I existed on this earth, — for 25 of which all the amount was sin, vanity, and rebellion against God; the last six, though spent differently, yet for every day in them I am persuaded I have sinned in heart, so as justly to merit condemnation of that God whose mercy I trust. Surely then I should sing loudly of His mercy for ever, but the remembrance of my sins seems properly now to call for humiliation and more strict self-examination, that I may note now the chief, and should another year be allotted to me here (which I rather expect than desire), I may see which is subdued and which remains in equal strength. This year, and to the present time, I have been much under the influence of a proud and passionate temper, apt to take offence and show, though not by any act of revenge, yet by a haughty manner and contemptuous look, the pride of my heart; this is my chief offence against my fellow creatures known to me. I fear too I must add I am not careful enough to avoid repeating everything to the disadvantage of another, which is a breach of the law of love. I have often, though not designing to deceive, detected myself afterwards in deviating from the exact truth in relating, which pains me greatly. I accuse myself of not showing that honour to my parents required by God. And now what a catalogue of sins might I enumerate, committed against God, — all against my fellow-creatures, all likewise against him, but in the hidden recesses of my heart, oh! what hateful evils against God are there, — indifference, ingratitude, forgetfulness, sloth, discontent,

unbelief, and ten thousand evils continually showing themselves
there. This is my state, and whither shall a leprous soul repair but
to Him, whose touch can remove the disease? Where shall the
dying sinner fly but to Him who is the life of the world? For Thy
all-conquering grace and abounding mercy I call, O God of my
salvation, that past iniquities may be pardoned, and Thy
subduing power be exerted over me. My motto for this year shall be
"Be thou faithfull unto death and I will give thee a crown of life."

This entry reveals so much about Lydia's character and her relationship with her parents, her former suitor, whom she blames herself for having hurt, and Henry Martyn, whom she is perhaps guilty of deceiving about her true feelings and motives in their relationship.

Central to her life is her guilt at ending a previous relationship which will cast a long shadow over both her own and Henry's happiness. In her Diary, prior to Henry's arrival on the romantic scene, Lydia expresses all her remorse for the hurt she has caused by breaking off her engagement in 1800,[12] to a local solicitor, a Mr. Samuel John of Penzance, who would later cause a financial scandal and flee to Paris to escape the law. Whether this decision was hers alone or whether her mother considered he was not socially of the Grenfells' standing is not clear. In her Diary Lydia confides the effect on her, and her feelings of remorse, and a continuing and apparently unnecessary sense of responsibility for Samuel John's happiness — who was presumably very attractive to women — and with whom she was clearly very much in love. She writes on October 26th, 1801: *Awoke early by a dream about my dear injured friend, and the impression kept me awake, I have reason to be humbled for having indulged my imagination so long and so improperly. O that I could think of him only to pray for him, and regard him only with the affection of a friend. I do desire this. Lord hear and enable me.* On April 24th the following year the effects of a broken heart are still rawly apparent: *I have suffered this week in mind from the illness of him, from whom I am separated on earth, perhaps for ever, yet to whom my heart is more closely united than to any*

---

[12] Henry Martyn Jeffery puts the date of her engagement as June 1800 in his *Preface to Extracts from The Religious Diary of Miss L. Grenfell.*

earthly object. God knows the truth of all I say, and alone is acquainted with the feelings of my heart. I desire that my affection may be regulated, and submit to the will of God for him, as well as what regards myself, but it is harder to do so. On May 2nd: *A worldly object this evening fills my mind, an object I can never long forget, nor cease to lament having injured — O what punishment do I merit! But I trust my punishment awaits me here.* On June 23rd, 1802 she marks the anniversary of breaking off the engagement: *I am thankful that sin has not so hardened me, as to destroy my feeling sorrow at the return of this memorable day. I do hate and abhor myself for my conduct towards a tender friend. O may I be watchful now, that I do not again transgress.* She again expresses her remorse three days later: *Oh what a week this was two years ago. What mischief did one false step lead me into. I hate and abhor my conduct towards a tender friend. Yet I will hope for pardon, even for the sins of departure from God and broken vows to man. ... I feel guilty and my sad conduct two years ago often weighs down my spirit. I am separated from him on earth, perhaps forever, yet my heart is more closely united to him than to any earthly object. God knows the truth of all I say. When I sleep it is he that engrosses my last thoughts. The idol is not destroyed and I lament that still my heart is given too much to him.* Her remorse and pain are all too evident. Her Diary from July 11th, 1802 until October 19th, 1803 has not been preserved but when it does resume she is still trying to come to terms with her action and the effect it will have on her and her reputation.

Of her seven siblings Lydia's oldest brother, Pascoe, 1761 – 1838, was the most successful but to Lydia he inhabited an alien world of which she wanted no part. August 6th, 1807: *My eldest and best brother arrived on Monday from London. Much as I love him, still O how impossible I find it to enjoy his society. This wretched world and its concerns cannot now interest me. O that he felt the vanity of the things he now pursues.* His view on the Methodists however, is robustly socially sympathetic as reported by Farington [13] in his entry dated Monday October 6th, 1806: *Mr Grenfield [Grenfell] yesterday said Methodists abound in Cornwall & well it is so, He sd. As the people wd. otherways be **savages** — many are situated far from a Church, & wd. Have no*

---

[13] Joseph Farington's Diary: see p. 2881 in *The Diary of Joseph Farington:*(eds Garlick & Macintyre).

religion but for the Methodist Preachers, who on Sunday evening drew them together & engage them from that time which they wd. spend at the Ale House. By 1807 he had become a highly successful businessman and had been a Member of Parliament for five years (he was MP for Great Marlow 1802 – 1820, for Penryn 1820 – 1826).

Pascoe Grenfell's keen brain was to make him an authority on fiscal matters and he became a watchful critic of the Bank of England. Prior to embarking on a commercial career as a partner in the Grenfell family copper business in London, he had served, as preparation, an apprenticeship in banking through a chance encounter between his father and Thomas Hope of the Amsterdam banking house Thomas and Adrian Hope: *The elder Pascoe Grenfell came across Thomas Hope just after the latter had been relieved of all his cash and valuables by a highwayman; Hope expressed his gratitude for Grenfell's kindness in providing him with the funds he needed to continue his journey by taking the younger Pascoe as an apprentice in his bank in Amsterdam.*[14] While there he made himself useful to the copper magnate Thomas Williams of the Anglesey mines, and went on to become the Welshman's right-hand man. Following Williams's death in 1802, he joined with the latter's son, Owen, in partnership as Williams & Grenfell, thereby inheriting a share of a copper and smelting empire that was to make him extremely wealthy. In 1806 his wealth was calculated by Joseph Farington to be some £20,000 per annum. After their father's death in 1810 he ensured that Lydia and her mother could live comfortably.

Pascoe's social standing had already been advanced when in 1798 he married for the second time —his first wife, his cousin Charlotte Granville, having died after four years of marriage. Giddy suggests that his sister, Mary, looked after the children of the first marriage during his widowhood. He was a generous brother and gave Mary £16,000 and his three other sisters £3,000 each. Georgina St. Leger, the daughter of the 1st Viscount Doneraile, became his second wife and bore him 12 children. Their youngest daughter, Frances, married Charles Kingsley in 1844.

---

[14] *The Life of a Soldier of Fortune; Colonel Grenfell's Wars*: Stephen Z Starr (1995) p. 16.

It seems likely that William 1765 —1844, his younger brother, the Grenfells' third child, followed Pascoe to Truro Grammar School. Like his older brother he went into the copper trade and joined the family business in London. In 1803, he joined the new firm of Williams & Grenfell. He married Frances Borlase in 1809 after having already fathered three illegitimate children by her: something one feels Lydia would have disapproved of strongly! They would separate in the late 1820s.

There were tensions between the four brothers over their various interests and involvement in tin and copper and it is John 1772 —1816, the third brother, who seems to have been a thorn in Pascoe's side. In Joseph Farington's Diary the entry for October 3rd, 1806 reads: *Lord Thomond spoke of the ungrateful conduct of a brother of Mr Grenfill* [sic.] *who Mr Grenfill had placed in a situation that wd have brought Him £3000 a year, & also advanced Him £5000. In this situation he endeavoured to undermine the interest of His Brother & being detected carried his malignity so far as to write letters to several persons to injure Mr Grenfill's character, among others one to Lord Granville who shewed it to Mr Grenfill to put him on His guard. Thus, it was observed the most prosperous situations may have their alloy, as in this instance is the case from singular ingratitude.* In 1813 Pascoe had dismissed his copper agent, John Vivian, which had led to bitterness on both sides. When, in February 1814, Vivian is looking for an agent himself he receives a letter from John Grenfell offering his services: *Giving him a salary is out of the question, but he is an active hand, with extensive connections, & I think would find sales for a great deal of copper... he is a plausible hand & for aught I know may not be worse than others.*

Lydia refers to John, to whom she was evidently not close, in her Diary on June 23rd, 1816 when he is dying and refers to the dissensions within her family — a topic which she refers to many times in her Diary: *Under family affliction, through the illness and expected death of my dear brother John. O heal the breaches in our much divided family, allay our animosities, and fill us with shame and sorrow for our divisions ... Little as we have known of each other on earth — for few days since my recollection have we passed together...*

Of her four brothers Lydia was closest to George her younger brother and she expresses her concerns for him often referring to him as 'Dear

George'. Born in 1778 he was the nearest in age and appears to have been her favourite brother. When Henry is organising Lydia's expected journey out to join him in India it is George he suggests that Lydia turn to in order to make the necessary arrangements as he, like his older brothers, had left Cornwall and moved to London. There in 1804 he married his first cousin once removed, Caroline Granville. They returned with their family to live in Penzance in 1815. George had wide interests: in finance, as a partner in Boase, Grenfell, Boase and Company, a banking house; and in the commercial world, in two tin smelting firms: Grenfell and Boase and Geo. Grenfell & Sons, London and Paris. His two sons became partners in the latter firm. One of the sons, George St. Leger, was moved to the Paris office in the late 1820s as a result of his financial irresponsibility and extravagant lifestyle in London. Sadly for his father he did not remedy his ways and entered into speculations which proved disastrous when they failed, underwritten as they were by assets of the firm. George disinherited him but himself suffered financial ruin.

Previous to these concerns, George had become a partner in a copper smelting firm Fox, Williams & Grenfell, between 1821 and 1823 in Swansea. This caused upset and ill feeling with both William and Pascoe which Lydia notes in her Diary on April 6th, 1823: *all this heartrending business — brother with brother, waging a deadly war of hatred and ill-will; and alas, what errors and evils appear even in that one, from whom most was to be expected.* June 1st *As a family, how varied have been lately His judgements or chastisements! It is the time of trial, of difficulty, of sorrow. My dear mother is a source of anxious care. My poor brother's constitution seems broken, and my dearest George afflicted mentally.* But two weeks later she writes more optimistically: June 15th *Favoured with a change of such unexpected good ... My two dear brothers, Pascoe and George, reconciled, and by a peculiar influence on the mind of the former, which should lead me to hope it was divine.* Rather than openly opposing her mother, or her father's and oldest brother's commercial attitude to life with its attendant emphasis on things material and inter-family quarrels and rivalries, Lydia reports retreating into the privacy of her room and praying for them. In spite of most of her family's opposition to her new found faith, only Emma, and her youngest brother, George, were sympathetic to her religious views.

Of her three sisters Lydia looked for advice and solace to Emma 1771 – 1854 who was closest to her in age and to whom she was closest in her evangelical faith. Emma was, it would seem from the disapproving comments of Giddy,[15] already a Methodist by November 20th, 1789. Her husband, whom she married in her late twenties, the Reverend Thomas Martyn Hitchins, was incumbent of Stoke, Plymouth Dock,[16] Devon which by 1801 had a population of 23,747 due to the establishment of the naval dockyard at Devonport. This sizeable town where Lydia would sometimes stay, as did Henry when en route to or from Cornwall, is described as *Two miles from Plymouth, on the eastern side of the Tamar, stands the town of Plymouth Dock, almost united to the former by the village of Stonehouse & the numerous houses that extend along the road. From the bustle and continual passing of people we could fancy ourselves in the outskirts of London.*[17] Emma's father-in law was the Reverend Malachy Hitchins. Most importantly Emma's husband had been a friend of Henry's since boyhood and many of Henry's most revealing letters are written either to him or Emma. Emma corresponded with both Lydia and with Henry, her cousin through marriage. Lydia's view of her sister is summed up on August 4th, 1816: *Dearest Emma here. How meek, how Christianlike in her whole deportment.*

Lydia's sister Mary, who was the eldest of the eight siblings, was born in 1760 but did not marry until the age of 42. The Reverend Humphry Willyams's first wife died in 1802 and he married Mary in August of the same year. In spite of being in her forties she produced one child, a daughter called Charlotte. Mary and her husband lived scarcely three miles from Marazion, at Relubbus, in a sizeable leased property called Tregembo which is described as a mansion house in the deeds of the same in 1802. Tregembo was a large property for a curate to maintain and when in 1813, according to the deeds,

---

[15] *Davies Giddy's Diary* (DG /14) November 1789: CRO; Truro.

[16] Now Devonport, Plymouth Dock was three-quarters of a mile from the parish church of Stoke Damerel.

[17] *Observations on the Western Counties of England*: W.G. Maton (1794 – 6) [Early Tours].

the Borlase sisters inherited it from an uncle, they were advised that they could reclaim it from their tenants in 1814. There was strong criticism of the Willyams's failure to maintain the estate in good repair and especially the fact that ten fir trees had been cut down which was forbidden in the lease of 1802.

Lydia records many visits there, both alone, spending *some peaceful and happy days*, and with her mother. She also records saying goodbye to Pascoe at Tregembo on August 23rd, 1807: *O how I grieve that I have taken no opportunity of speaking to him of things of eternal moment.* Pascoe also records staying there on October 14th, 1809. The Reverend Humphrey Willyams was curate at St. Erth and then later at Breage where Lydia would be buried.

Lydia's least favourite sister was Phillis, born in 1768 and who married Captain Thomas Hill in 1797 when she was almost thirty. From Lydia's Diary there seems to have been little love lost between them partly because she did not share Lydia's religious zeal although Lydia refers to visiting Kingsbridge in Devon, where Phillis lived, for short holidays. Lydia also refers to problems between her mother and older sister: *My afflicted wretched sister driven away...The removal of Phillis is cause for acknowledging the hand of Providence; for at the closing of the scene it would be too much for my dear mother to bear.*

As well as many references to family, friends and acquaintances in Marazion and Penzance, she refers to a Colonel Sandys who lived at Lanarth on the Lizard, near Helston, who was a key figure when she sought advice on the advisability of travelling to India. She also refers to the married daughter of Malachy Hitchins, Mrs. Josepha Millett, who lived at Gurlyn in the neighbouring parish of St. Erth. All her references to visiting Gurlyn are very positive: it was there that much of Lydia's Diary was written and it was to be the scene of her final farewell to Henry.

Reverend Henry Martyn
1781 – 1812

Chapter 2 — Truro and Cambridge

Henry Martyn was born in Truro, a Stannary town — copper, tin, smelting and hallmarking — in Cornwall, on February 18th, 1781. John Martyn, Henry's father, who came from a mining background and was self-educated in mathematics, held a one twenty-fourth share in a local mine, Wheal Unity, where upwards of £300,000 was later divided. He became chief clerk to Thomas Daniell, 'a general merchant, tin smelter and an adventurer in mines on the largest scale.' At Wheal Virgin, a copper mine, he was chief cashier to Daniell's son, Ralph Allen Daniell of Trelissick, who was a mayor of Truro, High Sheriff for Cornwall and a Member of Parliament for seven years. Truro's prosperity in the 18th and 19th centuries was built on the tin and copper mining industry which employed thousands of men, women and children. The women, who were referred to as bal maids or spallers, wore large white traditional hessian aprons and worked on the surface breaking up the large pieces of tin ore and barrowing the ore for crushing for which they were paid the equivalent of ten pence per one hundred barrows in 1759. Children would start work at the tender age of eight, going underground at the age of ten if they were boys. The conditions in which the tinners worked underground were dangerous *with hardly any room to turn their bodies, wet to the skin ... by the glimmering of a small candle, whose scattered rays will barely penetrate the thick darkness of the place.*[18] The heat could be intense and there was the ever present threat of flooding and rockfalls. Illness was endemic and

---

[18] Clarke: *Tour through South England*; 1791.

many suffered ankylostomiasis, miners' anaemia, caused by a parasitic hookworm. Equally appalling were their living and social conditions. A doctor gives the following account of a patient's 'home': *full of naked children ... destitute of all conveniences, and almost of all necessities. The whole, indeed, is a scene of such complicated wretchedness and distress as words have no power to convey.*[19] It is hardly surprising that for so many alcohol offered solace in these hard and often violent mining and fishing communities where the established Church played no role but where John Wesley found a ready audience.

John Martyn was a Non-Conformist and heard John Wesley preach both at Gwennap Pit, near St. Day, which could hold 5000 people, at the centre of the mining industry, and at the Coinage Hall in Truro, opposite to where he lived. Wesley first visited Cornwall in 1743 and returned 30 times subsequently to preach to huge gatherings of tin miners and fishermen who were won over by the fiery sermons, community singing and the humane attitude to the poor and needy. Accounts of the gathering at Gwennap Pit in 1773 to hear Wesley preach reflect his popularity. His skill as a preacher is shown by this account of how when using the image of a stricken ship beaten by a storm, his audience was carried away: *How the waves arise and dash against the ship! Our masts are gone! The ship is on her beam-ends! What next?* Back came the response from his enraptured congregation: *The long boat, take to the long boat!* Wesley remained a member of the Church of England but the attitude of many in the established Church was hostile to these large open air gatherings and Wesley's mission to preach the Gospel of Christ to every creature. Wesley created a highly organised system of 'class meetings' which were led by a class teacher and took place mid-week. Class tickets were awarded to those who were able to demonstrate that they were theologically and experientially Wesleyans. Wesley travelled down to Cornwall nearly every year. The missionary zeal with which Wesley and his followers delivered their message of salvation was unpopular with the High Anglicans. The Evangelical Movement in the Church of England, which reflected this greater humanity for the poor and dispossessed as well as a desire to save the heathen in Africa and India and abolish the slave trade, was also unpopular with some

---

[19] Pryce, *Mineralogia Cornubiensis*, 1778.

High Anglicans. Henry would become a Simeonite Evangelical and believe that Lydia, with whom he was to fall so deeply in love, would join him in his mission to India.

Henry's mother, Elizabeth, was his father's second wife. She died of tuberculosis, which Henry refers to as *the family complaint*, when Henry was just two years old, leaving three children of that marriage, Laura, Henry and Sally, and one son by her husband's first marriage, John, who was 15 years older than Henry.

In 1788, at the age of seven, Henry (known as "little Harry Martyn") was sent to Truro Grammar School in St. Mary's Street, a short walk along one of the many 'opes' or narrow passage-ways from his home. The school had been founded in 1549 and usually had between 60 and 100 boys. It was referred to as 'the Eton of Cornwall.' The headmaster was the Reverend Dr. Cornelius Cardew, appointed in 1771 at the age of 23. He became Chaplain to the Prince of Wales in 1790 and was Mayor of Truro in 1780 and again in 1797. Cardew charged a one guinea entrance fee and two guineas for a classical schooling. He doubled the latter in 1792. Cardew describes Henry: *his proficiency in the classics exceeded that of most of his schoolfellows ... for he was of a lively cheerful temper, and as I have been told by those who sat near him, appeared to be the idlest among them; being frequently known to go up to his lesson with little or no preparation, — as if he had learned it by intuition.* In 1798 Henry became a Macarmick medallist, an award for the best declamations of prose and verse given in Latin and English and judged by former members of the school. A fellow pupil, Clement Carlyon, recalls Henry's physical attributes rather than any sign of outstanding academic ability: *Harry Martyn, the familiar name by which best I remember him, was as a schoolboy not at all remarkable for any precocity of talent, or unusual proficiency in learning; neither was he particularly studious. He is best remembered as a good-humoured, plain little fellow, with red eyelids, devoid of eylashes [sic.] and indicative of a scrofulous habit; and with hands so thickly covered in warts, that it was impossible for him to keep them clean.* Henry, who was small for his age and rather delicate, was unfortunately the target of bullying. An older student, Kempthorne, who was the son of an admiral from Helston, a small market town between Marazion and Falmouth, was appointed as a kind of guardian to protect him from the unwanted attention of bigger and stronger boys. A strong friendship grew between them which was to continue after Henry followed him up to Cambridge. By the time he was 14 Henry was showing gifted academic ability and was put forward to try for a scholarship to Oxford. Henry refers to it in a Prefix to his Journal in 1803: *In the Autumn of 1795, my father, at the persuasion of many of his friends, sent me to Oxford, to be a candidate for the vacant scholarship at Corpus Christi. I entered at no college, but had rooms at Exeter College ... I passed the examination, I believe tolerably well; but was unsuccessful, having every reason to think that the decision was impartial.* He recognised that in fact this decision had saved him as he continues: *Had I returned, and become a member of the University at that time, as I should have done in case of success, the profligate acquaintances I had there would have introduced me to scenes of debauchery, in which I must, in all probability, from my extreme youth, have sunk for ever.* Instead he returned to school in Truro until 1797. Henry was just 16 and because of his outstanding academic brilliance his life was about to change. He left Cornwall, first for Cambridge, then for India and finally for Persia.

Henry followed Kempthorne, who continued to act as a mentor to the young man, up to St. John's College, Cambridge in the autumn of 1797 to read mathematics like him. However, because of his classical education in Truro at first the switch to mathematics proved very difficult for him. During his first year at St. John's he became so depressed by his lack of progress that he seriously thought about returning to Cornwall. But with the help of a second year student called Shepherd he succeeded in breaking through the concept barrier. Shepherd describes it as follows:

> *Henry Martyn had just entered the College as a*
> *Freshman under the Rev. Mr Catton. I was the year above him;*
> *i.e. a second year man; and Mr Catton sent for me to his rooms,*
> *telling me of Martyn, as a quiet youth, with some knowledge of*
> *classics, but utterly unable as it seemed to make anything of the*
> *First Proposition of Euclid, and desiring me to have him into my*
> *rooms, and see what I could do for him in this matter.*

Accordingly, we spent some time together, but all my efforts
appeared to be in vain; and Martyn, in sheer despair, was about to
make his way to the coach office, and take his place the following
day back to Truro, his native town. I urged him not to be so
precipitate, but to come to me the next day, and have another trial
with Euclid. After some time light seemed suddenly to flash upon
his mind, with clear comprehension of the hitherto dark problem,
and he threw up his cap for joy at his Eureka. The Second
Proposition was soon taken, and with perfect success; but in truth
his progress was such and so rapid, that he distanced everyone in
his year, and as everyone knows, became Senior Wrangler.[20]

Although Henry was generally known for being quiet and studious as an
undergraduate he was prone to outbursts of temper, possibly caused by the
bullying he had endured at school. One well documented incident describes
how he nearly killed a friend of his, Cotterill, when during an argument he
flung a knife at him in College. Fortunately the knife missed its intended
target and was left trembling in the wood panelling. He graduated in 1801
with the title 'Senior Wrangler' which is awarded to the candidate achieving
the highest marks of those placed in the first class division of the
Mathematical Tripos. Two months later he became the first Smith's Prize
man. A contemporary at Cambridge wrote: *Martyn was perhaps superior in
mental capacity to any of his day in the University.* This double academic
triumph in mathematics appears to have brought him little joy. He writes: *I
had obtained my highest wishes but was surprised to find I had grasped a
shadow.*

Henry was admitted a Fellow of St. John's on April 6th, 1802 and with
some spare time available entered and won the first Members' Prize for Latin
prose which, bearing in mind he had transferred from classical studies to
mathematics at 16, was a reflection of his outstanding ability and his interest
in languages which was later to play such an important part in his life. He
remained at St. John's where as a Fellow he occupied the set of rooms on the

---

[20] George Smith: *Henry Martyn, Saint and Scholar*, p 19.

Library Staircase (E, Second Court) on the top floor, then numbered 64.[21] He is said to have used a diamond ring to cut the following words in Greek on a pane of glass in his window: Εγειραι, ο καθευδων, και αναστα*(Awake, thou that sleepest, and arise)* and his initials. (He seems to have been fond of decorating panes of glass with inscriptions as he had done so at Truro Grammar School apparently on his birthday February 18th, 1801 shortly after he was made Senior Wrangler at Cambridge.[22]) He was busy tutoring students, conducting examinations and taking walks along the River Cam. But increasingly he was wrestling with a new problem — his evangelical calling. With his fine academic record he was well placed to follow his original plan and go in for the law or to remain in academia. Yet he chose not to do either.

Although his younger sister, Sally, was extremely religious and had taken it upon herself to be responsible for Henry's spiritual welfare by trying to encourage him to read the New Testament, it was not until 1800 that he did so. Henry's father, whom he described: *What an example of patience and mildness he was, and I love now to think of his excellent qualities,* last saw his son in October 1799 while he was on vacation in Cornwall. His father died suddenly in 1800 and it was his unexpected death that led Henry to begin studying the Bible: *At the examination at Christmas 1799 I was first, and the account of it pleased my father prodigiously, who I was told was in great spirits. What then was my consternation when in January, I received from my brother an account of his death! As I had no taste at that time for my usual studies, I took up my Bible, thinking that the consideration of religion was rather suitable to this solemn time; nevertheless I often took up other books to engage my attention, and should have continued to do so, had not K — advised me to make this time an occasion for solemn reflection. I began with the Acts as being the most amusing.* This must have delighted Sally, to whom he was close, and his mentor Kempthorne.

---

[21] *Admissions to The College of St John The Evangelist in the University of Cambridge,* Part iv, July 1767 – July 1802, Appendix p. 377.

[22] See full quotation before Chapter 4. Taken from a photograph of the pane of glass — held in St John's College Library, Cambridge.

Reverend Charles Simeon
1759 – 1836

Chapter 3 — 'Giving Light to the Heathen'

Henry had found academic success at Cambridge but he had also found religion and his evangelical calling which was to take him away from an academic life and set him on a very different course. The man who was largely responsible was Charles Simeon, one of the most powerful and gifted preachers of the period. He came from a wealthy family and had been educated at Eton and King's College, Cambridge where he was a Fellow. In 1782 he was ordained at Ely Cathedral before becoming Vicar of Holy Trinity Church in Cambridge in November the same year. The appointment was a contentious one as his parishioners preferred the other candidate, a Mr. Hammond, but fortunately for Simeon his father knew the Bishop of Ely in whose see it lay and so it was his!

In 1788 a group of Evangelicals — the Reverend David Brown, Mr. Grant, Mr. Chambers and Mr. Udny — had contacted Simeon with the view to establishing a mission to East India: *From the enclosed papers you will learn the project of a mission to the East Indies. We understand such matters lie very near to your heart, and that you have a warm zeal to promote their interest. Upon this ground we take the liberty to invite you to become agent on behalf of the intended mission at home. We humbly hope you will accept our proposal, and immediately commence a correspondence with us, stating to us, from time to time, the progress of our application.* Simeon accepted their invitation. A year later on February 24th, 1789 Brown proposes that two young clergymen should be sent out as missionaries to Bengal and should remain in Calcutta with Brown for a few months before moving to Benares to learn languages and further their study: *After which they may begin their glorious work of giving light to the heathen, with every probability of success.* He specifies that the two selected must be good at languages and be able to converse easily with the learned Brahmins. The pay would be 300 rupees per month, which was about £300 per annum: *therefore they must have zeal. He also proposes setting up native schools as most proper for the introduction of the main business.* The Governor-General of India, Lord Cornwallis, made no objection to these plans for missionary activities as he took the view that they must be ineffectual.

In 1789 Simeon became Dean of Divinity at King's. He had instituted evening lectures at Holy Trinity Church. However, his evangelical style of preaching had met with opposition from 'gownsmen' who had intimidated those attending by insulting them and throwing stones at the windows. So heated did the situation become that the Vice Chancellor intervened at Simeon's request and the culprits had to read out a public apology. He was also one of the founder members in 1799 of The Society for Missions to Africa and the East, with which Wilberforce became involved, and which later became the Church Missionary Society. Simeon saw his task as *to humble the sinner, to exalt the Saviour, to promote holiness.*

Simeon hosted weekly Conversation Parties for Cambridge under-graduates in his rooms in King's on Friday evenings when he greeted each student individually by shaking his hand before taking up his position in an imposing chair to the right of the fireplace while his audience sat on benches in front of him or perched on the window seats as waiters handed round tea. Simeon would invite questions on moral or religious matters such as: *What is the way to maintain a close walk with God?* to which he would reply, sometimes at great length. Then an often heated debate would follow. It was here that Henry first encountered him and his style of preaching, which he would desperately try to emulate later. In the summer vacation of 1801 Henry became much more closely acquainted with Simeon and his circle among whom was John Sargent, who like Simeon was from a privileged background. Sargent was one year Henry's senior and about to leave Cambridge for The Temple and a legal training, at his father's insistence, in order to administer his family's Sussex estate. They were to remain lifelong friends.

In 1802 William Carey, a Baptist Minister and shoe cobbler who had sailed for India with his family in 1793, impressed Simeon with his reports on India. He, and David Brainerd, who had preached to the North American Indian, became the two missionary models who were to inspire Henry and by the end of 1802 he made up his mind to emulate Brainerd, of whom he wrote: *I long to be like him. Let me forget the world and be swallowed up in a desire to glorify God.* He applied to The Society for Missions to Africa and the East to become a missionary and began preparing himself for ordination the following year although his sister, Sally, had her misgivings and described him as unfitted to the type of work.

In a letter to Sargent dated September 19th, 1803 he describes being busy drilling the university corps in the Fellows' Garden, known as the Wilderness. Henry was an officer in the College Company of Volunteers. One of his fellow officers at this time was Henry John Temple, third Viscount Palmerston who would later become Prime Minister.[23] War with France seemed to draw ever closer and the threat of invasion by Napoleon's troops was present and much in the forefront of everyone's mind although Henry was preoccupied with other pressing thoughts: *amidst the din of arms. I give our drilling this lofty title because a little is sufficient to disturb me. Too many resident friends in the university have contributed not a little to the frittering away of my time. I mean, however, to leave the university corps forthwith, as the day of my ordination (OCT.23) is drawing near.* On October 22nd, 1803 Henry took a gig and travelled across the flat and featureless fenland to Ely Cathedral to prepare for his ordination as deacon, an option which was open to Fellows of John's. His entry in his Journal reveals that he is beset by doubts and is in very low spirits after meeting the examining chaplain in the Bishop's Palace and *had nothing to think of, but the weight and difficulty of the work which lay before me, which never appeared so great at a distance. At dinner the conversation was frivolous. After tea I was left alone with one of the*

---

[23] *Admissions to The College of St John The Evangelist in the University of Cambridge,* Part iv, July 1767 – July 1802, Appendix.

deacons, to whom I talked seriously, and desired him to read me the ordination service, at which he was much affected. Retired to my room early, and besought God to give me a right and affecting sense of things. I seemed to pray a long time in vain, so dark and distracted was my mind. The next day he gets up early and goes for a walk but is still searching for an inner peace prior to his ordination which took place at ten-thirty that morning. After dinner (lunch) he walks the 15 miles back to Cambridge where he goes straight to Holy Trinity Church. A week later he discusses his plans to become a missionary and is deeply hurt to be told that he has *neither the strength of body or mind for the work*. The former is to prove all too true but it is the latter comment which really hurts.

He and his friend, Thomas Thomason, who was seven years older than Henry, both became assistant curates to Simeon who was always looking to direct the best of his curates into missionary work and both Henry and his friend were eager to follow that path. In 1803 Henry was licensed Curate of Lolworth, near Cambridge, with a stipend of £30 per annum. However, his preaching was not a success with his rural congregation and he admits at times to despising their ignorance. He writes somewhat dispiritedly in his Journal: *I began to see for the first time that I must be content to take my place among men of second-rate ability.*

At the beginning of 1804 his hopes of becoming a missionary were dashed when he received the shattering news that his patrimony had been appropriated and that it would prove almost legally impossible to reclaim it. His relatively independent financial situation was lost and with it any hope of missionary work as the stipend of a missionary would be insufficient to support himself and Sally, who was still unmarried and for whom he had become partially financially responsible since the death of his father in 1800. He refers to this in a letter to Sargent dated January 9th, 1804: *I thank you for the kind interest you take in my missionary plans. But unless providence should see fit to restore our property, I see no possibility of my going out.* Instead he was persuaded to apply to become a chaplain of the East India Company which would offer financial security with an excellent stipend of £1,200 per annum. Enough to offer Sally financial security and also enough to support a wife and family, although the prospect of being so financially secure led to some soul searching on Henry's part: *Nevertheless, I could have been infinitely better pleased to have gone out as a missionary, poor as the Lord and His Apostles.* Henry's name was duly put forward to the Board of Directors to fill a vacancy.

By the late 18th century the role of the East India Company [24] had changed from a trading enterprise with its three trading bases at Calcutta, Bombay and Madras, each with its own Governor, to a body responsible for governing the people of much of India. In 1774 Warren Hastings became the first Governor General and Calcutta assumed the most prominent role of the three former Indian Presidencies. The British presence in India by the end of the 18th century was more that of colonial rule under successive Governor-Generals with a military presence to deal with local disturbances. The East India Company had gained control of Bengal in 1764 at the decisive Battle of Buxar (Baksar) and held absolute authority throughout it. By 1798, when Richard Wellesley was Governor General, the policy of subduing warlike states enabled the East India Company to extend its power and influence and with this 'Forward Policy' the British exerted their supremacy in India.

The East India Company respected and did not interfere with the indigenous Hindu or other religions and officially banned any overt missionary activities until 1813. However, in 1794 the neglect of places to worship for soldiers and their families in Bengal was brought to the attention of Sir John Shore, who had succeeded Cornwallis as Governor General in 1793, by a Lieutenant White and a recommendation *to fix on spots where chapels shall be erected* made it possible for covered places set aside for worship to be created at the great military stations. At this period the Evangelical Movement was growing in England and Evangelicals saw the spiritual division in the world not just as a division between Christians and heathens but between evangelical Christians and the rest: *While they did not set rigid limits to God's mercy, Evangelical missionaries shared the basic belief of their party that all those who did not have the right type of faith, were to say the least,*

---

[24] In 1600 Queen Elizabeth 1 had signed the Royal Charter which gave rights of 'trading into the East Indies' to the Governor and Company of Merchants in London, later to be known as the East India Company.

in serious danger of everlasting damnation, and they felt bound to do all they could to rescue men from this awful fate.[25]

The Clapham Sect, part of this evangelical movement, developed close ties with India. Their dual targets were the abolition of the slave trade and the opening up of India to missionary enterprise. Both Sir John Shore and Charles Grant, two of the founder members had served with the East India Company in India and at this time Charles Grant was Chairman of the Board of Governors. Grant's view of the Hindus was uncompromisingly negative: *universally and wholly corrupt ... depraved as they are blind, and wretched as they are depraved.*[26] Charles Simeon was his confidential adviser in the appointment of chaplains and recommended his evangelical young protégé for one of the vacant chaplaincies. Henry records how he travelled up to London and met Grant at India House in Leadenhall Street. He and Grant then walked to Clapham where he was introduced by Grant to William Wilberforce, a distinguished Fellow of St. John's, a friend of William Pitt, and a well-known member of Parliament, which he had for many years tried to persuade to abolish the slave trade. In 1810 he would be instrumental in bringing about the East India Company's change of policy regarding missionary activity in their territories. Henry was in the company of great and powerful men. While walking with Henry to visit Wilberforce at Clapham, Grant not only gave Henry valuable though somewhat biased insight into India but also advised Henry *that the language spoken by the natives who lived in the English settlements, was the Hindostanee, which was a mixture of several languages, Arabic, Persic, Sanscrit, a sort of lingua franca; but that the Bengalee was the vernacular tongue of the bulk of the native inhabitants and must be acquired by missionaries among the Hindoos; that it would be absolutely necessary to keep three servants, for three can do no more than the work of one English; that no European constitution can endure being exposed to mid-day heat.* Unfortunately Henry was not to heed the last piece of advice. He dined with Wilberforce and Grant who took this opportunity to check out

---

[25] M.A. Laird: *Missionaries and Education in Bengal 1793 – 1837*, 1972.

[26] Quoted in William Dalrymple: *White Mughals*, 2002, from Marshall: *The British Discovery of Hinduism*.

Simeon's recommendation for the vacancy. Back in Cambridge, Henry, fired with enthusiasm, set about studying Bengali, Arabic and Hindustani. Simeon also impressed upon him how important language was to understanding another culture, a concept which was ahead of its time.

Having received his M.A. from Cambridge in July 1804 he visited London en route for a holiday in Cornwall to say goodbye to family and friends. He could not legally receive full ordination, which would enable him to take up a chaplaincy, until he was 24 the following year. He dined with Wilberforce in the evening and went with him to the House of Commons where he was surprised and charmed by Pitt's eloquence. He next broke the journey at Stoke, Plymouth Dock, Devon, where he stayed for three days from Friday till Monday with a cousin, the Reverend Thomas Hitchins, and his 'amicable' wife, Emma, whose younger sister was called Lydia Grenfell. Henry was about to fall in love.

'Loves that come to us in excess bring no good name or goodness to men'

Translated from the Greek quotation as inscribed by Henry Martyn, with his name in English and Persian, which he dated February 18th, 1801, on a pane of glass in Truro Grammar School:–

~~Εροτεσ~~ υπερ μεν αγαν
Ελθοντεσ ουκ ευδοξιαν
Ουδ αρεταν παρεδωκαν
Ανδρασιν.

From Euripides *Medea* at lines 629–30

The whereabouts of the glass is not known but a framed photograph is held in the library of St. John's College, Cambridge.

Note that George Smith in *Henry Martyn, Saint and Scholar* suggests that this was inscribed on Henry's farewell visit to Truro — which was in 1804 — and that his name was in English and Hebrew: the evidence of the photograph belies the latter suggestion.

Chapter 4 — 'Striving against this attachment'

No doubt Lydia would have been aware of Henry's stay with Emma and her husband en route for Cornwall and of his subsequent arrival in Truro later on July 16th. He and his sister, Sally, went on to Lamorran, near Truro. Laura, his older sister was married to the Reverend William Curgenven, curate of Kenwyn and Kea, nephew of the Vicar of Lamorran and St. Michael Penkevil, some five miles outside Truro. Woodbury, where they lived, next to Kea Church with its picturesque detached belfry perched above the creek, stands at the edge of Lamorran woods and is set among beautiful and tranquil countryside on the Fal river. Henry was to refer to it later in his letters to Lydia as an idyllic place. On this visit he describes it: *The scene is such as is frequently to be met with in this part of Cornwall. Below the house is an arm of the sea, flowing between the hills, which are covered with wood. By the side of this water I walk in general in the evening, out of the reach of all sound but the rippling of the waves and the whistling of the curlew.* He describes in a letter dated August 1st[27] how the following day he visits his half-brother John in Truro. He comments on the unexpected succession of heavy financial losses his brother has incurred and makes reference to *the present plan seems to be for us to accept of a share in a mine or an equivalent for our legacies. With the remainder of his property he will be able to pay his debts & then will remove to London to begin the world anew tho not in a way of trade.*

---

[27] Letter dated August 1st, 1804; written from Redruth in Cornwall to his friend John Hensman: MAR 1/4 Henry Martyn Centre, Cambridge.

Henry preached at his brother-in-law's two small churches, Kenwyn and Kea, and also at St. Michael Penkevil, then with its panels with plaster mouldings. He records, on August 5th that both his sisters *heard me for the first time* at St. Michael's where they were among the congregation. He was disappointed not to preach at St. Mary's in Truro,[28] where he had been baptised. The clergy of Cornwall had united to exclude Henry from preaching in their churches, his old headmaster the Reverend Dr. Cardew even offering his services at any time to pre-empt Martyn from preaching. Their objection was: *Mr Martyn is a Calvinist preacher in the dissenting way.* Henry describes the ban in a letter on August 8th to a friend in Cambridge: *The following Sunday it was not permitted me to occupy the pulpit of my native town but in a neighbouring church I was allowed to testify the Gospel of the grace of God. But that one sermon was enough. The clergy seem to have united to exclude me from their churches, so that now I must be contented with my brother-in-law's two little churches about five miles from Truro.*

It is during this farewell tour of family and friends in Cornwall that Henry first mentions Lydia Grenfell in his Journal on July 29th: *At St Hilary Church in the morning, my thoughts wandered from the service, and I suffered the keenest disappointment. Miss Lydia Grenfell did not come. Yet in great pain, I blessed God for having kept her away, as she might have been a snare to me ... Called after tea on Miss Lydia Grenfell, and walked with her ... All the rest of the evening, and at night I could not keep her out of my mind. I felt too plainly that I loved her passionately ... but in my dreams her image returned and I awoke in the night with my mind full of her.* It is clear that he was hoping to see her and harboured deeper feelings than friendship for her. Indeed he refers to visiting Lydia in his letter to Hensman on August 1st: *Last Sunday I officiated near Marazion. In the evening walked there to see Miss L.G. The consequence might be expected. There is no saying how much I was charmed with her, nor what a tumult of contending claims was excited in my bosom. ...I trust that it is in my heart to live & to die in the work of a missionary.* These conflicting thoughts may have been caused by news of Sargent's forthcoming marriage. He came from a wealthy background and under parental pressure

---

[28] Truro Cathedral built 1880 – 1910 now stands on the site.

had given up any hopes of following Henry to India. With his own thoughts turning to the subject of matrimony Henry writes to Sargent on August 6th from Lamorran: *Respecting your approaching union with that excellent lady, I have nothing to add at present, but that you have my prayers.* Sargent was to get married in November to Mary Smith of Hull, the daughter of a well-known banking family, who was a wealthy woman in her own right. They would name their son, who died in 1836 before coming of age, Henry Martyn Sargent.

During August he records his obsession and growing love for Lydia in the beauty of the wild Cornish landscape, memories which both haunted and sustained him later. In retrospect this was an idyllic time for Henry for he often refers to their walks and rides together near Marazion, Perran and inland at Gurlyn, near St. Hilary. On August 26th he writes: *Walked in the evening with Mr Grenfell, and Lydia, up the hill, with the most beautiful prospect of the sea ... but I was unhappy from feeling the attachment to Lydia, for I was unwilling to leave her.* His increasing obsession with this woman, who is five years older than he is, is evident from the entries in his Journal up to the end of that August when he leaves Cornwall to return to Cambridge: *Aug. 27th Walked to Marazion — Reading in the afternoon to Lydia alone; Aug. 28th I walked on dwelling on the excellence of Lydia; Aug. 29th — I walked to Truro with my mind almost all the way taken up with Lydia; Aug. 31st — In conversing on the subject of India with Major Sandys,* (who had first hand experience of India and was later to advise Lydia) *I could not help communicating the pain I felt at parting with the person to whom I was attached; but by thus dwelling on the subject my heart was far more distressed than ever.* On his way back to London Henry once again stays with Emma and *learns that my attachment to her sister was not altogether unreturned, and the discovery gave me both pleasure and pain.*

However, Lydia's Diary entry for August 26th gives no hint that she is falling in love with Henry: *Heard H.M. on 'Now we are ambassadors for Christ, as though God did beseech you by us ...' and a farewell address. A precious sermon. Lord bless the preacher and those that heard him.* She clearly had no idea of Henry's growing obsession with her and, having known him so long, perhaps viewed him only as a much younger man who was a friend of the family. She also still feels that she is responsible for Samuel John until he marries and would be painfully aware of any gossip which a relationship with Henry would give rise to in Marazion and Penzance. It seems that Henry has fallen in love but Lydia is more attracted to Henry's Simeonite Evangelicalism. Henry may well have been the first evangelical she had met.

Although Henry is increasingly preoccupied with his growing love for Lydia he is torn between his love for her and what he sees as his religious duty and mission in life and he cannot equate the two: *At night I continued an hour and a half in prayer, striving against this attachment. I endeavoured to analyze it, that I might see how base, and mean, and worthless such a love to a speck of earth, was, compared with divine love.* His attraction to her was based in part *on the highest admiration of piety and manners,* and he can *think of nothing but her excellencies and spent two hours reasoning with my perverse heart.*

Poor Henry, his mind was in tumult; his evangelical calling was soon to take him to India many thousands of miles away from Lydia. His entry for August 26th when he had to say goodbye to her reveals the depth of his feeling for her: *Parted with Lydia, perhaps for ever in this life, with a sort of uncertain pain, which I knew would increase to greater violence afterwards, on reflection.*

He then walked to St. Hilary and from there travelled to Helston where he preached at Helston Church and *greatly offended some ladies, who said they would not go again to hear such doctrine; accordingly in the afternoon, the genteel part of the congregation was smaller, but the poor more numerous.* Although Henry was approached by a Methodist to preach at their chapel, Henry reports *I refused of course.* He then continued to Truro where he saw his sister Sally before setting off for Plymouth Dock on September 8th. He reached Exeter on September 11th where *My thoughts were almost wholly occupied with Lydia, though not in a spirit of departure from God, for I considered myself as in his hands, and reposed with confidence and peace on his unerring wisdom.* By September 14th he was in London and contemplating the interior of the dome of St. Paul's and is clearly still preoccupied with Lydia and his evangelical calling. He writes to John Hensman on October 3rd from Cambridge: *Having occasioned to stop at a friend's house by the seaside, I walked out alone with Lydia G. and listened with no small delight, as you may suppose, to the remarks which the beauty and grandeur of the scene drew from her pious heart. In the afternoon we read together some of Watts, but the gloomy moment arrived when I parted with her perhaps for ever in this life.* He left London for Cambridge the following day and he remained there preparing for his new calling, apart from visits up to London, until February 1805 when he would be 24 and could be ordained as a priest before receiving confirmation of his appointment as chaplain to Bengal. He learns in November that his stipend would indeed be £1,200 if he is appointed; more than enough to support a wife and family but he notes: *At present I feel no desire after riches of the world.*

Neceffaries,

FOR A
WRITER to INDIA,
SOLD BY
WELCH AND STALKER,
(Late EVANS AND WELCH,)
No. 134, LEADENHALL-STREET, LONDON.

A COT.
Hair mattrafs and bolfter.
Feather pillow.
Blankets.
Quilt.
White fheets.
Pillow-cafes.
A fet of cot-curtains.
Callico fhirts.
Night-fhirts.
White neck-handkerchiefs.
Black filk ftocks.
Towels.
Pocket-handkerchiefs..
Cotton caps.
Net-caps.
White filk hofe.
White cotton ditto.
Brown cotton ditto.
Worfted ditto.
Cotton focks.
Brown cotton gloves.
White filk ditto.
Mufquetto trowfers.
Striped gingum ditto.
Pantaloons.
Surtout-coat.
Boat-cloak.
Coats of thin cloth.
Fancy-waiftcoats.
Cafimere breeches.
Thin waiftcoats with fleeves.
Thin breeches.
Callico drawers.
Flannel drawers.
Cloth and trimmings for two coats, to make in India.
Cafimere and trimmings for breeches.
Dreffing-gown.
Foul-clothes bag.
Needles, thread, &c.
Pieces of hair-riband.
Pieces of fhoe-riband.
Fine hats.
Sea-hats.
Travelling-cap.
Shoes.
Boots.
Boot-jack.
Silver-hilted fword.
Silk belt.

Fowling-piece.
Pair of piftols.
Saddle and bridle.
Stationary.
Travelling-cafe.
Moorifh grammar.
Perfian ditto.
Ditto dictionary.
Ditto interpreter.
Oufley's Perfian Mifcellanies.
Carlifle's Arabian Poetry.
Razor-cafe complete.
Hair-powder and pomatum.
Powder bag and puff.
Boxes of fhaving-powder.
Combs and brufh.
Pounds of Windfor foap.
Pounds of common foap.
Pewter bafon.
Clothes-brufh.
Set of fhoe-brufhes and blacking-balls.
Silver tea-fpoons and tongs in a cafe.
A mahogany knife-cafe, containing fix large filver fpoons, twelve table knives and forks, and fix defert ditto.
Quart tin mug.
Pint ditto.
Tea-kettle or tin boiler.
Pounds of wax candles.
Flat candleftick.
Sciffors.
Pen-knives.
Cork-fcrews.
Small looking-glafs with flider.
Buckles.
Sleeve-buttons.
Cafe of inftruments.
Tin fugar-canifter and padlock.
Pounds of lump-fugar.
Tea, coffee, and chocolate.
Portable foup.
Sage and balm.
Pounds of tobacco.
Folding camp-ftool.
Hamper of wine.
Liquor-cafe.
Liquor.
Box for books.
Trunk,
Cheft.

Chapter 5 — 'Let her live happy and useful in her occupation'

But how was Lydia feeling about this young man who was not yet 24 while she was 29? Although they had known each other through the Hitchins family since childhood they make no mention of the other until 1804 though they must have met or at least had news of each other when Henry came down to Cornwall in his vacations. However, Lydia's continuing sense of remorse over breaking off her previous engagement would preclude her feeling free to enter into another romantic relationship until Samuel John actually married. Jeffery describes her feelings towards Samuel John: *She felt the attachment of a widow with the responsibility of a wife.* In fact it is not until February 3rd in 1804, three years after breaking off the engagement, that Lydia actually visits Penzance, only two miles away from Marazion, which would have held memories of happier days with Samuel John, in order to see her father: *found my mind composed and free from fears. O that more gratitude were excited at what the Lord has done for me since I last entered that place! how great a deliverance has been wrought for me, so weak, so sinful a creature.* On February 25th she records that John is to marry: *My slumbers last night were distracted on his account, and through the day he has much occupied my thoughts, — too much — but now duty will, I trust, compel me to turn from one, who will soon be united to another. Sanctify this event to me, make it the means of drawing my thoughts and settling my affections above. Bless him and give him a blessing in her he has chosen. My heart says bless them.*[29] Samuel John was to

---

[29] Jeffery notes that three lines of the previous page and four lines of this page have been torn off.

have married in London but for some reason he did not in fact marry until the beginning of 1810 and then the marriage was short lived. While John remained unmarried Lydia felt she was morally not free to marry and by 1810 it would be too late. In the summer of 1804 when Henry comes down to Cornwall she still regards herself as tied to her former fiancé and her feelings for Henry are those of sisterly affection, admiration and respect for this younger man who appears to have dedicated his life to serving God. Poor Lydia, her distress as she tries to come to terms with John marrying someone else continues to haunt her in spite of her resolution on March 5th: *to resist the temptation of employing my thoughts on one, whom I must cease to love, or I should sin. O Lord help me, and when I fail, pardon.* With all this emotional turmoil it is hardly surprising that when she first hears Henry preach on August 26th that year her remarks on both the young man and on his sermon were brief and give no hint that she will fall in love with him. Whereas Henry appears smitten by her.

Lydia is much preoccupied with trying to convert her mother to her faith at the beginning of 1804. Her entry on February 7th refers to her mother's opposition to her going to Wesleyan meetings: *I have to record to my shame how haughty and angry I have felt today, while contending with my dear mother about going to Meeting. O! it was not the meek spirit of Christ that led me say all I did. I should have been silent before a parent.* This tension between mother and youngest daughter over their differing expression of faith remained throughout her mother's life and much to Lydia's distress she makes no headway in converting her. The fact that Lydia went against her mother's wishes reveals how strong-minded she could be at least when it came to religious matters.

Henry is preoccupied also. On January 11th, 1805, while waiting to be ordained and for his official appointment as chaplain of the East India Company he writes from 18 Brunswick Square, London, a long letter to Emma in which he opens his heart to her about his feelings for her sister:

> *My dear Mrs Hitchins, — How unaccountable must my long silence appear to you after the conversation that passed between us in the carriage! You may well wonder that I could*

forbear, for three whole months, to inquire about the 'beloved Persis.[30]*' Indeed, I am surprised at my own patience, but in truth, I found it impossible to discount what it is which I wish or ought to say on the subject, and therefore determined to defer writing till I could inform you with certainty of my future destination.*

He then describes the probability of his being based near Calcutta before turning to the real reason behind this letter:

But you will easily conceive that the increasing probability of my being settled in a town rather tends to revive the thoughts of marriage, for I feel very little doubt in my own mind, that in such a situation it would be expedient for me on the whole to marry, if other circumstances permitted it. It is also clear that I ought not to make any engagement with any one in England, till I have ascertained by actual observation in India, what state of life and mode of proceeding would be most conducive to the ends of my mission. But why do I mention these difficulties? If they were removed, others would remain still more insurmountable. The affections of the beloved object in question must still be engaged in my favour, or even then she would not agree to leave the kingdom, nor would any of you agree to it, nor would such a change of climate, it may be thought, suit the delicacy of her constitution.

Must I then yield to the force of these arguments, and resolve to see her no more? It shall certainly be my endeavour, by the help of my God, to do it, if need be; but I confess I am very unwilling to go away and hear of her only accidentally through the medium of others. It is this painful reflection that has prompted a wish, which I do not mention without some hesitation, and that is my wish of corresponding with her. It is possible you may instantly perceive some impropriety in it which escapes my notice, and

---

[30] Romans 16:12: Persis was a Christian woman who St Paul saluted at Rome: *'Salute the beloved Persis which laboured much in the Lord'*.

43

indeed there are some objections which I foresee might be made,
but instead of anticipating them I will leave you to form your own
opinion. In religion we have a subject to write about of equal
interest to us both, and though I cannot expect she would derive
any advantage from my letters, it is certain I should receive no
small benefit from hers. But I leave it with yourself; if you
disapprove of the measure, let the request be forgotten. It will be
best for her never to know I had made it, or if she does, she will I
hope, pardon the liberty to which I have been drawn only by the
love of her excellence.

Emma is now placed in the role of confidante and, moreover, is entrusted by Henry with the power of vetoing his request to correspond with Lydia but more importantly Henry has taken a key decision: he notes in his Journal: *I was in some doubt whether I should send the letter to Emma, as it was taking a very important step and I could scarcely foresee all the consequences. However, I did send it, and may now be said to have engaged myself to Lydia.*

Henry has found a woman of great piety who is attracted by the strength and direction of his belief and who, he hopes, would be the ideal partner to share his life in India. Once he became a chaplain of the East India Company, Henry would be financially secure and would be in a position to marry. Also his financial responsibility for Sally has now ceased as she has married. He acknowledges in this letter that it would be better for him first to establish what the local conditions would be like before entering into an engagement. This was common practice and fiancées would follow later, usually chaperoned by a married woman who was going out to join her husband. The subject of marriage and advice which Henry gets as to its expediency continues to trouble him throughout the period he is awaiting his appointment which finally comes on April 24th.

Henry is ordained priest on March 10th, 1805 at the age of 24 in the Chapel Royal of St. James in London and admitted to the Bachelor of Divinity degree by special mandate on April 5th. The following day he records walking in the Fellows' Garden at St. John's: *Passed most of the morning in the Fellows' Garden. It was the last time I visited this favourite retreat where I have often enjoyed the presence of God.* Two days later, accompanied by many of his *young friends* he caught the coach and left Cambridge for ever on *a thick, misty morning, so the University with its towers and spires, was out of sight in an instant.* On April 24th he meets Grant and *found that I was that day appointed a chaplain to the EIC, but that any particular destination would depend on the government in India.* His formal appointment as Chaplain on the Bengal establishment by the Directors of the East India Company was made at a meeting held on May 22nd chaired by Grant who also took the opportunity to remind Henry of the dangers of the Indian climate. While waiting to go to India he is preparing himself for his new life by learning Hindoostanee from Gilchrist's *Grammar* and *Dictionary*. He refers to meeting Gilchrist who helps with pronunciation and advises him against attempting translation of the scriptures: *till I knew much more of the language, by having resided some years in the country. He said it was the rock on which missionaries had split, that they had attempted to write and preach, before they knew the language.*

He becomes an assistant to the Reverend Richard Cecil at St. John's Chapel, Bedford Row in London but is still having problems with his style of preaching and confides to Emma in a letter dated June 24th:[31] *Mr Cecil has been taking great deal of pains with me. My insipid inanimate manner in the pulpit he says is intolerable. Sir, said he, it is cupola painting not miniature, that must be the character of a man that harangues a multitude.*

Whether a correspondence was permitted between himself and Lydia after his application to Emma is uncertain as the only reference is to his keen disappointment at not receiving a letter from her on April 24th, the same day he heard of his appointment as chaplain. Lydia makes no reference to any correspondence between them in her Diary. Social etiquette at this time would have frowned upon their corresponding with each other without an attachment so it was Emma who acted as an important go-between. Both Emma and her husband respond to his letters with references to Lydia and her interest in his welfare and Emma goes so far as to write *Lydia, whom I*

---

[31] *Two Sets of unpublished letters of the Rev. Henry Martyn, B.D.*, ed. Henry Martyn Jeffery, 1813.

heard lately from, is well, and never omits mentioning you in her letters, and, I may venture to say, what you will value still more, in her prayers also. Even when they do begin a correspondence Lydia is torn with guilt about the possible impropriety of writing to Henry especially as she still regarded herself as having a moral responsibility for Samuel John's happiness until he was actually married.

It is during this period that Henry is seeking the advice of other ministers on the subject of marriage which is occupying much of his time. Still it is Lydia he thinks of although he is prescient when he writes: *though I confess I think she will not consent to go (to India), I shall then have the question finally settled.* And on June 1st: *Yet tonight I have been thinking much of Lydia.* Mr. Cecil offers his advice on the subject two days later: *He said I should be acting as a madman if I went out unmarried. A wife would supply by her comfort and counsel the entire want of society, and also be a preservation both to character and passions amidst such scenes. I felt as cold as an anchorite on the subject as to my own feelings, but I was much perplexed all the rest of the evening about it. I clearly perceive my own inclination on the whole was not to marriage. The fear of being involved in worldly cares and numberless troubles, which I do not now foresee, makes me tremble and dislike the thoughts of such connection.* He then turns to examining great missionaries who remained celibate but then he acknowledges that he needs a companion to share his experiences with and marriage to Lydia would be the solution, although he admits *voluntary celibacy seems so much more noble and glorious, and so much more beneficial in the way of example, that I am loth to relinquish the idea of it ... In short I am utterly at a loss to know what is best for the interests of the Gospel. But happily my own peace is not much concerned in it. If this opinion of so many pious clergymen had come across me when I was in Cornwall, and so strongly attached to my beloved Lydia, it would have been a conflict indeed in my heart to oppose so many arguments. I hope I am not seeking an excuse for marriage, nor persuading myself I am indifferent about it, in order that what is really my inclination may appear to be the will of God. But I feel my affections kindling to their wonted fondness, while I dwell on the circumstances of an union with Lydia.*

Henry decides to ask Simeon for advice on June 5th: *Most of this morning was employed in writing all my sentiments on the subject of marriage to Mr Simeon. May the Lord suggest something to him which may be of use to guide me, and keep my eye single … Mr Cecil said today, he thought Lydia's decision would fully declare the will of God.*

On June 24th in the letter to Emma quoted above he describes the discussions he has been having on the subject of marriage and India with other ministers: *Mr Cecil speaking of celibacy said, I was acting like a madman in going out without a wife — a view shared by the ten other ministers present.* He continues *At last I wrote to Simeon stating to him the strongest arguments I heard in favour of marriage in my case. His answer decided my mind. He put it in this way. Is it necessary? To this I could answer no. Then is it expedient? He here produced so many weighty reasons against its expediency, that I was soon satisfied in my mind. My turbulent will was not so easily pacified. I was again obliged to undergo the severest pain in making that sacrifice which had cost me so dear before.* It is somewhat ironic that Simeon was later to change his opinion and intercede on Henry's behalf.

Henry then expresses the hope that he may now concentrate on serving Evangelicalism through his work, and continues: *The present wish of my heart is that (there may be never a necessity of marriage, so that) I may henceforth have no one thing upon earth for which I would wish to stay another hour, except it to be to serve the Lord my Saviour in the work of the ministry. (Once more, therefore I say to Lydia, and with her to all earthly schemes of happiness, farewell. Let her live happy and useful in her present situation.)* But a few lines later he is writing *(The only objection which presented itself to my advisers to marriage was the difficulty of finding a proper person to be the wife of a missionary. I told them that perhaps I should not have occasion to search a long time for one. Simeon knows all about Lydia. I think it very likely that he will endeavour to see her when she comes to town next winter).* Henry vacillates between being disposed to let Simeon act on his behalf and leave the rest to God's will, and yet at the same time he is obviously in love with Lydia and feels that she is the right wife for him.

On July 8th he gave his final sitting for his miniature for Sally and said his farewells to Daniel Corrie, who would later follow him to India. The following day he went to Midhurst to say farewell to Sargent and records an incident affecting his health that evening: *Though I was in good health a moment before, yet as I was undressing I fainted and fell into a convulsive fit; I lost my senses for some time, and on recovering a little found myself in intense pain ... Slept very little that night, from extreme debility.* But, in spite of this, the next day he continued to Portsmouth where Simeon and other friends were waiting to say goodbye. He went aboard *Union* but because of looming war and danger of interception by the French the fleet was delayed at Portsmouth for a week.

Britain and France were challenging each other for supremacy at sea and in Europe. By 1805 Napoleon had amassed a large army at Boulogne with the purpose of invading England so that he could continue with his European expansionism. In order to carry out this invasion a fleet of flat bottomed transport boats was now waiting off Boulogne. He ordered the French and Spanish fleets to sail for the West Indies to draw the British fleet away from the Channel. After rendezvousing the strategy was to sail back to Toulon where they would wait before breaking Nelson's blockade and invade. There was a sense of controlled panic and English phlegm reflected by Admiral Jervis's statement to the Upper House: *I do not say, my lords, that the French cannot come, I only say they cannot come by sea.* In May 1805 Nelson had left the Mediterranean and followed the French fleet, under Villeneuve, to the West Indies where he realised what Napoleon's plan was. He dispatched a fast brig to forewarn the Admiralty of the planned invasion. Hence the delay at Portsmouth while the fleet waited for Nelson's return and further instructions.

The decisive naval Battle of Trafalgar, off Cadiz, when Britain would achieve supremacy at sea, if not on land, over its old enemy, would not take place until October 21st. It would be one of the bloodiest British naval battles with more than 12,000 dead or wounded in total of British, French or Spanish forces. *The Times* dated Thursday, November 7th, 1805 reported a dispatch dated October 27th: *that on the 19th instant, it was communicated to the Commander-in-Chief from the ships watching the motions of the enemy in Cadiz, that the combined fleet had put to sea; as they sailed with light winds westerly, his Lordship concluded their destination was the Mediterranean, and immediately made all sail for the Streights' entrance, with the British Squadron, consisting of twenty-seven ships ....* The combined fleet of the enemy was 33 ships, 18 French and 15 Spanish.

Henry writes about the delay in a letter to his cousins on July 15th: *I went on board on Friday, expecting to sail immediately, but we have since been informed that the government will not suffer us to depart till tidings shall have been received from Lord Nelson.* The following day, aboard *Union* under the command of Captain Byng in a fleet of 15 ships under convoy of *Belliqueux*, Henry, as official chaplain, finally set sail for India.

Union was an EastIndiaman of 723 tons, a large, hybrid merchant vessel and warship. She was the Company's fifth with that name. Built in Bengal, with 11 gun ports on her upper deck, she had sailed for England in 1804. The journey that now lay ahead was dangerous with not only the very real threat of war but also natural hazards of storms, the Cape of Good Hope to be rounded, pirates in the Indian Ocean, illness and possible death at sea where burials were *always before breakfast.* Passengers aboard these vessels needed to negotiate with the captain who could often prove to be the most difficult obstacle they faced on the journey out to India. Conditions were spartan for most. Cabins were a luxury and on these boats passengers might have to sleep in a hammock slung overnight above a cannon with water from the bilges slopping on the floor. They could be cooped up for weeks on end if conditions were dangerous. One relief was afforded by regular services on Sundays at which everyone, both crew and passengers, were expected to attend and at which Henry would be expected to officiate.

Simeon, who had travelled down to Portsmouth to say his farewells to his protégé, presented him with a silver compass from his congregation in Cambridge to guide him in his new work. Henry suffered his first bout of the sea-sickness which would plague him on all his voyages. But there was to be further delay when two and a half days later the fleet anchored at Falmouth. At first strong gales keep them in harbour and then the fleet is ordered to be ready to muster *to oppose the Brest fleet, which it was supposed would soon out,* writes Henry and he begins to wonder if he will ever see the shores of India especially as: *The belief generally prevails amongst us, that the troops on board are intended to co-operate in taking the Cape of Good Hope; and that we are to wait off Ireland to join another fleet. These reports have set the minds of our young men afloat; and I cannot walk the deck without interfering with knots of consulting politicians.* Henry also notes with great disapproval: *The evening is a time of great idleness and noise on board, all are talking and laughing. The soldiers do nothing but jeering one another, and swearing. The passengers, lounging about, are sitting in chairs under the poop, the drums and fifes constantly playing ... my ears are constantly assailed and shocked by the most horrid oaths, and I see no method of putting a stop to it, except by perseverance and preaching the Gospel to them.*

Henry hears news of Lydia on July 20th, by which time Villeneuve and the combined fleet are lying off Corunna, in letters from Thomas and Emma Hitchins: ... *Lydia, from whom we heard about ten days ago, is quite well. She is much interested in your welfare:* Henry writes back to Emma, who has been in poor health, the same day:

> *My Dear Cousin,*
>
> *We sailed from St Helen's at daybreak last Wednesday morning, and to my no small surprise, I found we were bound to Falmouth. After a pleasant passage down the channel, we came to this harbour yesterday evening, and are ordered to continue until accounts be received of the combined fleets. You will easily conceive my feelings at being thus brought close to my friends; what the design of God is in this providence, I am at a loss to understand. May it be for the mutual establishment and comfort both of them and me! I have sent a short letter to my cousin at Marazion ... How happy should I be, if my cousin should be able to come part of the way to Falmouth to see me! But I pray that my heart may not again rove in pursuit of earthly comfort, and so subject me to new affliction.*

The temptation to see Lydia again is too much for Henry to bear and two days later ... *after much deliberation, I determined to go to Marazion on the morrow. Went to bed with much thought about the step I was going to take, and prayed that if it was not the will of God it might be prevented.* He then writes to his uncle, the Reverend Malachy Hitchins:

> *At daybreak last Wednesday the signal gun was fired by the Commodore, and the whole fleet, consisting of 15 sail under convoy of the Belliqueux, Capt. Byng, got under weigh from St Helen's and sailed down the channel with a fine breeze from the N.E. When we got on board at Portsmouth, I expected to have set foot on the shores of England no more, but found to my no small surprise and pleasure that the fleet was to wait at Falmouth, till tidings should be received of the motions of the combined fleet.*

Then follows family news before he adds a postscript:

> *Wednesday Evening. — I have taken my place in the coach for Marazion, so that if no dispatches arrive from London, I shall be with you almost as soon as my letter. I should be before it, only that I wish to pass some part of the morning at Mrs Grenfell's.*

The next few weeks were to prove decisive and dramatic in the love affair. Henry is only too well aware that before the order to sail comes, which may happen at any moment, he must use this borrowed time to persuade Lydia to follow him out to India.

How miserable did life appear without the hope of Lydia!
Oh, how has the discussion of the subject opened all my wounds
afresh! I have not felt such heartrending pain since I parted with
her in Cornwall. But the Lord brought me to consider the folly
and wickedness of all this. Shall I hesitate to keep all my days in
constant solitude, who am I but a brand plucked from the
burning? I could not help saying: Go Hindoos, go on in your
misery, let Satan still rule over you, for he that was appointed to
labour among you is consulting his ease. No, thought I, hell and
earth shall never keep me from my work.

Quoted in *Church Quarterly Review* in October 1881 from Henry Martyn's *Journal* for June 7th, 1805.

Henry's gift of a tea caddy
containing two copies of *Pilgrim's Progress*
June 24th, 1805

54

Chapter 6 — Time and Tide

Henry caught the morning mail coach and arrived in Marazion in time for breakfast. His love and attachment to Lydia are clear when he describes their meeting in his Journal entry for July 22nd:

> *I arrived in time for breakfast, and met my beloved*
> *Lydia. In the course of the morning, I walked with her, though not*
> *uninterruptedly; with much confusion I declared my affection for*
> *her, with the intention of learning whether, if I ever saw it right in*
> *India to be married, she would come out; but she would not*
> *declare her sentiments, she said the shortness of the arrangement*
> *was an obstacle even if all others were removed.*

This reference on Henry's part to an *obstacle* to their relationship reflects Lydia's sense and no doubt her parents' sense of propriety governing the question of marriage. She would also have been only too aware that with one broken engagement she could not enter into another without being absolutely certain of her feelings. Henry records how he then walked *in great tumult* along the lanes to St. Hilary, where the Reverend Malachy Hitchins lived, and, after dining, returned to Marazion with the purpose of speaking to Lydia again *but on account of the number of persons being there, I had not the opportunity of being alone with Lydia.* He returns to Falmouth in the company of 'G' and confides in his Journal: *was more disposed to talk of Lydia all the way, but roused myself to a sense of my own duty, and addressed him on the subject of religion.*

The following day he is plunged into melancholy *at what had taken place between Lydia and myself, and at the thought of being separated from her.* When he writes to Charles Simeon on July 26th he reveals his mental torment: he starts by describing his feelings once the fleet sailed from Portsmouth before turning his attention to his family and preaching, and then finally gets to the heart of the matter — his relationship with Lydia:[32]

> *My dear brother. It was a very painful moment to me when I awoke on the morning after you left us, & found the fleet actually sailing down Channel. Tho it was what I had been anxiously looking forward to so long, yet the consideration of being parted for ever from my friends almost overcame me. My feelings were those of a man who sh^d suddenly be told that every friend he had in the world was dead ... We continued our course with very fine weather & a fair breeze for two days & half, & on the Friday came to in Falmouth harbour. I was ill the whole time with the motion of the ship so that I could neither sit in my cabin nor walk the deck, but I succeeded in checking the sickness by sitting in the air on the poop. Want of employment thus laid me more open to carnal regret & desires after the enjoyments I had left. But the Lord in mercy upheld my sinking faith when I had scarcely power to pray. Here I am once more in the bosom of all my relations. My sisters came hither immediately & the younger is still with me. On the last Lord's day, the morning being unfavourable for divine service on deck on account of the rain & wind, I went ashore & preached for my cousin Mr Hitchins at Falmouth Church without notes & was assisted to speak for nearly an hour without any hesitation. In the even^g I went aboard again & preached with more life & power than I ever experienced since I have been in the ministry. Such is the kindness of God in giving me every encourag^t to labour vigorously in the work. Wednesday morn^g I preached at Falmouth Church on the three last verses of St Matthew.*

---

[32] Letter dated July 26th, 1805 to Charles Simeon: Henry Martyn Centre, Westminster College, Cambridge: MAR 1/10.

But I have something else to say at which you will not be so well pleased. Miss L.G. lives not more than 20 miles from this place at Marazion. Thither after five days hesitation I determined to go in order to know in what light I might consider her if after my arrival in India I sh^d see it right to be married. To this question I obtained no decisive answer — nor indeed could it be expected. But the worst is that I have returned more attached to her than ever — on leaving her the whole creation seemed to be a blank — such was my idolatry! Sometimes I think I cannot live without her, so necessary does she seem, but so is the right eye necessary & a right hand — I have no doubt about cutting it off, at the command of God — but it is far more painful than ever. If she w. prove a real blessing I have no right to complain at her being withheld, because I deserve nothing at the hands of God. … I am now walking in pain & sorrow. Sometimes I endeavour to count it all joy at falling into divers temptations, in hopes that the trial of my faith may be precious — but in general I am in Heaviness. Our great high Priest is touched with the feeling of our infirm^s. & to Him I find consolat^n in opening my heart. Do you my dearest brother, pity my weakness, & tho this attachment may well seem unworthy of a missionary, yet pray that it may be neither injurious to my soul, nor a hindrance to me in my great work.

He writes to Emma an undated letter between July 27th and August 5th which is more pragmatic in tone:

The consequence of my Marazion journey is that I am enveloped in gloom; but past experience assures me it will be removed. I have taken every step that I conceive right, and now I leave the whole matter with the Lord. May he give me grace to turn cheerfully to my proper work and business, in respect of which all others sink into comparative insignificance. If she would prove a real blessing, it is not for me to complain of God, or of her, that

she is withheld. Another consequence of my journey is, that I love
Lydia more than ever.

The sudden and totally unexpected reappearance of this young man into her
life was to cause Lydia much indecision and heartache. Her Diary entries for
July 1805 record seeing her brother George for the first time in three years
and her concern about the impression she is giving him as she berates herself
for *this lightness of mind by discoursing with too much levity and gaiety.* On
July 23rd she records at some length the effect on her of the death of a young
man and of another friend's illness. She tries to reconcile her grief with her
belief in salvation and ends with a prayer: *Heaven, Heaven is his! Should not
all who knew him rejoice? Rejoice, oh my soul! I do congratulate thee, my
brother, freed from the load of mortality; we long to join you in beholding and
adoring God. O Lord, give me grace to endure unto the end. Amen.* Two days
later her entry refers to Henry's unexpected appearance:

> *I was surprised this morning by a visit from H.M. I have
> passed the day chiefly with him. The distance he is going, and the
> errand he is going on, rendered his society particularly interesting.
> May the Lord moderate the sorrows I feel at parting with so
> valuable and excellent friend. Some pains have attended it, known
> only to God and myself. May we each pursue our different paths
> and meet at last around our Father's throne.*

The tone is one of resignation but by the following day her feelings for Henry
become all too apparent yet she is desperately trying to subsume them:

> *O how has this day passed away! nothing done to any
> good purpose. Lord help me; I feel Thy loved presence withdrawn;
> I feel departing from Thee. O let Thy mercy pardon, let Thy love
> succour me. Lord, deliver me from this temptation, set my soul at
> liberty, and I will praise Thee. I know the cause of all this
> darkness, this depression; — dare I desire what Thou dost plainly,
> by the voice of Thy providence, condemn? O Lord, help me to
> conquer my natural feelings, help me to be watchful as Thy child.*

*O leave me not, or I fall prey to this corroding care. Let me cast
every care on Thee.*

She refers to *depression* and *to conquer my natural feelings* revealing the
torment she is in and perhaps her fear that she will become ill again as she did
after breaking off the previous engagement. Lydia placed her duty to her Lord
foremost and she clings to this although it is clear that she is strongly
attracted by Henry — *this temptation* — who is offering her a second chance
of personal happiness and marriage.

Meanwhile Henry has returned to Falmouth and life aboard *Union*.
Even as his emotional life was in turmoil he was also taking up his duties as
chaplain to the fleet and seems to find them to his liking. Much to his delight
the Lascars aboard *Union* understand him when he speaks a few sentences in
Hindustani. He writes to the Reverend Malachy Hitchins on July 23rd, 1805
while off Falmouth:

> *A great work lies before me, and I must submit to many
> privations, if I would see it accomplished. I should say that poverty
> is not one of the evils I shall have to encounter, the salary of a
> chaplain, even at the lowest, is 600 rupees a month. My situation
> on board ship is very pleasant; the mess, which consists of some
> officers of the 59th, and some young cadets and writers,[33] is very
> orderly, and my cabin is large and commodious. My audience on
> Sundays is between two and three hundred.* But later in the same
> letter he writes: *The consequence of my Marazion journey is that
> I am enveloped in gloom and that I love Lydia more than ever.*

Now there begins a correspondence between Henry and Lydia starting at
Falmouth and ending at Tabriz, in what was then Persia, some seven years
later in 1812. 17 of his letters to her were first published in 1862 in an
Appendix to Sargent's *The Life and Letters of Henry Martyn*. The originals
have disappeared. Her replies have not been traced and may well have been

---

[33] See illustration *Neceffaries, for a Writer to India*

destroyed. Henry's letters reflect all the growing heartbreak and frustrations of conducting a long distance courtship by letter at that time.

Henry writes to Lydia on July 27th, 1805 asking her to copy out a hymn:

> *As I was coming on board this morning, and reading Mr Serle's Hymn you wrote out for me, a sudden gust of wind blew it into the sea. I made the boatman immediately heave to, and recovered it, happily without any injury, except what it had received from the sea. I should have told you that the Morning Hymn, which I always kept carefully in my pocket-book, was one day stolen, with it and other valuable letters, from my rooms in College. It would be extremely gratifying to me to possess another copy of it, as it always reminded me most forcibly of the happy day on which we visited the aged saint. The fleet, it is said, will not sail for three weeks, but if you are willing to employ any of your time in providing me with this or any other MS hymns, the sooner you write them the more certain I shall be of receiving them. Pardon me for thus intruding on your time; you will in no wise lose your reward ... The love which you bear to the cause of Christ, as well as motives of private friendship, will, I trust, induce you to commend me to God ... To His gracious care I commend you. May you long live happy and holy, daily growing more meet for the inheritance of the saints in light.*
>
> *I remain, with affectionate regard,*
>
> *Yours most truly,*
>
> *H. Martyn.*

The tone of the letter belies his true feelings for her but the subject matter of the lost hymn sheet maintains the propriety of writing to an unmarried woman of 29. However, he makes a reference to a visit they made together the previous year which holds happy memories for him and then tells her that the fleet will be in Falmouth for a possible further three weeks. He confides his real feelings when he responds on July 30th to a letter from Emma in which he writes about the affair. He recognises that the shortness of Lydia's and his acquaintance is an obstacle to Lydia but, although he expresses gratitude to Emma for suggesting that he could return from India to marry Lydia, he feels that his work must come first:

> *But when your letter came, I found it so sympathizing, so affectionate, that my heart was filled with joy and thankfulness to God for such a dear friend, and I could not refrain from bowing my knees immediately to pray that God might bless all your good words to the good of my soul, and bless you for writing them. My views of the respective importance of things continue, I hope, to rectify. The shortness of time, the precious value of immortal souls, and the plain command of Christ, all conspire to teach me that Lydia must be resigned — and for ever, — for tho' you suggest the possibility of my hereafter returning and being united to her, I rather wish to beware of looking forward to anything in this life as the end or reward of my labours. It would be a temptation to me to return before being necessitated. The rest which remaineth for the people of God is in another world, where they neither marry nor are given in marriage. But while I thus reason, still a sigh will ever and anon escape me at the thought of a final separation from her ... if I should return and other obstacles were removed — which opinion of yours, is, no doubt very pleasing to me, — but if there were anything more than friendship, do you think it all likely she could have spoken and written to me as she has?* and continues: *If in India I should be persuaded of the expediency of marriage, you perceive that I can do nothing less than make her the offer, or rather propose the sacrifice. It would be almost cruel and presumptuous in me to make such an application to her, especially as she would be induced by a sense of duty rather than personal attachment. But what else can be done? Should she not be warned of my intention before I go? If you advance no objection, I shall write a letter to her notwithstanding her prohibition. When this is*

done no further step remains to be taken, that I know of. The shortness of our acquaintance, which she made a ground of objection, cannot now be remedied. The matter, as it stands must be left with God — and I do leave it with him very cheerfully.

On July 30th Lydia goes to stay with Mrs. Josepha Millett, a close friend and daughter of the Reverend Malachy Hitchins, at Gurlyn, near St. Hilary, where much of her Diary was written. Lydia writes: *Blessed Lord, I thank Thee for affording me the retirement I so much delight in; here I enjoy freedom from all the noise and interruption of a town and watch against the intrusions of vain thoughts.* However, she is preoccupied with Henry and his impending departure with all its uncertainties. August 4th: *This evening my soul has been pained with many fears concerning my absent friend.* She continues by comparing her own emotions with the raging storm outside: *It is a stormy and tempestuous night ... I hear the voice of God in every blast, — it seems to say "Sin has brought storm and tempest on a guilty world."*

As the fleet remains delayed off Falmouth, Lydia comments on her relief on August 5th with: *My mind is relieved today by hearing the fleet, in which I thought my friend had sailed, has not left the port.* But the entry ends with: *Oh, it is a state of conflict indeed.* It is evident from the entries in her Diary for this period that she is increasingly torn by the conflict within her as to the right decision. A decision which would affect both their lives irrevocably. Two days later she refers to her inward corruption and that *I have yielded to temptation in mind and body, losing myself in imaginary scenes, having an earthly object to fill my heart.* It is now five years since she broke off the relationship with Samuel John and she is almost thirty. Yet her assumed moral responsibility for his marital happiness is to be one of the major obstacles to her seizing this chance of marriage. She is now clearly attracted to Henry which must have made her only too painfully aware of her isolation and her mother's opposition to her religious views. She is being pressed to leave her life in Marazion, and go out to India by this ardent young man of 24. The temptation to leave her mother and marry Henry so that together they could unite in their mission to save the souls of the unbeliever also presented her with the possibility of escaping from her mother's disapproval and starting a new and very different life to that which she led in the small Cornish fishing village of Marazion.

However, there were several other obstacles to their marriage which, in a letter to her after he reached India, Henry would later try to overcome by forceful argument. Lydia feels constrained by social etiquette governing unmarried young women making the long and often hazardous journey by sea out to India which at that time would take upwards of five or six months. There were also inherent dangers in the voyage as well as the very present danger posed by the French, Dutch and Spanish fleets. The EastIndiamen with their guns were best able to cope with some of the dangers which Henry describes later in letters home. East India Company policy, which had once banned women on its posts, now encouraged women to travel out to India and settle. In the first part of the 18th century the keeping of a bibi or Indian mistress had been viewed benignly but this had changed with the advent of Richard Wellesley as Governor-General, who was opposed to inter-racial relationships. Although properly chaperoned fiancées, wives and other female relations now regularly travelled out, as Mary Corrie was to do later, to be reunited with their menfolk, the voyage was viewed with foreboding. Mrs. Sherwood, who later became a close and good friend to Henry, wrote in her Diary *Those who have not been to sea can never conceive the hundredth part of the horrors of a long voyage to a female in a sailing vessel.* Lydia may also have been aware that unattached and unchaperoned women who were unkindly referred to as *the fishing fleet* were also beginning to travel out in the hope of finding a husband the growing number of European men in India who far outnumbered women. Their arrival would be carefully timed for the cooler weather in the autumn as there were dire warnings about the effect of the blistering heat on delicate European constitutions.

Henry does not leave the matter with God. He takes the opportunity of paying another visit to Lydia to press his case again for her to join him in India. On August 7th having preached at Falmouth Church he sets off on foot for St. Hilary. As he walks the 20 miles he is in high spirits at the prospect of seeing Lydia again. He spends a pleasant evening and the next day walks across to Gurlyn to see Lydia. She was out: *So I walked to meet her, and when I saw her coming up the hill I was almost induced to believe her more interested in me than I had conceived.* He returned to St. Hilary only to be called back to Falmouth. A message had come of the fleet's imminent departure.

Lydia, after this second unexpected visit, writes on August 8th: *I was surprised again to-day by a visit from my friend, Mr. Martyn, who contrary to every expectation, is detained, perhaps weeks longer. I feel myself called on to act decisively, — O how difficult and painful a part — Lord assist me. I desire to be directed by Thy wisdom, and to follow implicitly what appears Thy will. May we each consider Thy honour, as entrusted to us, and resolve, whatever it may cost us, to seek Thy glory and do Thy will. O Lord, I am so weak that I would fain fly from this trial. My hope is in Thee — do Thou strengthen me, help me to seek, to know and resolutely to do, Thy will; and that we may be each be divinely influenced, and may principle be victorious over feeling.* But the signals that Henry is getting — *I was almost induced to believe her more interested in me and her apparent need to act decisively* — conflict. There is further delay when the orders to sail are once again cancelled which gives Henry more time to press his suit and increases Lydia's emotional turmoil.

On August 9th he calls at Gurlyn where Lydia is staying with her mother, to find that Lydia is again out so he leaves a message that he will return the next day and goes to St. Hilary to spend the night. Lydia writes:

> *What a day of conflict has this been! I was much blessed, as if to prepare me for it, in the morning, and expected to see my friend, and hoped to have acted with Christian resolution. At Tregembo I learnt he had been called off by express last night. The effect this intelligence had on me shows how much my affections are engaged. O Lord, I lament it, I wonder at myself, I tremble at what may be before me, — but do not, O Lord, forsake me. The idea of his going, when at parting I behaved with greater coolness and reserve than I ever did before, was a distress I could hardly bear, and I prayed the Lord to afford me an opportunity of doing away the impression from his mind. I saw no possibility of this — imagining the fleet must have sailed — when, to my astonishment I learnt from our servant that he had called this evening and left a*

message that he would be here tomorrow. O I feel less able than
ever to conceal my real sentiments, and the necessity of doing it
does not so much weigh with me. O my soul, pause, reflect, — thy
future happiness, and his too, the glory of God, the peace of my
dear mother, all are concerned in what may pass tomorrow; I can
only look and pray to be directed aright.

Lydia is already regretting her coolness to Henry when she is offered this further unexpected meeting with him. It also suggests that Lydia was expecting a formal proposal with the reference to their future happiness. However, she also includes her filial duty for her mother's happiness: this did not include Henry.

The following day Henry records: *Rose very early, with uneasiness increased by seeing the wind northerly; walked away at seven to Gurlyn, feeling little or no pleasure at the thought of seeing Lydia; apprehension about the sailing of the fleet made me dreadfully uneasy.* He and Lydia spent a short time alone before her mother joined them for breakfast. They all planned to walk along the coast together later. Henry was fully aware of Mrs. Grenfell's disapproval of his being an Evangelical and of her objections to his relationship with Lydia too. Her strong opposition was also founded on social position. She felt, according to one of her nieces, that the Martyn family was socially inferior to the Grenfell family and her family. Also, selfishly, she did not want to be deserted by her last remaining daughter at home in spite of having Mary close at hand at Tregembo.

Henry had just finished reading Psalm 10 and, as Lydia was handing him the Bible to read Genesis 10, they were suddenly interrupted by a messenger to say the fleet was about to sail. Henry describes the dramatic scene in a letter to Emma Hitchins on August 10th:

This morning at nine o'clock, I had just finished reading
'Horne on the Psalms' to Lydia and your mother at Gurlyn, when
a messenger brought an account of an express from Falmouth; how
delusive are our schemes of delight. It was but yesterday that I
went to St Hilary; this morning Lydia and myself were to have

*taken a walk to view the grounds, and then to have gone to T — ;
and tomorrow I was to have preached at St Hilary and Marazion,
but four hours only have elapsed, and the shores of England are
receding from my sight. But I bless God for having sent the fleet
into Falmouth; I go with far greater contentment and peace than
when I left Portsmouth; the Lord will do all things well, and with
him I cheerfully leave the management of this and every other
affair for time and eternity through Jesus Christ.* Henry describes
his farewell to Lydia: *Lydia was evidently painfully affected by it;
she came out, that we might be alone at taking leave, and then I
told her that if it should appear to be God's will that I should be
married, she must not be offended at receiving a letter from me. In
the great hurry, she discovered more of her mind than she
intended; she made no objection whatever to coming out.
Thinking, perhaps, I wished to make an engagement with her, she
said, 'we had better go quite free', with this I left her.*

Henry subsequently expresses regret that he did not extract a promise from
her that she would join him by persuading her to agree to an engagement.
Lydia's apparent agreement to join him was no match for her mother's
determined opposition and time for face-to-face persuasion was against him.
What took place between them can only be conjecture. However, Lydia
writes after the third visit:

> *Much I have to testify of supporting grace this day, and of
> what I must consider divine interference in my favour, and that of
> my dear friend, who is now gone to return no more. My affections
> are engaged past recalling, and the anguish I endured yesterday,
> from an apprehension that I had treated him with coolness,
> exceeds my power to express, but God saw it, and kindly ordered it,
> that he should come and do away with the idea from my mind. It
> contributed likewise to my peace, and I hope to his, that it is clearly
> now understood between us that he is free to marry where he is*

66

going, and I have felt quite resigned to the will of God in this, and shall often pray the Lord to find him a suitable partner.

Far from being *clearly now understood between us that he is free to marry* Henry is convinced that she has agreed to come out to India. She continues by describing her distress at the thought that Henry may have missed the fleet. But after galloping back to St. Hilary, then transferring to a chaise sent for him and finally getting another horse he arrived back in Falmouth about midday and went straight on board. There is a terse account of his dramatic departure from the Reverend Malachy Hitchins:[34] *as the signal gun for sailing was fired at 5 that morning, and the fleet were to be under weigh that day at 9.a.m. By an accident which detained the* Union *a little longer than the other ships, Mr Martin* [sic.] *was on board in season.*

Lydia writes on the 10th: *Went to Meeting in a comfortable frame, but the intelligence brought me there — that the fleet had probably sailed without my friend — so distressed and distracted my mind, that I would gladly have exchanged my feelings of yesterday for those I was now exercised with; yet in prayer I found relief, and in appealing to God. How unsought by me was his coming here.* Lydia seems unable to reach a decision about their relationship and now is taking refuge in blaming Henry's ardour for the situation.

The following day, August 11th, on returning from church she finds Henry's letter from the *Union*. In this brief second letter dated August 10th from aboard *Union* he writes:

> *My dear Miss Lydia,*
>
> *It will perhaps be some satisfaction to yourself and your mother, to know that I was in time. Our ship was entangled in the chain, and was by that means the only one not under weigh when I arrived. It seems that most of the people on board had given me up, and did not mean to wait for me. I cannot but feel sensibly this instance of Divine mercy in thus preserving me from the great*

---

[34] Memorandum on the back of Martyn's letter dated July 23rd written in red ink probably by Rev. M. Hitchins.

trouble that would have attended the loss of my passage. Mount's
Bay will soon be in sight, and recal you all once more to my
affectionate remembrance ...

I bid you a long farewell. God ever bless you, and help you
sometimes to intercede for me.

H. Martyn.

There is now a tone of resignation and an acceptance on her part that her prayers have been answered yet tinged with regret: *O may my thoughts upon my bed be solemn and spiritual. The remembrance of my dear friend is at times attended with feelings most painful, and yet, when I consider why he is gone, and whom he is serving, every burden is removed, and I rejoice on his account, and rejoice that the Lord has such a faithful servant employed in the work. O may I find grace triumphant over every feeling of my heart.* Lydia's mother must have been relieved that fate had intervened and a snared chain had enabled this evangelical young man to finally embark for India. The danger of losing her last remaining daughter at home had seemingly passed.

Henry writes in his Journal: *So delusive are schemes of pleasure! At nine in the morning I was sitting at ease with the person dearest to me upon earth, intending to go out with her afterwards to see different views, to visit some persons with her, and to preach on the morrow: four hours only elapsed, and I was under sail from England.* Time was unfortunately not on Henry's side to press his suit.

On Sunday, August 11th, 1805 Henry writes:

I rose dejected, and extremely weak in body ... On
repeating the text a second time, I could scarcely refrain from
bursting into tears. For the Mount [St. Michael's Mount] *and St*
Hilary's Spire [35] *and trees were just discernible by the naked eye at*
the time I began my sermon, by saying, 'that now the shores of

---

[35] St Hilary, the 13th-century church which Henry knew so well, has a spire which acted as a landmark for Cornish sailors and fisherman This is unusual as most Cornish churches have towers. In 1853 the church was almost destroyed in a great fire but Henry's beloved spire survived.

England were receding fast from our view, and that we had taken
a long, and to many of us, an everlasting farewell ...' England had
disappeared and with it all my peace; ... Would I ever go back?

In an unpublished letter to Emma, dated June 24th, 1805, which Henry wrote from London while waiting to embark from Portsmouth he refers to a tea caddy in which he encloses two copies of *Pilgrim's Progress* — one for Emma and the other for Lydia. In subsequent letters he refers to having left the caddy and the key at his lodgings at 25, New Ormond Street in London. However, in a letter to Emma written in December 1807, he refers to the caddy and key as *I suppose are irrevocably gone as you have ceased to mention them*. It would be romantic to think that perhaps a beautiful ivory and tortoise-shell tea caddy with gold mounts[36] was a farewell gift to Lydia though he may have harboured a vain hope that before long they would be happily reunited and both enjoy tea from it together in India.

---

[36] Now in Royal Cornwall Museum, Truro and reputed to have been given to Lydia by Henry.

A Fleet of EastIndiamen at Sea
Nicholas Pocock 1803

Chapter 7 — The Passage to India

Off The Lizard, the most southerly point of Britain, famous for its fierce storms and wrecks, Captain Byng opened the sealed despatches. As a counter espionage measure the fleet's sailing orders would be sealed and only opened once the fleet was safely at sea. Though provisioned for a long voyage and carrying passengers en route for India even Captain Byng would not know his orders but he now discovered that once again the fleet was diverted, this time to Cork. Henry is already suffering from seasickness and missing Lydia:

> *Journal (Monday, August 12th;) A day of the most severe trial for me. England had disappeared, and with it all my peace; the memory of Lydia, and all the dear Christian friends in England, cut me to the heart every moment. Every wave produced vertigo and sickness in the body, and what was more painful, bore me farther and farther from Lydia ... Throughout the whole of this day, the want of Christian society, or of any friend with whom I could converse, made me scarcely doubt of sending for Lydia, immediately on my arrival in India. I almost think I should before that, only that I may perhaps never arrive.*

Henry was the only chaplain in a force of 8,000 soldiers which he describes filling the transport ships in preparation for an expedition *probably to the Cape of Good Hope, or the Brazils.* During the short voyage Henry is trying to make contact with soldiers and officers but much to his chagrin is told that *the officers and others did nothing but make objections to my sermons.*

71

Moreover, the captain has told him that one service a day at sea must suffice because *the men who had to keep watch in the night, were obliged to take rest in the evening.* Henry is also finding the company of officers in the mess room not to his taste and the lack of privacy in his shared cabin difficult as both preclude prayer and contemplation. On August 14th the fleet anchors at Cork from where Henry wrote to Emma on August 16th: *The beloved objects were still in sight, and Lydia I knew was about that time at St Hilary, but every wave bore me farther and farther away from them.* He continues by describing how the female members of his congregation were affected by his observation that *we had now bid adieu to England, and its shores were dying from the view.* The female passengers would be facing this long voyage with increased trepidation because of the fear of attack from the French and Spanish combined fleet. The last sight of Cornwall was: *The Mount continued in sight till five o'clock* and asks: *If you have heard from Marazion I should be curious to know whether the fleet was observed passing.* Next he turns to more pressing personal matters: *If it should please God to send me another letter from you, which I scarcely dare hope, do not forget to tell me as much as you can about Lydia. I cannot write to her, or I should find the greatest relief and pleasure even in transmitting upon paper the assurances, of my tenderest love.*

The vagaries of sending and receiving mail are apparent when, on August 28th just before the fleet left *under convoy of five men of war* for Madeira he writes again to Emma:

> My dearest Cousin, — I have but a few minutes to say
> that we are again going to sea — under convoy of five men of war.
> Very anxiously have I been expecting to receive an answer to the
> letter I sent you on my arrival at this port, bearing date August
> 16; from the manner in which I had it conveyed to the post-office, I
> begin to fear it never reached you. I have this instant received the
> letter you wrote me on the day on which we sailed from Falmouth.
> Everything from you gives me the greatest pleasure, but this letter
> has rather tended to excite sentiments of pain as well as pleasure. I
> fear my proceedings have met with your disapprobation, and have

therefore been wrong — since it is more probable you should judge
impartially than myself.

>*I am now fully of opinion that, were I convined [sic.] of*
>*the expediency of marriage, I ought not in conscience to propose it,*
>*while the obstacle of S.J. remains. Whatever others have said, I*
>*think that Lydia acts no more than consistently by persevering in*
>*her present determination. I confess, therefore, that till this*
>*obstacle is removed, my path is perfectly clear, and blessed be God!*
>*I feel very, very happy in all that my God shall order concerning*
>*me.*

The S. J. whom Henry refers to is Samuel John, who now lived in London. At this point Henry seems to accept that the subject of marriage to Lydia must be deferred until John marries. Henry is corresponding regularly with Emma from each port of call but Lydia is dependant on Emma for news:

>*September 3. — Still no letters from Stoke,* [where Emma
>lived] *and no intelligence whether the fleet has sailed — this is no*
>*small exercise of my patience, but at times I feel a sweet*
>*complacency in saying, 'Thou art my portion, O Lord.' I have often*
>*felt happy in saying this, but it is in a season such as this, when*
>*creature comforts fail, that we know whether we are sincere in*
>*saying so.*

On August 31st the fleet set sail from Cork for Madeira, from where he wrote from Funchal to Emma again on September 30th: *God knows how dearly I love you, and Lydia, and Sally, and all his saints in England, yet I bid you all an everlasting farewell, almost without a sigh.* Henry's thoughts are now turned to the torment he has gone through over parting with Lydia, and his even more immediate discomfort from seasickness, which was to continue to plague him on all his voyages:

>*To describe the variety of perplexing, heartrending,*
>*agonizing thoughts that passed thro' my mind, which united with*

the sickness and languor of my body to depress me, would be impossible. From day to day I continued in the same state, rising in the morning without strength or spirit to dress myself, vomiting quantities of acrid bile before breakfast. All the arguments of God's word came to me with irresistable force, but self-will is deaf to reason — the soul without the influence of grace is in a state of insanity. I felt disposed to throw away my honour, my integrity, my life, my soul, for what I did not know.

The fleet then sailed to San Salvador in Brazil. It was here that the officers were informed that the purpose of the expedition was, as had been rumoured, to recapture the Cape of Good Hope which was in the hands of the Dutch. Lydia was still very much on Henry's mind and in a letter to Emma dated November 15th, 1805 he requests the profiles of her, her husband and Lydia, adding: *If she would consent to it, I should wish for her miniature. The expense attending it should be defrayed by Simeon, who is good enough to be my agent.* Emma did not receive this letter until February 24th the following year.

Lydia makes references to the fleet in her Diary in September but her main preoccupation is seeking comfort in her religion and she is even contemplating her own death so that she will then enjoy *a state a of uninterrupted enjoyment of God.* Throughout the rest of the year she is struggling to reconcile the loss of Henry by seeking redemption through Christ. From Lydia's Diary we can follow the struggle she was going through tormented by her duty to her Lord, her duty to her mother, her strong moral feeling that she should not enter another engagement until Samuel John marries, her worries about her health and the propriety of travelling out to India. On November 16th, 1805 she makes a momentous decision to end her relationship with Henry: *I have been employed today in a painful manner (perhaps for the last time) to too-dear a friend. I have to bless God for keeping me composed whilst doing so, and for peace of mind since, arising from a conviction that I have done right.* Lydia has allowed her moral scruple over Samuel John's welfare, and her duty to her mother, who had steadfastly refused to give their relationship her blessing, to end the relationship. However, this letter never reached Henry. It was captured in the *Bell* Packet at sea so he remains blissfully unaware of her decision. Henry is still thinking of Lydia:

> *— December: 5 My mind has been running on Lydia and the happy scenes in England, very much; particularly that day when I walked with her on the sea-shore, and with wistful eye looked over the blue waves that were to bear me from her. While walking the deck I longed to be left alone, that my thoughts might run at random. Tender scenes on distant shores do not leave me indisposed for communion with God.*

A few days later she writes: *Yesterday brought me most pleasing intelligence from my dear friend, for which I have, and do thank thee, O Lord my God. He assures us of his being well, and exceedingly happy, — O may he continue so. I have discovered that insensibly I have indulged the hope of his return, which this letter has seemed to lessen. I see it is my duty to familiarize my mind to the idea of our separation being for ever ... and I look forward to our meeting only in another state of existence, and O how pure and exalted will be our affection then! here it is mixed with much evil, many pains, and great anxieties.* Lydia had clearly been harbouring hopes that Henry would return to Cornwall but now accepts that this is unlikely. Instead she has resigned herself to obeying her mother's wishes. Her social position will not be compromised by following this zealous young man out to India. Instead she will remain in the bosom of her family, isolated from some of them by her religious beliefs, and lead an unblemished life of prayer and good works among the dying and unbelievers in the known world of Marazion. However, Henry will not be willing to let this woman he loves so deeply slip from his grasp.

The fleet anchored between Robben Island and Blaauberg near Cape Town on January 4th, 1806. The British wanted to re-capture the Cape from the Dutch, who were in Napoleon's control after his invasion of Holland, to ensure an open sea route to the East to safeguard trade. They succeeded in doing so at the Battle of Blaauberg — a bloody battle — on January 8th. In a letter to Simeon Henry describes in graphic detail how he went ashore after the battle and saw first hand the aftermath with the wounded and dying left to their fate:

> *A little onward were three mortally wounded. One of them, on being asked where he was struck, opened his shirt, and showed a wound in his left breast. The blood which he was spitting showed that he had been shot through the lungs. As we spread a great coat over him, by the surgeon's desire, who passed on without attempting to save him, I spoke of the blessed Gospel, and besought him to look to Jesus Christ for salvation. He was suprised, but could not speak, and I was obliged to leave him, in order to reach the troops, from whom the officer, out of regard to my safety, would not allow me to be separated.*

His coolness in the aftermath of the battle and his zeal to save the souls of the dying shows in this description:

> *One poor Hottentot I asked about Dr Vanderkemp, I saw by his manner that he knew him; he lay with extraordinary patience under his wound on the burning sand; I did what I could to make his position comfortable, and laid near him some bread, which I found on the ground. Another Hottentot lay struggling with his mouth in the dust and the blood flowing out of it, cursing the Dutch in English, in the most horrid language; I told him he should rather forgive them, and asked him about God, and after telling him about the Gospel, begged he would pray to Jesus Christ; but he did not attend. While the surgeon went back to get his instrument in the hopes of saving the man's life, a Highland soldier came up and asked me in a rough tone, "Who are you?" I told him, "An Englishman;" he said "No, no, you are French," and was going to present his musket. As I saw he was rather intoxicated, and might in mere wantonness fire, I went up to him and told him that if he liked he might take me prisoner to the English army, but that I was certainly an English clergyman. The man was pacified at last. The surgeon on his return found the*

thigh bone of the poor Hottentot broken, and therefore left him to die. After this I found an opportunity of retiring, and lay down among the bushes and lifted up my soul to God. Victory was signalled when at sunrise on the tenth, a gun from the commodore's ship was instantly answered by all the men-of-war, as the British flag was seen flying on the Dutch fort.

Later in a letter to Reverend Malachy Hitchins, dated May 30th, from Serampore Henry refers to a drawing that Fortescue Hitchins, the son of the Reverend Malachy Hitchins, who was a solicitor, had given him of the vicarage at St. Hilary and how much comfort it had brought him during that time: *In the tempestuous nights off the Cape, when I was almost dying with sickness, and could do nothing but gaze round the sides of my cabin, the sight of the picture often made me long to exchange my rolling prison for that little parlour, and regret that I could not stroll thro' the walks of the garden instead of going out only to slide down the lee side of the quarter deck.* Perhaps Lydia was wise to have had second thoughts about joining Henry although in letters to her from India he plays down the discomforts and dangers of the voyage. Henry was only too well aware how diseases such as dysentery from which many of the crew and the captain had died from en route, could decimate passengers on the voyage out.

The fleet remained at the Cape for five weeks and while there Henry met two missionaries: a Mr. Read and the Dutch missionary, Dr. Vanderkemp, whom Henry had questioned the dying Hottentot about, and whom he had much admired while he was at Cambridge. As he stands talking to Read he remembers Lydia: *Talking with Read on the beach, we spoke of the excellency of missionary work. The last time I stood on the shore with a friend, speaking on the same subject, was with Lydia at Marazion, and I mentioned her to Read. However, I felt not the slightest desire for marriage and often thank God for keeping me single.* Yet, a few months later he will be proposing to Lydia, unaware that she has decided not to join him in India. Henry vacillates between devoting his life to carrying out his missionary work in India alone and yearning for Lydia to be his wife and join him.

His love and fascination with languages was to stand him in good stead and during this voyage he continued to read both Latin and Greek and he had time to continue with his studies in Urdu, Arabic and Persian as well as practising his Hindustani on the Laskars. He also kept a fascinating account of his journey; the countries and people he encountered and his often less than successful attempts to persuade them of his evangelical Christian views. His evangelical preaching on board was not well received either and at times he is full of self-doubt and self-loathing.

Henry finally reached Madras on April 22nd, 1806 some ten weeks after leaving the Cape and nine and half months after leaving Falmouth. He records his first impressions as he went ashore: *At sunrise we anchored in Madras roads. Several doolbashees or interpreters came on board, dressed in white muslin. I went ashore in one of the country boats, made very high in order to weather the surf ... On shore I was surrounded by an immense crowd of coolies, I suppose two hundred, who caught up one box after another, and were going off in different directions, so that I was obliged to run instantly, and stop them. ... Nothing as yet struck me as remarkable in the country, for the novelty of it had been anticipated in what I had seen in St Salvador.* This landing at Madras which had no natural harbour was viewed with alarm by Europeans, especially the women passengers who were confronted by near-naked native boatmen controlling the outriggers through the boiling surf to the relative safety of the beach, where they would be carried ashore. Madras was ceded by treaty in 1639 to the East India Company and for Europeans it had a relatively healthy climate. Administration and military matters were housed in Fort St. George, started in 1640, which had taken over 150 years to build. More importantly for Henry the oldest Anglican Church in India, St. Mary's, built in 1680, was also there and Madras was held to be the site of the martyrdom of St. Thomas.

He was now 25 years old and about to begin a very different life from his life in England. While dining he comments on the Indians around him: *The elegance of their manners I was much taken with; but in general one thought naturally occurred, — the conversion of their poor souls. I felt a solemn sort of melancholy at the sight of such multitudes of idolaters. While the turbanned Asiatics waited upon us at dinner, about a dozen of them, I could not but help feeling as if we had got into their places.* His evangelical zeal to save the souls of the heathen and his Eurocentric moral certitude give him assurance that he occupies the religious high ground: *Now that I am actually treading on Indian ground, let me bless and adore my God for doing so much for me; and if I live let me come hither for some purpose.* A different mood is reflected when he reports on a visit to his servant Samee's village, Chindapur: *Here all was Indian — no vestige of anything European ... I thought of my future labours among them with some despondency; yet I am willing, I trust through grace, to pass my days among them, if, by any means these poor people may be brought to God.*

While at Madras he preached a sermon at Fort St. George before the Governor of Madras. However, the Europeans in the congregation were not enamoured by Henry's somewhat severe style of preaching. After two weeks lying off Madras *Union* sailed under convoy of *Victor,* a sloop of war, to the treacherous Hooghli river and, after being almost wrecked on a sandbar on May 13th, Henry finally reached Calcutta, and the East India Company's magnificent symbol of British Imperial power — Fort William. Calcutta had taken precedence over Madras and Bombay with the arrival of Warren Hastings who became the first Governor General of India in 1774. On May 16th Henry writes with some relief after his eventful and dangerous voyage: *My long and wearisome voyage is concluded, and I am at last arrived in the country in which I am to spend my days in the work of the Lord.* Henry then records how *with some difficulty* he finally met his role model from Cambridge days, William Carey.

For the final part of his journey he was rowed further up the Hooghli river, for about an hour and a half on the tide, the 16 miles to Aldeen, a suburb of Serampore in Lower Bengal to stay with the Reverend David Brown and his family. Mr. Brown, who had been the first chaplain sent out by the East India Company in 1786, was by then a senior chaplain, and was to prove a good friend and mentor to this somewhat unworldly young man and Henry took much comfort from his contact with the family, especially with the children. He was charmed by his accommodation: *My habitation is a pagoda, which Mr Brown fitted up as a sort of summer house in his garden, when it was forsaken by its God Bulhub some years ago. Notwithstanding the vicissitudes of life, who could have guessed a few years ago, that I should have at last found a house in an Indian pagoda.* Henry appears to suffer no scruples about living in a disused Hindu temple in the grounds of the mission house, indeed there is a tone of triumphalism in the following: *Thither I retired at night, and really felt something like superstitious dread at being in a place once inhabited, as it were, by devils, but yet felt disposed to be triumphantly joyful that the temple where they were worshipped was become Christ's oratory.*

When Daniel Corrie, an old friend from Cambridge days, arrived in Calcutta in the autumn of 1806 Henry went down from Aldeen to meet him. Corrie would later become Bishop of Madras. Henry remained at Aldeen until October 1806, while waiting for his appointment to a military station. He was in the company of Baptist missionaries and had close contact with Carey, his missionary model. At this period he is very busy in adjusting to his new life and is shocked at times by the local religious festivals. He is excited by a vast project under discussion to translate the New Testament into eastern languages by a group of missionaries. Marshman, a Baptist, was translating it into Gujarati and Sanscrit. They were keen for him to join them so that the word could be spread among the heathens. However, Henry's duties to the East India Company did not make him an entirely a free agent as his *'official duties as a chaplain of The Honourable East India Company were strictly confined to ministry to the Company's officials, British soldiers, and their families*[37]*'* although he remains resolute in *going among the heathen as a missionary,* having firmly rejected a plan for him to remain in Calcutta. Nevertheless, it was decided that it would be Henry's task to study Sanscrit and continue with Hindustani and begin work on translating the New Testament into Urdu[38]: *23rd May: Spent the morning with Mirza Phitrut, who read over with me the Hindoostanee (Urdu) translation of the first two chapters of Genesis. I knew enough to point out several errors which he corrected.* He is also in discussion with Marshman as to his role in India: *Had a long conversation at night with Marshman, whose desire now is that I should stay at*

---

[37] Brian Stanley, *An Ardour of Devotion: The Spiritual Legacy of Henry Martyn*, The Henry Martyn Centre, Westminster College, Cambridge.

[38] Hindi v. Urdu: linguistically there is little difference. Yule in *Hobson Jobson* refers to Hindostanee and comments *it is also called Oordoo....This language was for a long time a kind of Mahomedan lingua franca all over India.*

Serampore, give myself to the study of Hindoostanee (Urdu) for the sake of the Scriptures, and be ready to take the place of Carey and Marshman in the work, should they be taken off; and for another reason that I might awaken the attention of the people of God in Calcutta more to missionary subjects ... could not see that it was the path God designed for me. The distribution of tracts brought the missionary activities to the notice of the authorities and in August Carey was instructed *not to dispense any more tracts nor send out more native brethren, or in any way interfere with the prejudices of the natives.*

While at Serampore Henry would travel down to Calcutta on Sundays to collect mail. He receives letters from England on July 12th. Amongst them are one from Lydia dated December 1805 to which Henry refers to in his reply and one from Simeon. This letter from Lydia was written after the one she sent in November 1805 in which she had ended his hope of her coming out to India but which he never received. This suggests that she had decided to continue writing to Henry as a friend in affectionate terms. What Lydia said in this letter is not known except for Henry's reference to its tone as *affectionate* which Henry interprets as a signal that she is in love with him. Lydia blames herself later for expressing her affection and regard for *him too freely.* Encouraged by the tone of her letter and also by a reference to her in a letter from Simeon in which *even he seemed to regret I had gone without her* Henry decides to act decisively. The following day he broaches the subject to David Brown and goes so far as to read her letter to him: *Talked to Mr Brown about Lydia, and read her letter to him. He strongly recommended the measure of endeavouring to bring her here and was clear that my future situation in the country would be such as to make it necessary to be married.* A letter from Colonel Sandys, which he opened afterwards, spoke in the highest terms of her. *The subject of marriage was revived in my mind, but I feel rather reluctant to.*

The expediency of Henry's being married is now in the forefront of the minds of: ironically, Simeon, who had earlier argued for celibacy; Colonel Sandys, who thought so highly of her, yet as a friend of the family would have been aware of Mrs. Grenfell's opposition; Brown, who no doubt would be aware of how lonely a young chaplain could be and understood how useful a wife would be, especially as he had observed how much Henry enjoyed the company of his own wife and children; and the other ministers in Calcutta and Serampore who encouraged him to marry. Henry, in spite of further vacillation on the subject is persuaded: *'Mr B's arguments appear so strong, that my mind is almost made up to send for Lydia. I could scarcely have any reasonable doubts remaining that her presence would most abundantly promote the ends of the mission.'* He writes a long letter to Lydia.

Landing on the North Beach, Madras
Charles Hunt after Sir James Buller East, 1856

Chapter 8 — 'Come out to me in India'

Henry's letter dated, July 30th, 1806, is the third letter he has written to Lydia. It is a formal proposal of marriage.

> *My dearest Lydia,*
>
> *On a subject so intimately connected with my happiness and future ministry, as that on which I am about to address you, I wish to assure you that I am not acting with precipitancy or without much consideration and prayer while I at last sit down to request you to come out to me in India.*
>
> *May the Lord graciously direct His blind and erring creature, and not suffer the natural bias of his mind to lead him astray. You are acquainted with much of the conflict I have undergone on your account. It has been greater than you or Emma have imagined ...*

He then explains that during the long sea voyage

> *God in great mercy gave me deliverance, and favoured me throughout the voyage with peace of mind, indifference about all worldly connections, and devotedness to no object upon earth but the work of Christ. I gave you up entirely — not the smallest*

expectation remained in my mind of ever seeing you again till we should meet in heaven.

He goes on to say that he continued to feel the same after his arrival in India. What then changed his mind?

> *... my own opinions began to change, and when a few weeks ago we received your welcome letter, and others from Mr Simeon and Colonel Sandys, both of whom spoke of you in reference to me, I considered it even as a call from God to satisfy myself fully concerning his will. From the account which Mr Simeon received of you from Mr Thomason, he seemed in his letter to me to regret that he had so strongly dissuaded me from thinking about you at the time of my leaving England. Colonel Sandys spoke in such terms of you, and the advantages to result from your presence in this country, that Mr. B. became very earnest for me to endeavour to prevail upon you. Your letter to me perfectly delighted him, and induced him to say that you would be the greatest aid to the Mission that I could possibly meet with. I knew my own heart too well not to be distrustful of it, especially as my affections were once again awakened.* He emphasises then how he must follow his duty and having weighed up the advantages and disadvantages of their marrying: *My reason is fully convinced of the expediency — I almost say the necessity of having you with me. It is possible that my reason may still be obscured by passion;– let it suffice to say that now, with a clear conscience and the enjoyment of the Divine presence, I calmly and deliberately make the proposal to you.*

He then refers to her letter which has further persuaded him to prepare:

> *Your letter dated December, 1805, was the first I received, and I found it so animating that I could not but reflect on the blessedness of having so dear a counsellor always near me. I can truly say, and God is my witness, that my principal desire in*

this affair is that you may promote the kingdom of God in my own heart, and be the means of extending it to the heathen. My own earthly comfort and happiness are not worth a moment's notice. I would not, my dearest Lydia, influence you by any artifices or false representations ... Come, and the Lord be with you. It can be nothing but a sacrifice on your part, to leave your valuable friends.[39]

He follows with an appeal to her: *I ask it not of you or of God for the sake of my own happiness, but only on account of the Gospel.*

He turns to the practicalities of the voyage out and other arrangements and in spite of his above protestation of not misrepresenting anything he does, however, allow poetic licence to get the better of him, when he says: *You will meet no hardships. The voyage is very agreeable. The climate is fine. The dreaded heat is really nothing. The whole country is a land of peace and plenty, multitudes of simple people sitting in the shade listening to the words of eternal life.* He does not confide his abhorrence at some of the Hindu religious practices nor does he mention the discomfort of seasickness on the voyage out, the mosquito bites he has suffered, his high fevers and the intense heat of India. He assures her that she will not be left isolated from the European community *because no chaplain is stationed where there is not a large English society:* a reference to the cantonments which were built close to towns, organised in military fashion for they were primarily a barracks but also a microcosm of life in Europe with a church, shops, bungalows and social gatherings where the British memsahib was beginning to hold increasing sway. He also assures her that his salary *is abundantly sufficient for the support of a married man.* He will go into more detail on this subject in his subsequent letter.

He then turns to the practicalities of the voyage out and reveals that he is fully aware that he and Lydia must make sure that there is no impropriety in the arrangements for her journey out. He suggests she comes in February 1807: *This letter will reach you about the latter end of the year, — it would be*

---

[39] See Part Two for complete letters.

very desirable if you could be ready for the February fleet, because the voyage will be performed in far less time than at any other season. George (Lydia's brother) will find out the best ship; one in which there is a lady of high rank in the service would be preferable. You are to be considered as coming as a visitor to Mr Brown, who will write to you or Colonel Sandys, who is best qualified to give you directions about the voyage. The 'lady of high standing' would be chaperone thereby hopefully forestalling any arguments about the propriety of travelling alone. He goes on to further re-assure her, and Mrs. Grenfell, that she will be received by Mr. Brown and looked after when she arrives if he is not available to do so because of his duties. He also advises her to take Gilchrist's *Indian Stranger's Guide,*[40] *and occasionally on the voyage learn some words.* He then writes about his enthusiasm for his work and that his posting will probably be to Patna *a civil station, where I shall not be under military control.* Such is his optimism that he even says that he is going to write to his cousin, Thomas, and suggests he and Emma come out as missionaries. However, fully aware that letters get captured or lost in transit he proposes sending this letter in duplicate or even triplicate to ensure that she does receive his proposal. He then turns to correspondence with his family and Emma revealing the reason he has not written to her before:

> *I did not know it was permitted me to write to you — or I fear she would not have found me so faithful a correspondent on the voyage. As I have heretofore addressed you through her, it is probable that I may now be disposed to address her through you — or what will be best of all, that we both of us address her in one letter from India. However, you shall decide, my dearest Lydia ...*

and he makes reference to her decision being directed by *that spirit of simple looking to the Lord* and with this guidance she will make the right decision. He thanks her for remembering him in her prayers *frequently and every day.* He ends this long and eloquent proposal:

---

[40] John B. Gilchrist: *The Strangers' East Indian Guide to the Hindoostanee:* Calcutta, 1802.

Dearest Lydia, in the sweet and fond expectation of you being given to me by God, and of the happiness which I humbly hope you yourself might enjoy here, I find pleasure in breathing out my assurance of ardent love. I have now loved you most affectionately, and my attachment is more strong, more pure, more heavenly, because I see in you the image of Jesus Christ. I unwillingly conclude by bidding my beloved Lydia adieu.

H. Martyn.

The phrase *I did not know it was permitted me to write to you* suggest that it was Lydia who initiated the correspondence once Henry had set sail. Whether she acted independently of her mother or whether Emma had interceded on her behalf after she had sent the initial letter which was captured at sea is not known but clearly a woman in Lydia's social position would not have acted with any hint of impropriety. What is abundantly clear is the difficulty at that time for a young man to conduct a courtship by letter until family approval had been granted. Bearing in mind that Mrs. Grenfell was so opposed to Lydia leaving Marazion perhaps it was Emma who, as a respectably married woman, took it upon herself to encourage the correspondence between two people very dear to her.

True to his word, one month later on September 1st, Henry sends a duplicate letter[41] with the following letter from Serampore which he will leave in six weeks time for his new posting. It has still not been decided where he will be — Benares, which Henry favours as the holiest city in India, Patna or Moorshedabad. He is impatient for her reply but he would not receive Lydia's reply until October 24th, 1807, almost 15 months from the first letter proposing to her.

My dearest Lydia,

---

[41]George Smith, *Henry Martyn, (1892)* suggests that the first letter failed to reach Lydia and the duplicate carried in the *Sarah Christiana* packet was delayed. Henry refers to the two letters in a letter to Mrs. Brown at Aldeen dated July 21st, 1807.

With this you will receive the duplicate of the letter I sent you a month ago, by the overland despatch. May it find you prepared to come! All the thoughts and views which I have had of the subject since first addressing you, add tenfold to my first opinion ... I sometimes regret that I had not obtained a promise from you of following me, at the time of our last parting at Gurlyn; as I am occasionally apt to be excessively impatient at the long delay. Many, many months must elapse before I can see you, or even hear how you shall determine. The instant your mind is made up you will send a letter by the Overland Despatch.

Henry suggests that Lydia's brother George will be able to organise it. The overland route from Alexandria in Egypt to the Red Sea had been safeguarded at the Battle of the Nile in 1798 with Nelson's victory over Napoleon. The advantage of the route lay in the fact that it was shorter and did away with the tedious and dangerous long sea route. However, it involved travelling to Italy, then by boat across the Mediterranean before travelling via Cairo across Egypt to the Red Sea and then embarking to cross the Indian Ocean to India. Although quicker it still presented dangers and discomforts to the European traveller with extremes of temperature in the desert. This route would not become an effective alternative until Thomas Waghorn improved it later in the 19th century. The letter continues: *It is a consolation to me during this long suspense, that had I engaged with you before my departure I should not have had such a satisfactory conviction of it being the will of God.*

Henry is full of confidence that she will come, guided by God to accept his proposal:

By the fleet which will sail hence in about two months, they [Emma and Sally] *will receive longer letters. You will then, I hope, have left England. I am very happy here in preparing for my delightful work; but I should be happier still if I were sufficiently fluent in the language to be actually employed; and happiest of all if my beloved Lydia were at my right hand, counselling and animating me. I am not very willing to end my letter to you; it is difficult not to prolong the enjoyment of speaking, as it were, to one who occupies so much of my sleeping and waking hours; but here, alas! I am aware of danger; and my dear Lydia will, I hope, pray that her unworthy friend may love no creature inordinately.* He then praises God and refers to her as *my beloved sister and friend, dear to me on every account, but dearest of all for having one heart and one soul with me in the cause of Jesus and the love of God.*

He ends the letter:

> *Now, my dearest Lydia, I cannot say what I feel — I cannot pour out my soul — could not if you were here; but I pray that you may love me, if it be the will of God; and I pray that God may make you more and more his child, and give me more and more love for all that is Godlike and holy.*
>
> *I remain, with fervent affection,*
>
> *Yours, in eternal bonds.*
>
> *H. Martyn*

Henry writes a third love letter to Lydia almost two weeks later in which he tries to reconcile the dream of having Lydia by his side being realised and at the same time respecting her right to turn down his proposal. The thought of the latter is painful but he regards her decision as showing God's will.

> *How earnestly do I long for the arrival of my dearest Lydia! Though it may prove at last no more than a waking dream that I ever expected to receive you in India, the hope is too pleasing not to be cherished till I am forbidden any longer to hope. Till I am assured of the contrary, I shall find pleasure in addressing you as my own. If you are not to be mine, you will pardon me; but my expectations are greatly encouraged by the words you used when we*

parted at Gurlyn, that I had better go out free, implying as I thought, that you would not be unwilling to follow me if I should see it to be the will of God to make the request. I was rejoiced also to see in your letter that you unite your name with mine, when you pray that God would keep us both in the path of duty; from this I infer that you are by no means determined to remain separate from me. You will not suppose, my dear Lydia, that I mention these little things to influence your conduct, or to implicate you in an engagement. No, I acknowledge that you are perfectly free, and I have no doubt that you will act as the love and wisdom of our God shall direct. Your heart is probably far less interested in this business than mine, in all probability.

Henry is full of optimism hoping that Lydia has already left England to join him by the time this letter arrives and mentions his other letters to her: *If these shall have arrived safely you will perhaps have left England before this reaches it. But if not let me entreat you not to delay a moment. Yet how will my dear sister Emma be able to part with you and George — but above all, your mother? I feel very much for you and for them, but I have no doubt at all about your health and happiness in this country.* Henry continues by giving her news that he has been appointed chaplain to the cantonment at Dinapore, near Patna and although he is disappointed that he is not going to Benares — *the heart of Hinduism* — there is much to recommend Dinapore: *The air is good, the living cheap, the salary £1,000 a year, and there is a large body of English troops there.*

Reference to the troops is a reminder that although Bengal was under British authority other areas were not and there were frequent skirmishes and battles with the warlike Marathas until 1818. With an income of £1,000 Henry would have been quite well off and it is possible that he includes this information so that Mrs. Grenfell will be impressed at his new improved financial position. Another piece of good news is that two other Bengal chaplains will be stationed close by at Benares and Moorshedebad. One of these chaplains is Daniel Corrie.

Having told Lydia in an earlier letter that India is a pleasing country he perhaps unwisely breaks off this letter and resumes with *I have just been interrupted by the blaze of a funeral pile, within a hundred yards of my pagoda; I ran out, but the wretched woman had consigned herself to the flames before I reached the spot, and I saw only the remains of her and her husband.* A reference to the practice of suttee which someone of Lydia's delicate constitution might have preferred not to read even in the safe world of Marazion. It would probably have strengthened her mother's Eurocentric preconceptions and opposition to her travelling out to such a dangerous heathen country. He then condemns the Brahmins for allowing such a murder to happen: *I stammered out something to the wicked Brahmins about the judgements of God upon them for the murder they had just committed, but they said it was an act of her own free will.* He comments that the missionaries have been forbidden to preach to the natives in the British territory and continues that unless this order is revoked then the Mission will be totally suppressed. Henry ends this letter, the last he wrote from Serampore, with praise and love to Lydia:

> *Surely, were you here, I should act with more cheerfulness*
> *and activity with so bright a pattern before me. If Corrie brings*
> *me a letter from you, and the fleet is not sailed, which however, is*
> *not likely, I shall write to you again. Colonel Sandys will receive a*
> *letter from me by this fleet. Continue to remember me in your*
> *prayers, as a weak brother. I shall always think of you as one to be*
> *loved and honoured.*
>
> *H. Martyn.*

This is his final letter to Lydia before setting out by river for Dinapore first on the Hooghli and then on the mighty Mother Ganges. His next letter to her is not until over a year later on October 24th, 1807 when she has received his proposal and replied.

This sense of optimism about Lydia coming is reflected in a letter dated September or early October 1806 which he writes on the Hooghli River to Emma from his *budgerow or barge about 100 miles up the river from Calcutta, proceeding to my station — and for the first time alone with the natives.* After mentioning letters he has received from her and Lydia on September 20th and letters he had sent at the beginning of the same month to Lydia, Sally, Mr. Grant and Simeon and the one above to Lydia on the 14th he continues:

> *Much of my time is spent, perhaps too much, in thinking*
> *of Lydia. I think so long and so fondly of her, that I generally find*
> *that at the conclusion of my reveries, that I have been only*
> *employed with idolatrous industry in setting her up on a pedestal,*
> *and then comes the painful work of taking the idol down again. I*
> *suppose from what you said that you saw dear Lydia's letter. The*
> *avowal of her regard affected me so strongly that I could not forget*
> *it day or night. How it justifies the propriety of my application to*
> *her, if that needed any justification! Since the receipt of that letter,*
> *I have scarcely a doubt left of our Father's having designed her for*
> *me, or rather for this country ... Of all who will feel pain at her*
> *departure from England, you will suffer most ... As I expect that*
> *she will have left England two months before this reaches you, I*
> *think it is needless to address any more letters to her ... As soon as*
> *she arrives in the river, Mrs Brown (a most sensible and zealous*
> *woman) will go down 50 or 60 miles to bring her up, so that she*
> *will not have the least trouble, and in ten or twelve days I can be*
> *down from Dinapore ... I please myself with the idea of visiting*
> *these places the next time in company with Lydia, and of walking*
> *with her morning and evening on these delightful banks ...*
> *Marriage, with all its consolations, opens new sources of care, and*
> *is reserving one or the other for the severest of all temporal*
> *afflictions. While keeping these sorrowful certainties in view, there*
> *will be less danger of our expectations being excessive.*

This letter from Lydia to which he refers and which Emma has seen has made him openly optimistic about Lydia leaving England to marry him. The phrase *the avowal of her regard* suggests that Henry has misinterpreted her feelings. In her Diary Lydia expresses her regret at using the phrase and feels she has been guilty of misleading him. It seems strange that Emma did not draw her attention to the danger in expressing her feelings in these terms if she did not wish to encourage Henry's plan to marry her. A possible explanation could be that Lydia found solace in writing to Henry from the privacy of her room, away from the disapproving comments of her mother, and perhaps allowed her pen to run away with her emotions towards this young man who espoused his religious views with such zeal. In her isolation within her immediate family in Marazion she perhaps created an idealised Henry, to whom she was sexually attracted, but who was now safely out of physical reach in India, and disguised the fact under a relationship based on shared religious zeal.

Henry left for the military garrison of Dinapore, near Patna and Bankipore, where civil administration was based, on October 15th, 1806 by barge or "budgerow", which was hauled for about 20 miles per day when the weather and river conditions were good, first up the Hooghli, which could be a treacherous river with sandbanks and flooding, to Berhampore and then on to the great military station at Moorshedabad before joining the holy river Ganges and then up to Dinapore. While visiting the hospital at Berhampore on October 27th he meets by chance an old school friend from Truro who is the surgeon there. He greets him with *Bless me, it is Martyn! I soon recognised my old schoolfellow and townsman, John Marshall.* They spent a happy evening together on the budgerow no doubt reminiscing about their schooldays and Dr. Cardew, their old headmaster. However, Henry's attempts the following day to preach to the 150 patients at the hospital did not meet with success: *after waiting a long time, wandering through the wards, hoping the men would get up and assemble, I went away amid the sneers and titters of the common soldiers.*

The whole journey took about six weeks and Henry spent his time continuing learning Sanscrit and Arabic and translating the Acts into Urdu. For the first time he was alone in the company of Indians and isolated from other Europeans while travelling until he reached the military station at Dinapore on November 26th. Henry was responsible for the spiritual care of two European regiments as well as the Europeans at the East India Company's civil station at nearby Bankipore. Patna, the second city in Bengal with half a million native population was also close. He describes a visit there on December 1st:

> *Early this morning I set off in my palanquin for Patna.*
> *Something brought the remembrance of my dear Lydia so*
> *powerfully to my mind that I could not cease thinking of her for a*
> *moment. I know not when my reflections seemed to turn so fondly*
> *to her; at the same time I scarcely dare to wish her to come to this*
> *country. The whole country is manifestly disaffected. I was struck*
> *by the anger and contempt with which multitudes of the natives*
> *eyed me in my palanquin.*

Henry is feeling depressed and isolated in his new posting and vents his feelings towards the local Muslims with this outburst:

> *Let men do their worst, let me be torn to pieces, and my*
> *dear Lord torn from me. Here every man I meet is an enemy,*
> *being an enemy to God, he is an enemy to me also on that account;*
> *but he is an enemy too to me, because I am an Englishmen. What*
> *a wonderful place heaven must be, where there are none but*
> *friends. Indeed England appears almost a heaven upon earth,*
> *because there one is not viewed as an unjust intruder.*

Yet he had written at Berhampore: *It is extraordinary, that I seldom or ever meet with contempt on account of religion except from Englishmen, and from them invariably. A prophet is not without honour, save —. An English saint is undoubtedly one of the greatest characters on earth. His native solidity softened by grace makes him venerable; but the pride and contempt of God so remarkable in the bulk of the nation seem to be the forerunners of a humbling stroke.* Although Henry's faith is unshakeable even though his extempore preaching did not go down well with his European flock and *it was intimated to him, by letter, that it was their wish that he should desist from extempore preaching* it is perhaps now more than ever Henry needed a wife to share these problems of anomie as he adapted to life at Dinapore cut off from his former circle of missionaries at Serampore and Calcutta. Henry is only too aware that the year

1807 could be a watershed in his personal life and writes on January 1st: *And since this year will determine whether Lydia shall be given to me or no, let the Lord order it, so that whatever the event be, it may be finally good for all souls!*

It was while he was at Dinapore that he first met Captain and Mrs. Henry Sherwood. He was paymaster to the 53rd Regiment of Infantry and they were en route to Cawnpore where Henry would later meet up with them again. Mrs. Sherwood was a remarkable woman.[42] She was the same age as Lydia and was the daughter of a clergyman who became chaplain to George III. She had been educated under a strict and at times severe regime at home in Kidderminster: she was made to wear an iron collar and stand in stocks while having lessons. She became a prolific writer of tracts and pamphlets as well as writing moral tales for young children. In her Diary she describes the problems and perils of bringing up children in India which she knew to her cost only too well, and the day to day life and people she met, including Thomason, Brown, Corrie and Henry Martyn who was later to become a close friend in Cawnpore. She was deeply influenced by Henry's views on religion which she incorporated into an evangelical story which was published under the title *Little Henry and his Bearer.* She describes Henry Martyn as *Walking in this turbulent world with peace in his mind and charity in his heart.* However Henry's living arrangements at Dinapore were somewhat spartan even for Mrs. Sherwood and she describes how he invites them to spend two nights with him when she is unfortunately suffering from neuralgia: *there was no such thing as a pillow in the house. I could not find anything to lay my head on at night but a bolster, stuffed as hard as a pin-cushion. We had not, as is normal brought our own bedding from the boats. Probably the good man had given us his own room; but I could get no rest during the two nights of my remaining there, from the pain in my face.*

Henry is missing the solace of regular letters from his family. He writes to Emma's husband in 1807: *my dear faithfull Lydia has more than compensated for all the neglect of my own relations. I believe she has sent me more than all the rest in England put together. If I had not loved her before, her*

---

[42] Martha Mary Sherwood, 1775 – 1851: author of *Little Henry and his Bearer:* Edinburgh: 1814 (first published anonymously).

affectionate and constant remembrance of me would win my heart. Lydia is proving to be a good correspondent, she writes six letters to Henry before receiving his proposal. The first is lost in the *Bell* Packet but the others all seem to have been couched in affectionate terms and Henry's references to her are full of praise. He continues his letter with grumbles about his sister Sally being a poor correspondent and also refers to Laura, his sister, who is terminally ill and would die later that year from tuberculosis, the family complaint. He continues: *You mention the name of your last little one (may she be a follower of her namesake). It reminds me of what Mr Brown has lately written to me. He says that Mrs B. had determined that her expected one should be called after me but as it proved to be a girl, it was called Lydia Martyn Brown, a combination that suggests many reflections in my own mind.* Henry seems to have had a natural affinity with children and the reference to the Browns' new baby daughter leads him to daydream of having children himself with Lydia. He refers to playing with the Reverend and Mrs. Brown's children and clearly adored Mrs. Sherwood's infant daughter in Cawnpore. The Sherwoods later named one of their sons after him. Henry Martyn Sherwood, their second son, was born in 1813 at Meerut, after Henry had left for Persia. Daniel Corrie was his godfather. Corrie recounted how, when visiting the Sherwoods in Worcester several years later when he was on furlough, recovering from ill-health, he heard the voice of a child speaking Hindustani and realised that it was his godson.

Henry is now 26 and is busy setting up native schools, which he finances out of his own pocket, in Dinapore, Patna and Bankipore with a total of some 120 boys. He meets criticism from the European community on January 2nd, 1807: *Visited the place of the school to see how the building was going on, and in my way met many of the Europeans taking their evening exercise. They seem to hate to see me associating with the natives and — gave me a hint a few days ago, about taking my exercise on foot. But if our Lord had always travelled about in his palanquin, the poor woman, who was healed by touching the hem of his garment, might have perished. Happily I am freed from the shackles of custom; and the fear of man, though not extirpated, does not prevail.* He also meets opposition from some of the local schoolmasters who are critical of Henry for what they regard as the Europeanisation of native children by converting them to Christianity — a theme which Mrs. Sherwood would use in her book *'Little Henry and his Bearer'*. He is in close correspondence with Corrie who has set up similar schools at Chunar, near Benares. Henry decides to translate the church service into Hindustani so that the Eurasian women attached to the East India Company's regiment will understand it. Much to his joy he reports that on March 23rd 200 women attend. His health however, is not good and in April, with the approaching hot season, he records loss of appetite, sickness and pain yet he continues to make long journeys to marry officers, baptise children, visit hospitals and officiate at burials.

In a letter to Simeon dated April 26th his views on marriage seem to be very different from those when he wrote to Lydia proposing:

My Dearest friend and Brother,

All your letters, eight in number, have reached me and every of them demand my warmest acknowledgements. But I think I observe, that since my notification of my wishes to become a married man, your letters are not so affectionate. Know therefore that I rejoice in my celibacy; and am finally resolved to abide by my first determination, to be single like yourself, and for the same reason I trust that I may care only for the things of the Lord. Your proposal therefore, respecting some young lady coming out in the fleet, is highly unacceptable to me; for were my regard to Miss G. at all diminished, which it is not, yet I am so sick of the idea of all earthly connections so pregnant with sorrow, that it seems that I would rather die than marry.

His reference to a young woman being sent out to him as a prospective wife by Simeon reveals that Simeon must have been well aware by this time of Mrs. Grenfell's opposition to the marriage. Presumably in his position in England with his close connections to Grant and the Clapham Sect he could guarantee finding a suitable candidate who, with the backing of her family, would embrace the chance to spread the Gospel. Henry is clearly not about to give up on Lydia but his view on marriage is a very negative one here. He is now fully absorbed with working on the translation of the New Testament into Urdu and in June he is asked by David Brown to commence on overseeing the translation of the New Testament into Persian. From Henry's comments in his Journal it is clear that he finds the translation work enjoyable: *The time fled imperceptibly, while so delightfully engaged in the translations; the days seemed to have passed like a moment.* When he is offered the opportunity to return to Calcutta he refuses, preferring to stay in Dinapore. He responds to the invitation from Brown: *If ever I am fixed at Calcutta, I have done with the native.*

Henry still burns to convert the Hindus and from his Journal for 1807 he seems to have adapted to his solitary life at Dinapore on which he comments to Corrie *a long residence in college has rather prepared me for it.* Although he is finding the heat at 92°F almost unbearable and comments on his complete loss of appetite he appears relatively content: he is working hard studying Arabic, translating, distributing tracts, setting up schools and ministering to the sick at the hospital. But by July he is longing to receive Lydia's reply to his proposal. His optimism that she will come is undiminished. He refers to having received Lydia's profile and in a letter to Emma requests *her miniature picture, and you must draw on Mr Simeon, my banker, for the expense ... I need not assure you and Cousin T. of my unceasing regard, nor Lydia of my unalterable attachment. God bless you all, my beloved friends. Pray for me, as I do also for you. Our separation will soon be over*

On July 3rd he refers to receiving *two Europe letters — one from Lydia, and the other from Colonel Sandys.* However, they have been written before Lydia has received his proposal. The tone of Lydia's letter does nothing to dispel Henry's expectations of her coming out to him although he expresses disappointment that she does not express her love for him as ardently as he would wish: *The tender emotions of love and gratitude, and veneration for her, were again powerfully awakened in my mind, so that I could with difficulty think of anything else; yet I found myself drawn nearer to God by the pious remarks of her letter. Nature would have desired more testimonies of her love to me, but grace approved her ardent love to her Lord.* Henry has now waited a year for Lydia's reply. In a letter to Mrs. Brown at Aldeen dated July 21st the reason for this delay is explained: *It appears that the letter by the overland despatch did not reach Lydia. Again the* Sarah Christiana *packet, which carried the duplicate, ought to have arrived long before the sailing of these last two ships from England, but I have no account of her. It is probable that I shall have to wait a considerable time longer in uncertainty.* This would suggest that in fact Lydia received first, his third letter from Serampore dated September — approximately September 14th — as he refers to his second duplicate letter of proposal which he wrote on September 1st: *About a fortnight ago I sent you a letter accompanying the duplicate of the one I sent overland in August* — on March 2nd, 1807 to which she replies on March 5th. Henry receives this on October 24th, 1807. This would explain why when she received the duplicate letter of proposal, written on September 1st, 1806, on April 23rd, 1807, it triggers a meeting with Simeon at Sandys's house at Lanarth on April 25th and the following day she writes a second letter of farewell to Henry.

Henry receives another packet of letters from Europe, including another letter from Lydia on July 30th: *still kept in ignorance about the Lord's purposes respecting Lydia, and likely to remain so some time.* In the same packet is a letter from his sister Sally with the news that his eldest sister, Laura, has died which affects him deeply. She has succumbed to tuberculosis which will later also kill Sally. Her death makes him begin to question his isolation from his remaining family. His life is further shattered when Lydia's reply finally arrived in October, some 15 months after he had sent his first proposal.

Lydia did not receive his proposal, dated July 30th, 1806, until nine months later in March 1807. Up till then she has been in regular correspondence with Henry. Life for her in Marazion during 1806 is dominated by her increasing introspection and piety, periods of illness and discord within the family: August 2nd, 1806: *My family's unhappiness preys on my mind, — sister against sister, brother against brother, a father against his children. O what a picture! Let me not add to the weight of family sin; August 28th: Went to Marazion, and had the salvation of seeing my mother and Phillis spend the day affectionately together, and being received myself kindly by my father; October 3rd: I thought a week ago that to spend some hours every day with my poor and unhappy father must rob me of comfort in the Lord ... but seeing it as a plain command to spend time with my father, and by seeking the Lord's blessed help in performing my duty, I have found the most delightful peace, both in and after doing it.* She refers to letters she has written to *dear*

Henry or as on May 30th simply: *Wrote to dear H.* and records receiving news of him through Emma. But, on March 2nd, 1807, when she returns from spending a few days with her married sister, Mary, at Tregembo, a letter from Henry is waiting for her. *My return was marked by two events, long to be remembered — seeing John* [a brother] *and hearing from H.M. Great has been my distress, but peace is returned, and could I cease from anticipating future evils, I should enjoy more. The Lord has been gracious in affording me help, but He made me first feel my weakness, and suffered Satan to harass me. I am called upon now to act a decisive part. Lord, Thou knowest I desire only what Thou shalt command, — teach me to do Thy will.* As his first letter never reached Lydia and his second letter with duplicate was delayed it seems likely that this letter was in fact his third letter from Serampore in which he is confidently expecting her to have possibly already embarked. Henry refers in this third letter from Serampore of having sent Colonel Sandys a letter by the same fleet.

Lydia finally writes to Henry on March 5th refusing him. The pain and tormented anguish she is going through are evident in her entry on March 8th in her Diary. It reads:

> *Twice have I been called on to act* — (here a line has been erased by a subsequent writer)[43] *in a way few are tried in, but the Lord's goodness towards me is so manifest in the first, that I have come to wait in silence and hope the event of this. I am satisfied I have done now what is right, and peace has returned to me, — yet there is need of great watchfulness to resist the enemy of souls, who would weaken and depress my soul, bringing to remembrance the affection of my dear friend, and representing my conduct as ungrateful towards him. Today I have had many distressing feelings on his account, yet in general I have been looking to things invisible and eternal, and therefore enjoyed peace; I must live more in the contemplation of Christ and Heavenly things. O come, fill and satisfy my soul, be my leader*

---

[43] Footnote by Jeffery.

and guide, dispose of me as Thou wilt. The pain of writing to him
is over, and I feel satisfied I wrote what duty required of me.

In her letter, which Henry received on October 24th, the content can be pieced together from Henry's reply. Lydia refused his proposal and blamed herself for giving him encouragement in the belief that his attachment was returned. She also blames *present circumstances* which Henry will refer to as *obstacles* and does his pragmatic best to find answers to in his reply. The key obstacle is the indomitable Mrs. Grenfell.

Lydia reports the arrival of letters on April 23rd, 1807. Henry's first letter proposing, dated July 30th, 1806, sent overland, failed to reach Lydia so it would suggest that here she refers to the arrival of his second letter from Serampore, dated September 1st, 1806, together with a duplicate of his first letter. These letters had been delayed in the *Sarah Christiana* Packet. Having taken the painful decision in March to turn down his proposal this second appeal to her upsets her deeply: *April 23rd. Today my mind has been painfully affected by the receipt of letters from —* [44]. *I found in the presence of my mother I dared not indulge the inclination I feel to mourn.* Poor Lydia she is under such emotional constraint that she feels unable to express her grief over the whole affair in the presence of her mother who is one of the major reasons why she felt unable to join Henry in India. Instead she wrote *what duty required me.* Mrs. Grenfell seems to have won her way by insisting that her youngest daughter fulfil her filial duty and remain at home to look after her in her advancing years.

The following day none other than Charles Simeon arrived to intercede for Henry and Lydia takes strength from his calm and logical approach to the situation: *The arrival of dear Mr Simeon has been a cordial to my fainting heart.* Four days later she refers to going to Helston with Simeon when they visited Colonel Sandys, who lived at Lanarth, near St. Keverne, on the Lizard Peninsula, for further discussion and advice on the matter, especially as he had also received a letter from Henry in March in which the main topic would most likely have been Lydia. On April 29th she writes: *The state of my*

---

[44] Letters written in September 1806 from Serampore.

mind lately has led me to fill too much of my Diary with expressions of regard for an earthly object, and now I am convinced of the evil of indulging this affection. O may the Lord enable me to mortify it, may this mirror of my heart show me more of love to God and less to anything earthly. This morning was a sad one, and to the present I have to mourn over the barrenness of my soul, its indisposedness to any spiritual exertion. Almost constantly do I remember my dear absent friend, may I do so with less pain. Lydia then hears a rumour which unsettles her further: *May 2nd: Today and yesterday I have found more composure of mind than of late; once indeed the enemy (whose devices I am too ignorant of to meet them as I ought) succeeded in distracting my mind, and excited many sinful passions from the probability that a Miss Corin, [sic.], who is going to her dear brother, may be the partner appointed for my dear friend. This continued for a short time only, and I found relief at a throne of grace. It is a subject I must not dwell on, — when the trial comes, grace will be given; but at the moment I have none to meet it; yet I have prayed the Lord to provide him a suitable help-mate. Deceitful is my heart, how little do I know it! O Thou bleeding Saviour, let me hide myself in Thee from deserved wrath, and O speak peace once more to my soul.*

The rumour that Miss Corrie was going out to become Henry's wife was totally without foundation but at this difficult time for Lydia it must have added to her heartbreak. Henry refers to this rumour in a letter to Simeon on April 26th, 1807 and in his letter to Lydia, August 14th, 1810. Poor Lydia is suffering the grief of having broken off the relationship. Coupled with it is the realisation that all her romantic dreams are dashed on the shore of her mother's wilful intransigence. Alone in her torment she confides to her Diary on May 5th that she is seized *with a violent depression of spirits and a sadness of heart, hard to be concealed. I have not as before, fallen into a long train of vain imaginations, drawing scenes improbable and vain, but my soul has lost its spiritual appetite. I am looking forward to distant and uncertain events with anticipations of sorrow and trial impending. O my Lord and my God, come to my relief.* A reference to Henry receiving her refusal which would put an end to their correspondence. A further cause for her distress seems to have been *a dread of dishonouring the name of the Lord by appearing to have acted deceitfully in the eyes of the family, and some pride is at the bottom of this (I like not to be thought ill of), and also pain for the disappointment my dear friend will soon know. His situation grieves me infinitely more than my own.* Lydia is torn by guilt that she has deceived her family as to Henry's true feelings towards her, which had become only too apparent with the arrival of his letter, and anguish for Henry when he receives her letter.

On May 20th Lydia expresses concern that she has *not given too much reason for my dear friend's hoping I might be prevailed on to attend to his request, and I feel the restraint stronger than ever, that, having before promised, I am not free to marry. I paint the scene of his return, and, which ever way I take, nothing but misery and guilt seems to await me.* It is clear from this that Lydia still feels that she is duty bound by her former engagement to Samuel John not to marry until he has done so. Her guilt is compounded further by the thought of meeting Henry when he returns to England. She then continues by giving an insight into her behaviour towards him: *that when I regarded him otherwise than as a Christian brother, I believed myself free to do so, imagining him I first loved to be united to another. When I consider this circumstance my mind is relieved of a heavy burden, and yet I must lament the evils that have flown from this mistake.* She had wrongly assumed that John would marry in 1804 or soon thereafter and so had permitted herself to see Henry in a different light as an attractive, unattached man who most importantly would provide the spiritual companionship and guidance for which she yearned so deeply. In a cruel turn of fate the obstacle of Samuel John's marrying was not resolved until 1810.

For the rest of 1807 Lydia continues to suffer with uncertainty over how Henry will react to her refusal and vacillates between an acceptance that she will never see him again and the pain that this gives her: *I chide myself for every painful feeling of the probability of our meeting no more occasions, yet they return again and again, when I have fancied myself wholly resigned to it.* She is now 32, well into middle-age for a woman of that time, and has broken off two relationships.

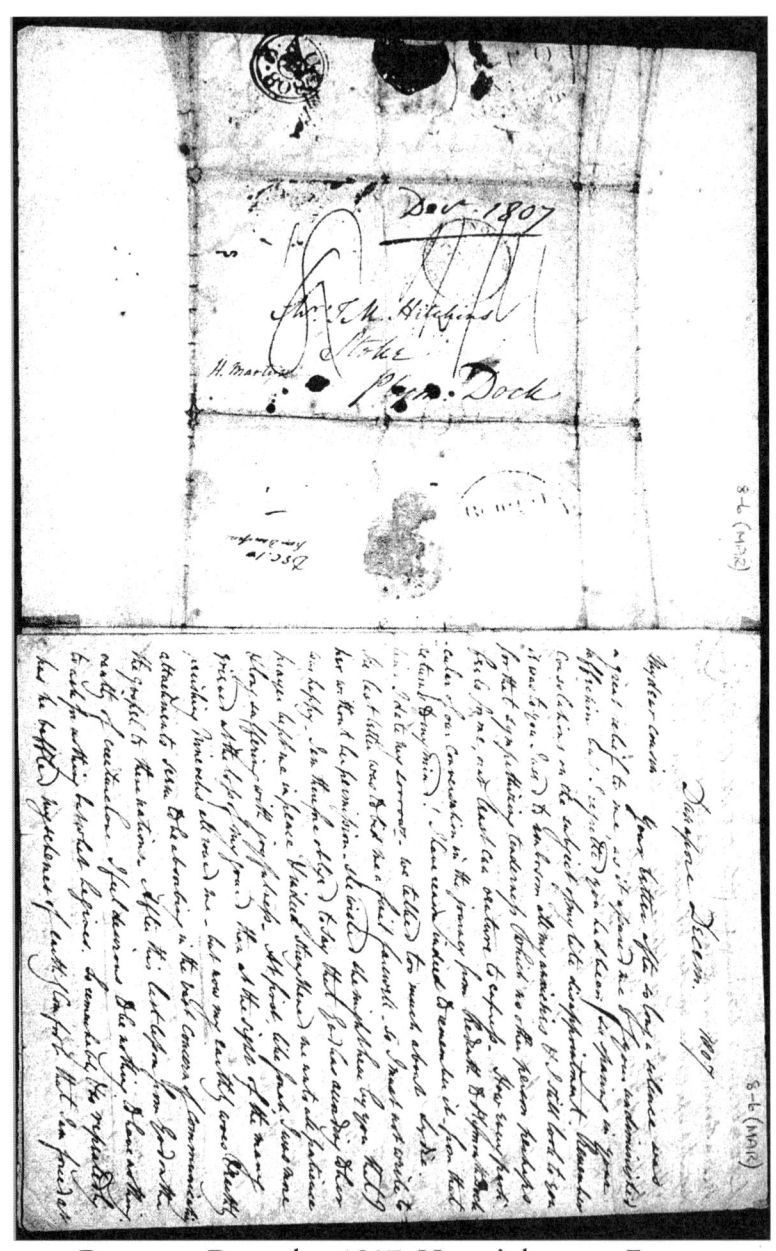

Dinapore, December 1807: Henry's letter to Emma

Chapter 9 — 'I write not to blame you'

Henry did not receive Lydia's refusal[45] until October 24th, 1807 almost 15 months after his proposal of July 30th, 1806. It is a shattering blow: *An unhappy day; received at last a letter from Lydia in which she refuses to come because her mother will not consent to it. Grief and disappointment threw my soul into confusion at first; but gradually, as my disorder subsided, my eyes were opened, and reason resumed its office. I could not but agree with her, that it would not be for the glory of God, nor could we expect his blessing, if she acted in disobedience to her mother. As she has said, "They that walk in crooked paths, shall not find peace;" and if she were to come with an uneasy conscience, what happiness could either of us expect?* Mrs. Grenfell had intervened and reminded Lydia of filial duty as the last remaining unmarried daughter at home, in spite of the probability that Mary would continue living close to Marazion.

The difficulties and frustrations of conducting a courtship by post from India with long delays between sending a letter and receiving a reply are only too apparent. Henry wasted no time and began his reply the same day in a long, eloquent and well-reasoned letter. In it he responds to all the obstacles perceived or real that Lydia has put forward against joining him in India. This is the full text:

TO MISS L. GRENFELL.

Dinapore, Oct. 24. 1807.

---

[45] Written March 5th, 1807 and received by Henry October 24th, 1807.

MY DEAR LYDIA,

*Though my heart is bursting with grief and
disappointment, I write not to blame you. The rectitude of all your
conduct secures you from censure. Permit me calmly to reply to
your letter of March 5, which I have this day received.*

*You condemn yourself for having given me, though
unintentionally, encouragement to believe that my attachment
was returned. Perhaps you have. I have read your former letters
with feelings less sanguine since the receipt of the last, and I am
still not surprised at the interpretation I put upon them. But why
accuse yourself for having written in this strain? It has not
increased my expectations, nor consequently embittered my
disappointment. When I addressed you in my first letter on the
subject, I was not induced to it by any appearances of regard you
had expressed, neither at any subsequent period have my hopes of
your consent been founded on a belief of your attachment to me. I
knew that your conduct would be regulated, not by personal
feelings, but by a sense of duty. And therefore you have nothing to
blame your-self for on this head.*

*In your last letter you do not assign, among your reasons
for refusal, a want of regard to me. In that case I could not in
decency give you any further trouble. On the contrary, you say that
'present circumstances seem to you to forbid my indulging
expectations.' As this leaves an opening, I presume to address you
again; and till the answer arrives, must undergo another eighteen
months of torturing suspense.*

*Alas! my rebellious heart, what a tempest agitates me! I
knew not that I had made so little progress in a spirit of
resignation to the divine will. I am in my chastisement like the
bullock unaccustomed to the yoke, like a wild bull in a net, full of
the fury of the Lord, the rebuke of my God. The death of my late*

most beloved sister almost broke my heart; but I hoped it had softened me and made me willing to suffer. But now my heart is as though destitute of the grace of God, full of misanthropic disgust with the world, and sometimes feeling resentment against yourself and Emma, and Mr. Simeon, and in short, all whom I love and honour most. Sometimes in pride and anger resolving to write neither to you nor to any one else again. These are the motions of sin. My love and my better reason draw me to you again.

But now with respect to your mother, I confess that the chief and indeed only difficulty lies here. Considering that she is your mother, as I hoped she would be mine, and that her happiness so much depends on you; considering also that I am God's minister, which amidst, all the tumults of my soul I dare not forget, I falter in beginning to give advice which may prove contrary to the law of God. God forbid therefore that I should say, disobey your parents where the divine law does not command you to disobey them; neither do I positively take upon myself to say that this is a case in which the law of God requires you to act in contradiction to them. I would rather suggest to your mother some considerations which justify me in attempting to deprive her of the company of a beloved child.

26. A sabbath having intervened since the above was written, I find myself more tranquillized by the sacred exercises of the day. One passage of Scripture which you quote has been much on my mind, and I find it very appropriate and decisive, — that we are not to "make to ourselves crooked paths, which whoso walketh in shall not know peace." Let me say I must be therefore contented to wait till you feel that the way is clear. But I intended to justify myself to Mrs. Grenfell. Let her not suppose that I would make her, or any other of my fellow-creatures miserable, that I might be happy. If there were no reason for your coming here, and the contest were only between Mrs. Grenfell and me, that is between her happiness and mine, I would urge nothing further, but resign you to her. But I have considered that there are many things that might reconcile her to a separation from you (if indeed a separation is necessary, for if she would come along with you, I should rejoice the more). First, she does not depend on you alone for the comfort of her declining years. She is surrounded by friends. She has a greater number of sons and daughters honourably established in the world, than falls to the lot of most parents — all of whom would be happy in having her amongst them. Again, if a person worthy of your hand, and settled in England, were to offer himself, Mrs. G. would not have insuperable objections, though it did deprive her of her daughter. Nay I sometimes think, perhaps arrogantly, that had I myself remained in England, and in possession of a competency, she would not have withheld her consent. Why then should my banishment from my native country in the service of mankind, be a reason with any for inflicting an additional wound, far more painful than a separation from my dearest relatives?

I have no claim upon Mrs. G. in any way, but let her only conceive a son of her own in my circumstances. If she feels it a sacrifice, let her remember that it is a sacrifice made to duty; that your presence here would be of essential service to the church of God, it is superfluous to attempt to prove. If you really believe of yourself as you speak, it is because you were never out of England.

Your mother cannot be so misinformed respecting India and the voyage to it, as to be apprehensive on account of the clime or passage, in these days, when multitudes of ladies every year, with constitutions as delicate as yours, go to and fro in perfect safety, and a vastly greater majority enjoy their health here than in England. With respect to my means, I need add nothing to what was said in my first letter. But alas! what is my affluence good for now? It never gave me pleasure, but when I thought you were to share it with me. Two days ago I was hastening on the alterations in my house and garden, supposing you were at hand; but now every object excites disgust. My wish upon the whole is, that if you perceive it would be your duty to come to India, were it not for your mother, — and of that you cannot doubt, — supposing I mean that your inclinations are indifferent, then you should make her acquainted with your thoughts, and let us leave it to God how he will determine her mind.

In the mean time, since I am forbidden to hope for the immediate pleasure of seeing you, my next request is for a mutual engagement. My own heart is engaged, I believe indissolubly.

My reason for making a request which you will account bold, is that there can then be no possible objection to our correspondence, especially as I promise not to persuade you to leave your mother.

In the midst of my present sorrow I am constrained to remember yours. Your compassionate heart is pained from having been the cause of suffering to me. But care not for me, dearest Lydia. Next to the bliss of having you with me, my happiness is to know that you are happy. I shall have to groan long perhaps with a heavy heart; but if I am not hindered materially by it in the work of God, it will be for the benefit of my soul. You, sister beloved in the Lord, know much of the benefit of affliction. O may I have grace to follow you, though at a humble distance, in the path of patient suffering, in which you have walked so long. Day and night I cease not to pray for you, though I fear my prayers are of little value.

But as an encouragement to you to pray, I cannot help transcribing a few words from my journal, written at the time you wrote your letter to me. (7th March.) 'As on the two last days (you wrote your letter on the 5th), felt no desire for a comfortable

111

settlement in the world, scarcely pleasure at the thought of Lydia's coming, except so far as her being sent might be for the good of my soul, and assistance in my work.' How manifestly is there an omnipresent, all-seeing God, and how sure we may be that prayers for spiritual blessings are heard by our God and Father. 0 let that endearing name quell every murmur. When I am sent for to different parts of the country to officiate at marriages, I sometimes think, amidst the festivity of the company, Why does all go so easily with them, and so hardly with me? They come together without difficulty, and I am balked and disconcerted almost every step I take, and condemned to wear away the time in uncertainty. Then I call to mind that to live without chastening, is allowed to the spurious offspring; while to suffer is the privilege of the children of God.

Dearest Lydia, must I conclude? I could prolong my communion with you through many sheets; how many things have I to say to you, which I hoped to have communicated in person. But the more I write and the more I think of you, the more my affection warms, and I should feel it difficult to keep my pen from expressions that might not be acceptable to you.

Farewell! dearest, most beloved Lydia, remember your faithful and ever affectionate,

H. MARTYN.[46]

From this letter it is clear that the major obstacle to Lydia's coming out to India and joining him is her mother, and her reasonable anxiety for Lydia's safety, not only on the long and arduous voyage out but also once she had arrived in India. There is also the question of Lydia's true feelings for Henry. Henry first generously absolves Lydia from any guilt she may feel at having unwittingly encouraged him in her letters to believe her feelings for him were

---

[46]Henry's letter, October 24th, 1807 received by Lydia May 9th, 1808.

deeper than affection. He continues by acknowledging that he knew that her sense of duty would govern any decision but builds his hope of winning her round by the fact that she does not give *a want of regard for me* as a reason for turning him down. Henry's determination and optimism show themselves when he uses this argument to justify his request that she consider his proposal again. The time lapse involved in conducting a courtship by post between India and Cornwall is evident in his remark: *and till the answer arrives, must undergo another eighteen months of torturing suspense.*

Henry's sense of isolation from his family is revealed when he refers to the death of his elder sister Laura. With this in mind he then turns to the key subject of the letter — Mrs. Grenfell: *But now with respect to your mother, I confess that the chief and only difficulty lies here. Considering that she is your mother, as I hoped she would be mine, and that her happiness much depends on you.* Unfortunately for Henry any hopes he may have harboured of being welcomed into the Grenfell family were to be dashed in the face of Mrs. Grenfell's implacable opposition to his proposal.

Henry takes a break from his letter for a day, the Sabbath, and returns in a calmer frame of mind to try to answer all the points which Lydia has raised in her letter which have led to her refusal. Mrs. Grenfell is still uppermost in his mind. Although the tone is careful it is critical and implies that Mrs. Grenfell is acting selfishly in this matter when she has family and friends *for the comfort of her declining years.* Henry was not to know that she would outlive him to a ripe old age. He even tries to generously accommodate Mrs. Grenfell: *if indeed a separation is necessary, for if she would come along with you I should rejoice the more.* He must have known in his heart that this was a totally unrealistic proposal. He argues that had he remained in England he would have been deemed acceptable to her and then makes some rather terse remarks in his comments on Mrs. Grenfell's view of travelling out to India and life there: *Your mother cannot be so misinformed respecting India and the voyage to it, as to be apprehensive on account of the clime or passage, in these days when multitudes of ladies every year, with constitutions as delicate as yours, go to and fro in perfect safety, and a vastly greater majority enjoy their health here than in England.* But both Henry, who had faced the voyage, and Mrs. Grenfell would be only too well apprised of the discomforts and dangers facing women in the long voyage out. No doubt she would also be only too well aware of the dangers posed by disease and the intense heat once Lydia had arrived in India. Diseases such as cholera, tuberculosis, malaria and dysentery were all prevalent in India. If Henry and Lydia produced children there would be the very real threat of losing one or more children in infancy in an epidemic. Then there would be the heartbreaking decision of whether to send them home to England at a tender age to be educated. Often children hardly knew their parents when they finally were reunited as Mrs. Sherwood found to her cost with her eldest daughter. The terrible heat of the plains followed by the monsoon when rivers flooded and broke their banks would be very different from the natural hazards of gales and storms lashing the coast in Cornwall. Life in Marazion was a known and safer world, conducted within well-known social parameters. Moreover, Lydia had a close network of family and friends whereas in India, although she could have busied herself with good works as Mrs. Sherwood did, there would be times when boredom and the isolation from Europe would depress her.

Henry's appeal to Lydia and her sense of duty to God put her in agonising torment when she finally received this letter in May the following year. Although Henry argues that Lydia should make her mother *acquainted with your thoughts* it is evident from her Diary that their relationship makes this impossible. Henry then asks Lydia to agree to a mutual engagement so *that there can then be no possible objection to our correspondence* and further promising *not to persuade you to leave your mother.* He is prepared to settle for a long-term distant relationship based on correspondence rather than lose touch with her completely. A tone of self-pity is evident in his reference to his officiating at other people's weddings and his rhetorical question: *Why does all go so easily with them, and so hardly with me? They come together without difficulty, and I am balked and disconcerted almost every step I take, and condemned to wear away the time in uncertainty.* He finds the answer with *while to suffer is the privilege of the children of God.* He ends this moving letter with an expression of his deep frustration at being so far away from her with their only communication being by letter.

References in her Diary reveal the depth of Lydia's torment. She berates herself for vanity and deceitfulness yet she was clearly flattered by the attentions of Henry in 1805. Was she perhaps alarmed at the ardour of Henry but once he had set sail felt safe in continuing her correspondence with him — after her first letter which never reached him — safe in the knowledge of her self-imposed veto, that she was not free to marry until her former fiancé married, and fully aware of her mother's strong opposition? Did she allow her *imaginings* to carry into her letters and so offer poor Henry encouragement that her feelings for him were as strong as his for her? She must have been aware of his love for her from Emma in whom Henry had confided so much. No doubt she was flattered by his attention. Here was a young man whose Evangelicalism had led him to India and he was asking her to dedicate her life to the same cause. Their admiration for each other was rooted in their piety.

Unbeknown to Henry none other than Charles Simeon had interceded in April to try to persuade Lydia to go out to India. He visits her to try and persuade her by answering the obstacles she puts in the way of accepting Henry's proposal. These are Charles Simeon notes of his meeting with Lydia on April 25th:

> *With her mother's leave Miss Grenfell accompanied us to Col. Sandys; where I had much conversation with her about Mr Martyn's affair. She stated to me all the obstacles to his proposals; first her health; second the indelicacy of her going out to India alone on such an errand; third her former engagement to another person, which had indeed been broken off, and he had actually gone up to London two years ago to be married to another woman; but as he was unmarried, it seemed an obstacle in her mind; fourth the certainty that her mother would never consent to it.* Simeon answered: *On these points I observed that I thought the last was the only one that was insurmountable; for that, first, India often agreed best with persons of a delicate constitution, e.g. Mr Martyn himself and Mr Brown. Second, it is common for ladies to go thither without any previous connection, how much more therefore might one go with a connection already formed! Were this the only difficulty, I engaged with the help of Mr Grant*

*and Mr Parry, that she should go under such protection as should
obviate all difficulties upon this head. Third, the step taken by the
other person had set her at perfect liberty. Fourth, the consent of
her mother was indispensable; and as that appeared impossible,
the matter might be committed to God in this way; if her mother,
of her own accord, should express regret that the connection had
been prevented, from an idea of her being irreconcilably averse to
it, and that she would not stand in the way of her daughter's
wishes; this would be considered as a direction from God in answer
to her prayers, and I should instantly be apprised of it by her, in
order to communicate to Mr Martyn. In this she perfectly agreed. I
told her, however, that I would mention nothing of this to Mr M.,
because it would only tend to keep him in painful suspense. Thus
the matter is entirely set aside, unless God, by a special
interposition of His providence (i.e. by taking away her mother, or
overruling her mind, contrary to all reasonable expectation, to
approve of it) mark His own will concerning it.*

Simeon's reference *it is common for ladies to go thither without any previous
connection* is probably to the 'fishing fleet' which was the name given to
unattached ladies who travelled out to India in the hope of finding husbands.
By this time the practice was quite respectable whereas in the 1670s when the
East India Company introduced assisted passages for groups of unattached
females out to Madras some were disreputable! The 'fleet' would arrive in the
autumn to ensure that their fair complexions had not been spoilt by fierce
Indian sun: if they failed to find a husband they faced the ignominy of
returning to Britain labelled 'returned empty'. For the British men there was
also the practice of taking an Indian wife, or 'bibi' which was looked on
benignly until the arrival of Cornwallis who succeeded Warren Hastings as
Governor-General in 1786. By 1791 the Anglo-Indian male offspring of such
unions found themselves excluded from most positions in the Company.
Social exclusion was also taking place. By the early 19th century there was an
ever increasing number of European memsahibs travelling out to India. With
them they brought a stern reminder of European values and often an

arrogance in what they perceived as their intrinsic European superiority over the native Indian populace.

In spite of being able to put forward a pragmatic solution to three of the obstacles facing Lydia and Henry, Simeon has to accept that the obstacle of Mrs. Grenfell's opposition is insuperable. He commits the matter to God by stating that if Lydia's mother should at any time express regret at standing in the way of *her daughter's wishes* then this would be seen as a direction from God. Was he entirely governed by altruism or is he perhaps driven by a desire to ensure that Henry does not abandon his work and mission in India in order to return to England and Lydia? Whatever his motives were it would appear from these notes that Lydia would agree to marry Henry if her mother were to agree, *contrary to all reasonable expectation*, or if she were to die. Simeon is now clearly eager to promote the marriage whereas earlier he had expressed his doubts about its expediency. The accepted view on marriage and missionaries is very clearly expressed by George Smith in his book *Henry Martyn, Saint and Scholar*, published in 1892: *In these days the course followed by missionary societies as the result of experience is certainly the best. A missionary and a chaplain in India, should, in ordinary circumstances, be married, but it is not desirable that the marriage take place for a year or longer, until the young minister has proved the climate, and has learned the native language, when the lady can be sent out to be united to him. At the beginning of the modern missionary enterprise, a century ago, it was difficult to find spiritual men to go to India on any terms, and they did well in every case to go out married. All the conditions of time, distance, society, and Christian influence were then different. If the missionary's or chaplain's wife is worthy of his calling, she doubles his usefulness, notwithstanding the cares and the expense of children in many cases, alike by keeping her husband in a state of efficiency on every side, by her own works of charity and self-sacrifice — especially among the women, who can be reached in no other way — and by helping to present to the idolatrous Mussulman community, the powerful example of a Christian home. Henry Martyn's principles and instincts were right in this matter. As a chaplain, at any rate he was in a position to marry at once. As India or Bengal then was, Lydia, had she gone out with him, or soon after him, would have proved to be a much needed force in Anglo-Indian society.*

Lydia agreed to the arguments put forward by Simeon and she also agreed with Simeon's suggestion that Henry should not be told *because it would only tend to keep him in painful suspense* which reflects his empathy for him. In a letter from Henry to Emma, dated November 15th, 1805, an insight is given as to Mrs. Grenfell's relationship with Henry. He asks to be remembered to her mother: *if she considers me as now at sufficient distance.* However, Mrs. Grenfell may have had a more noble motive: that of safe-guarding her youngest daughter's mental health. This she could oversee while Lydia remained at home and in close contact with friends and family. But if she had agreed to her going to India then possibly Lydia's mental health could have deteriorated as it had in 1800, and would again in 1826, and she would have been thousands of miles from her family. Lydia seems content to put her trust in God for guidance and allows her mother's strong opposition and other arguments to over-rule her true feelings and persuade her against joining Henry. Was it perhaps that she was for some reason frightened of marrying and took refuge behind a smokescreen of difficulties feeling more fulfilled dedicating her life to God through prayer and good works, seeing her renunciation of marriage as a necessary sacrifice and duty by subsuming her own happiness if she was to attain her higher goal?

Henry refers to this setback repeatedly both in letters and in his Journal. In a letter to David Brown dated October 26th, 1807 the same day as he finished his impassioned letter to Lydia asking her to reconsider her decision, and characteristically empathising with her in his Journal by acknowledging the suffering this must be causing her, he writes:

> *My Dear Sir,*
>
> *I have received your last two letters of the 14th and 17th, the last contained a letter from Lydia. It is as I feared. She refuses to come, because her mother will not give her consent. Sir, you may wonder at my pale looks, when I receive so many blows to my heart.*

He includes a poignant domestic detail:

The queen's ware on its way out to me can be sold at an outcry or given to Corrie. I do not want queen's ware or anything else now. My new house and garden, without the person I expected to share it with me, excite disgust.

So certain had Henry been of Lydia joining him that he had ordered the Queen's Ware dinner service.

On November 25th Henry records receiving a second letter from Lydia which she had written in April to bid him a final farewell:

Letters came from Mr Simeon and Lydia, both of which depressed my spirits exceedingly; though I have been writing for some days past, that I might have it in my power to consider myself free, so as to be able to go to Persia or elsewhere; — yet now that the wished-for permission has come, I am filled with grief; I cannot bear to part with Lydia; and she seems more necessary than my life; yet her letter was to bid me a last farewell.

He records on November 26th in his Journal:

Received a letter from Emma, which again had a tendency to depress my spirits; all day I could not attain to sweet resignation to God, I seem to be cut off for ever from happiness in not having Lydia with me.

His response to Emma in December[47] underlines his growing sense of personal isolation:

My Dear Cousin,

Your letter after so long a silence was a great relief to me, as it assured me of your undiminished affection; but I regretted you had been so sparing in your consolations on the subject of my

---

[47] Original held at the Courtney Library, Royal Institution of Cornwall, Truro.

late disappointment. Remember it was to you I used to unbosom all my anxieties, and I still look to you for that sympathizing tenderness, which no other person perhaps feels for me, or at least can venture to express. How every particular of our conversation in the journey from Redruth to Plymouth Dock returns to my mind! I have reason indeed to remember it — from that time I date my sorrows — we talked too much about Lydia. Her last letter was to bid me a final farewell, so I must not write to her without her permission; she wished she might hear by you that I was happy ... Lydia allows me not the most distant prospect of ever seeing her; and if indeed the supposed indelicacy of her coming out to me is an obstacle that cannot be got over, it is likely indeed to be a lasting separation: for when shall I ever see it lawful to leave my work here for three years, when every hour is unspeakeably precious? I am beginning therefore to form my plans as a person in a state of celibacy, and mean to trouble you no more on what I have been writing so much. However, let me be allowed to make one request; it is that Lydia would at least consider me as she did before, and write as at that time. Perhaps there may be some objection to this request, and therefore I dare not urge it. I say only that by experience I know it will prove an inestimable blessing and comfort to me. If you really wish to have a detailed account of my proceedings, exert your influence in affecting this measure; for you may be sure, that I shall be disposed to write to her letters long enough, longer than any other, for this reason among others, that of the three in the world who have most love for me, i.e. Sally, Lydia, and yourself, I believe that, notwithstanding, all that has happened, the middle one loves most truly. If this conjecture of mine is well founded, she will be most interested in what befalls me, and I shall write in less fear of tiring.

He also refers to Lydia's profile which he has received and asks Emma: *I have now to request her miniature picture, and you must draw on Mr Simeon, my banker, for the expense.* Neither this plea for a mutual engagement nor plea for

120

a resumption of correspondence with Lydia met with any success immediately.

In January, 1808 Henry writes to Charles Simeon and this extract reveals that, although he now has accepted that celibacy will enable him to dedicate his life to God and has resigned himself to never seeing Lydia again, he still loves her:

> *My expectation of seeing Lydia here is now at an end —*
> *the affair which has cost me so many an anxious thought seems to*
> *be settled for me by God — for after such repeated and remarkable*
> *disappointments, I cannot doubt any longer what is the divine*
> *will, & I therefore bow to it. I have another & a stronger*
> *testimony within that celibacy is designed for me — for of late*
> *since I have been led to consider myself as perfectly disengaged from*
> *the affairs of this life, my soul has been filled with more ardent*
> *desires to spend & be spent in the service of God & tho in truth the*
> *world has now little to charm me, I think these desires do not arise*
> *from a misanthropic distrust to it. I beg therefore my dear brother*
> *[sic.] that nothing more may be said to Miss L.G. on the subject*
> *— for with the important plans I have in my mind & which*
> *marriage would entirely disconcert, I should be exceedingly sorry to*
> *hear she was coming. These my present feelings are in my*
> *judgement the suggestions of the Spirit & not of the flesh for I*
> *never loved, nor ever shall love, human creature as I love her.*[48]

Yet ironically it is during 1808 that rumours, which cause Lydia some disquiet, begin to circulate that Henry and Miss Corrie are planning to marry. David Brown writes a rather sharp response to Simeon: *How could you imagine that Miss C. would do as well as Miss L.G. for Mr Martyn? Dear Martyn is married already to three wives, whom I believe he would not forsake for all the promises on earth — I mean his three translations of the Holy Scriptures.* Henry was to receive two further letters from Lydia.

---

[48] Letter dated Dinapore January 1808, addressed to Charles Simeon at Ryde, Isle of White: MAR 1/16 Henry Martyn Centre, Cambridge.

In the early part of 1808 Lydia is teaching at the Sunday school which brings comfort to her and by March writes that she is reconciled to never seeing Henry again. However, this peace is shattered when in May she receives Henry's letter dated October 24th, 1807 from Dinapore *requesting me to come out.* Her letter dated May 9th, 1808, is in answer to his request in his letter for a mutual engagement, thereby hoping to ensure that the correspondence between them could continue. He notes on December 14th, 1808 in his Journal:

> *I received a letter from Lydia today which renewed my pain, though it contained nothing but what I expected. Prayer was my only relief and I found peace by casting my care on God. My mind was somewhat sorrowful that I was not to see her again till after death.*

Lydia is distressed that she has had to write again to Henry and worries about the effect it will have:

> *May 11th 1808 My mind distressed, perplexed, and troubled for my dear friend; much self-reflection for having suffered him to see my regard for him (and what it is).*

And on May 15th her torment is even greater:

> *What a week have I passed! never may such another pass over my head! my thoughts wholly occupied about my absent friend, — distressed for his distress, and full of self-reproaches for all that's past, — writing bitter things about myself, — my heart alienated dreadfully from God, — and the duties I am in the habit of performing, all neglected since I no way excuse myself, but am I trust, humbled for my imprudence in letting my friend know my state of mind towards him, and this is all I have injured him in. I accuse myself for want of candour with my family.*

Her want of candour must indicate that her mother had not been fully apprised of Lydia's true feelings. Lydia confides to her Diary on June 12th: *Prayed much for my father, and spoke to him of death and eternal judgement* and then reveals that:

> *My remembrance of God's dear saint in India is frequent, but I am still in this affair, and expect to know more of the infinite power, wisdom, and goodness of our God in it and by it than I have heretofore. My prayer for him constantly is that he may be supported, guided, and made in all things obedient and submissive to the will of his God. The school was pleasing employ today to me. Lord, bless this work and labour of love. Amen.*

However, on July 8th, 1808, she writes again to Henry, on the advice of Colonel Sandys, who knew them both and had been involved in the discussion on the subject of marriage with Simeon and Lydia on April 25th, 1807 at his home at Lanarth, which Lydia refers to in her Diary and of which Simeon kept the notes quoted above. There was obviously some anxiety back in Cornwall that the message that the relationship was at an end had not got through to Henry. Colonel Sandys felt the second letter was necessary so that there could be no further correspondence between them. *I trembled at the handwriting, but it was only more last words sent on the advice of Major Sandys in case the previous letter had not arrived* notes Henry when he received it on March 28th, 1809.

In August Lydia is staying at Kingsbridge in Devon with Phillis, but this holiday from Marazion brings little comfort as her anguished entries from August 10th reflect:

> *I have been under frequent and distressing dejection of mind of late from a sense of inward weakness, want of alertness of thought. I have seemed to myself almost an idiot not capable of any rational exertion of mind, a child in knowledge, understanding — the melancholy occasioned by this feeling has been less excessive than formerly. I have felt almost, or more resigned to it, if by the Lord's will my health is not good, and I believe this state of mind is*

occasioned by it. Lord, Thou art my refuge and stronghold. This
season reminds me of my absent friend, but the remembrance is
less distressing, I trust from my having gained more of a submissive
spirit, and being able to believe in the wisdom of God respecting
our separation.

Lydia turns to her religion for solace and expresses her contempt for family values and her isolation within the family, August 11th, 1808:

The society of my dear family is unproductive of
enjoyment, because God is not in all their thoughts, and the world
and its vanities their constant idols. Today it is a wilderness to me,
and I cannot be interested in its concerns further than duty calls
me.

Her depression deepens and on August 16th she writes:

The last 2 days endured considerable distress of mind
from an inward sense of weakness, unprofitableness, and concern
about H.M. My heart dreadfully alienated from God.

The following day:

I am obliged to resist the least rememberance of —, but in
prayer, for I cannot trust my heart again, I have sought grace from
the Lord to have no regard for him, but what is sanctioned by his
providence, — to think of him seldom is my duty, till this is the
case.

On August 29th, she refers to receiving a letter from Henry which has not survived but was probably written on November 7th the previous year according to Jeffery:

Heard of my absent dear friend by today's post, and was
strangely affected, though the intelligence was satisfactory in every

*respect. I sought deliverance in prayer, and the Lord spoke peace to
my agitated mind, and gave me what I desired, — liberty of soul
to return to himself, and the contemplation of Heavenly things,
though a sadness remained on my spirit. Heard three sermons, for
I thought it best to be less alone than usual, lest my thoughts
should wander.*

Lydia has bowed to duty but seemingly broken her heart in the process.

Although Lydia recognises that she must occupy her mind with other
matters in order to block out painful memories of Henry she continues to
suffer:

*September 11th. After some days of darkness and distress,
sweet peace and light returns, and my soul rests on God as my
all-sufficient help. O the idolatrous state of my heart! what painful
discoveries are made to me! I see the stream of my affections has
been turned from God and on ... ... An exertion must be made, like
cutting off a right hand, in order to give Thee, O Lord, my heart. I
must hear neither of or from the person God has called in His
providence to serve Him in a distant country. O be resolute,
knowing by woeful experience the necessity of guarding my
thoughts against the remembrance of one, though dear. As I value
the presence of my God, I must avoid everything that leads my
thoughts to this subject, — O Lord keep me dependent on Thee for
Grace to do so; Thou hast plainly informed me of Thy will by
withholding Thy presence at this time, and Thy word directed me
to lay aside this weight. Heard two most precious sermons to-day,
and my soul is strengthened and drawn nearer the Heavenly
world.*

In her entries for October she is castigating herself for *seeking too much the
esteem of man, and for my pains I have obtained what I deserve.*

Her mental torment continues as she blames her love for Henry as
sinfulness in the eyes of the Lord and is seeking to find her faith in the Lord
once again. On her birthday, October 19th, she writes that she has *entered*

into a covenant with the Lord to be His alone and by October 30th she has found hope:

> *Thought of my dear friend to-night with tenderness, but*
> *entire resignation to Thy will, O our God, in never seeing or*
> *hearing from him again; to meet him above is my desire.*

By November 1808 Lydia has become more reconciled to the fact she will not see or hear directly from Henry ever again. Instead she is rejoicing in the fact that her mother seems to be being uncharacteristically generous when on November 29th she writes: *The Lord seems doing a wonder in inclining my dear mother to give us a place of His worship. O how is His hand to be acknowledged in it.* A few weeks later she refers on December 20th: *I must notice the goodness of God in disposing my dear brother to give me a place, where I hope the glorious gospel of His grace will sound.* However, she is plunged into deep depression again at the end of the year when she contemplates her own death on December 27th:

> *Much indisposed, and my heart dull and lifeless. O let me*
> *not sleep as do others, but be up, my soul, and praise thy Saviour. I*
> *am weak and very poor ... ... Lord Jesus, my feeble frame seems*
> *tottering, and let it fall for any delight I have here, myself only*
> *considered. I can but exult in its decay, for it is a dull prison, a*
> *heavy clog to my soul. But as a child I wish to live for the sake of*
> *my parents, and to promote Thy cause and interest, here. I am*
> *loathe to die. The dear children — who will care for them?*

However, her Diary entry on December 30th is totally different in register: *Surprised today by a letter from my dear George, informing me of the blessed change wrought in his mind* reveals that Lydia has found a new equilibrium in her mental state and she continues, with insight later in the same entry:

> *I reckon among my mercies the Lord's having enabled me*
> *to choose a single life, and that my friend in India has been so well*
> *reconciled to my determination. The trial was a sore one, and I*

believe the effects of it will be felt as long as I live. My weak frame could not support the perturbed state of my mind, and the various apprehensions that would have assailed me on his arrival nearly wore me down. But the Lord removed them all by showing me he approved of my choice, and in granting me the tidings of his enjoying peace and happiness in our separation. Every burden now respecting him is removed, and my soul has only to praise the wise and gracious hand, which brought me through that thorny path. It was one I made to myself, by ever entering into a correspondence with him, and by expressing too freely my regard.

From this it seems that Lydia blames herself for agreeing to correspond with Henry and by unwisely expressing *too freely my regard* which Henry has interpreted as an indication that she would marry him. Instead she has accepted, or her family has persuaded her, against agreeing to a mutual engagement. Furthermore, following the dictates of social propriety, she has broken off her correspondence with the man she loves. Instead she is resigning herself to the role of spinster which contemporary society has assigned her and doing her duty by caring for her two parents as they approach old age. The contrast with Henry's pragmatic approach to the obstacles put in the way of their marriage is extreme. Lydia sees them as burdens which she is not physically or mentally strong enough to bear, yet when it comes to defying her mother over religion she is a strong and determined woman. She has now been forced to act decisively and must have realised that at almost 33 years of age her chances of marrying anyone else were unlikely. Her religion will increasingly become her source of solace. She also records in the same entry that: *by George's unexpected liberality, I have now sufficient to defray the expenses of the Meeting.* The affair is regarded as finished and their correspondence is seemingly over. Is this perhaps the reason that her mother and George finance the setting up of a Methodist Meeting House to placate Lydia for the sacrifice she has been forced to make? Or had Lydia had no intention of following Henry out to India to become his wife. Had she been flattered by the attentions of this ardent young man and perhaps had allowed her pen to run away with her so allowing him to think she would accept his proposal of marriage? If so then her mother may have provided an unassailable reason for preventing her marrying Henry which Lydia seized knowing full well that Henry would accede to her mother's wishes on filial duty.

Opinion is divided on her decision not to go out to India. Constance Padwick in her book published in 1922 *Henry Martyn: Confessor of the Faith* is less than sympathetic when she writes: *Had she been wise she would have left ill alone. But, Lydia for all her real goodness, was not of the heroic build.* Whereas George Smith is far more charitable in his view of her in *Henry Martyn, Saint and Scholar* published earlier in 1892: *As a chaplain, at any rate, he was in a position to marry at once. As India or Bengal then was, Lydia had she gone out with him, or soon after him, would have proved to be a much needed force in Anglo-Indian society, an influence on the native communities whom he sought to bring to Christ. Above all, as a man born with a weak body, with habits of incessant and intense application to study and to duty, Henry Martyn required one with the influence of a wife to keep him in life and to prolong his Indian service. It was the greatest calamity of his whole career that Lydia did not accompany him. But, since he learned to love her with all the devotion of his passionate nature, we cannot consider it 'a bitter misfortune', as some do, that he ever knew her. His love for Lydia in the fluctuations of its hope, in the ebb and flow of its tenderness, and in its transmutation of its despair into faith and resignation to the will of God, worked out a higher elevation for himself, and gives to his* Journals and Letters *a pure human interest which places them above the 'Confessions of St. Augustine'.*

When she next writes to Henry it is on an entirely platonic basis.

Missionary Influence or How to Make Converts
Rowlandson 1815

Infidels Barbarians! we are come to convert you to the european faith. by Order of the great Authority whose Image I bear on this shield. the benignant beams of whose countenance enliven the ignorant inhabitants of this country. therefore destroy to your Gods burn your books, be converted and be saved.

Master, you very fine Gentleman got very fine Topy[49] – but not speak too much good sense - Master I'm poor people all black fellow poor Man, all master slave - What for burra Sahib behauden Send Master for black man not become Christian; .... got one God already – What can I say more?

Wah! Wah! Topywalla

[49] Topy — hat

Chapter 10 — The Fierce Ishmaelite

The year 1807 had proved to be a turbulent year not only for Lydia but for Henry too with the news of the death of Laura, his eldest sister, which had depressed him, and then Lydia's letter which had shattered his dreams of marriage. He refers to this in letters dated October and November 26th to David Brown in Calcutta who sent mail from England on to Henry who was no doubt eager to hear of Lydia's response:

> *The other letter is from Lydia, to bid me a last farewell. I think now that I ought to urge it no more, since God so evidently forbids it. Mr Simeon went into Cornwall and had an interview with her — and from his account there appeared to be no great difficulty, but her own letter conveys a different impression.*

What differed from Simeon's report will never be known but it seems likely that Lydia's resolve to remain single and dedicate her life to God through prayer and good works has led Henry to finally accept her decision — their relationship and correspondence was at an end.

Fortunately for Henry he is fully absorbed in his work and studies which provide some solace. He is busy learning Hebrew and his translation work is occupying much of his time and energies not least because he was having to deal with the jealousy between his two translation assistants, Sabat and Mirza. At the request of the Baptist missionaries in Serampore Henry had begun work on translating the New Testament into Urdu, with the assistance of Mirza Muhammad Fitrat from Benares, and into Arabic and Persian, with the help of Nathaniel Sabat, *a man of good family in Arabia,* who had converted to Christianity. Henry regarded the Persian translation as being: *of incalculable importance. One may safely say, it is of more consequence than any three of the Indian languages, Sanscrit excepted — spoken as it is all the way from hence to Damascus.*

Henry gives news of Sabat's arrival at Dinapore in a letter to David Brown dated November 10th, 1807:

> *Sabat arrived last Saturday, and he now takes up so much of the time I am free from the moonshees* [interpreters and language teachers] *that I can hardly tell where to find a moment for writing a letter. But you are anxious to know what I think of him. Truly, not to esteem him a monument of grace, and to love him accordingly, is impossible: and yet with all, as you say, he is an Arab ... The very first day we began to spar. He would come into none of my plans, nor did I approve of his; but I gave way, and by yielding prevailed, for he now does everything I tell him.*

In his letter to Simeon, written in January, 1808 in which he accepts that Lydia will not be joining him, Henry describes the progress he is making with his native schools but regrets the lack of books for the children which he blames on Government interference delaying their printing. He heaps praise on Sabat describing him as a *Christian brother, a bosom friend & a thorough scholar in the languages I am learning.* Henry sees Sabat's work in translating the New Testament into Arabic as an important step *towards the ruin of Mohammedanism.*

However, Sabat turned out to be far from an easy assistant to work with. Mrs. Sherwood describes how *He would often contend for a whole morning about the meaning of an unimportant word; and Mr Martyn has not unseldom ordered his palanquin and come over to us, to get out of the sound of the voice of the fierce 'Ishmaelite.'* Sabat made life difficult for Henry with his petulance, threatening at one point to write to David Brown to have himself removed from the project:

The immediate cause of this vexation was, that some boxes which he had been making, at the expense of 150 rupees, all cracked at the coming of the hot weather. He was also extremely jealous of Mirza whose working relationship with Henry was excellent: *Mirza and myself go on steadily* although Henry felt he must be careful with Mirza, for *he is like a ball of wax, easy to be moulded into any shape; and whatever he sees me earnest for he will give up; so I alter as little of his translation as possible, lest through his absurd pliability he should give up the true idiom in my desire of having it literal.*

But Mirza could be equally devious causing trouble between Sabat and Henry who comments on the frustrations of dealing with both men after Mirza has entered Sabat's bungalow, which was close to Henry's, without removing his shoes, and had then told a pack of lies about him to Henry: *Oh, the hypocrisy and wickedness of an Indian. I never saw a more remarkable contrast in two men than in Mirza and Sabat. One is all exterior — the other has no outside at all. One a most consummate man of the world — the other an artless child of the desert.* Henry was caught in the middle between his two assistants. An insight into his working relationship with Sabat appears in a letter he wrote to Corrie dated May 9th, 1808:

> *Sabat having one of his headaches, leaves me at liberty to take a complete sheet. This week has passed as usual, in comparing the Persian and Greek; yet we are advanced no further than the end of the 15th Matthew. Notwithstanding the vexation and disappointment Sabat has occasioned me, I have enjoyed a more peaceable week than ever since his arrival.*

It was Sabat's grasp of Persian, referred to in a letter to Corrie dated June 6th, 1808, which was giving Henry cause for concern: *Today we have completed the Persian of St Mathew, and tomorrow it is to be sent off to be printed ... Sabat is prodigiously proud of it: I wish some mistakes may not be found in it, to put him to shame.*

He was uneasy about the translation as being *so high* that it would prove unusable for the evangelical purpose. His misgivings were later to prove to be right when they finished translating the New Testament into Persian on February 13th, 1810 and sent it to Calcutta for comment.

The church which Henry had worked so hard to get built at Dinapore opened on March 13th, 1809, much to his delight. Soon afterwards in April, at the beginning of the hot season, Henry set off overland, leaving Sabat and his wife to follow by boat with the baggage, and travelled the 400 miles up to Cawnpore, his new posting, in the burning heat. Henry's health, which was not good, suffered terribly as a result. At first things went well. He saw Corrie at Chunar but after Allahabad the group were forced to travel for two days and nights non-stop across *plains of immeasurable extent, covered with burning sand* and *with the wind blowing like a fire from a furnace.* By the time Henry arrived at Cawnpore on May 30th he was exhausted and dangerously ill. He writes to the Reverend Thomas Hitchins: *This part of the journey had nearly proved fatal to me; for as there was no European all the way between Allahabad and Cawnpore, a distance of 140 miles, I was compelled to travel by day, exposed to the hot winds and burning sand.*

Unfortunately Henry had a talent for choosing to travel on long journeys during the hottest parts of the year with appalling consequences for his health. It is now apparent from entries in his Journal that he is declining rapidly:

May 1st: seized with a fever — fainted twice.

May 22 –27: Constantly ill, a headache without intermission, day and night.

Cawnpore, with its hot winds sweeping the desolate lands and always hit by drought in the hot season, was possibly the worst station Henry could have been sent to in his delicate health. Fortunately for Henry the Sherwoods were now based at Cawnpore with the 53rd Regiment. The Eighth Light Dragoons and six companies of Artillery were also based there in readiness for battles and skirmishes with Marathas, Sikhs and Goorkhas. It was Mrs. Sherwood who nursed Henry back to health in their home. She describes his journey across the burning plain to Cawnpore in her Diary:

... no friendly cloud or verdant carpet of grass to relieve the eye from the strong glare of the rays of the sun, pouring on the sandy plains of the Ganges. Thus, Mr Martyn travelled, journeying night and day, and arrived at Cawnpore in such a state, that he fainted away as soon as he entered the house. When we charged him with the rashness of hazarding his life in this manner, he always pleaded his anxiety to get to the great work. He remained with us ten days, suffering considerably, at times, from fever and pains in the chest.

Because of the intense heat, at times up to 96°F indoors, and Henry's high fever the Sherwoods made up a bedroom for him in their central hall where it would be cooler. She nursed him lovingly and doubtless saved his life.

Henry loved being part of their domestic scene, talking to Annie, a foster child, whom Mrs. Sherwood had adopted at the end of 1807 when her first son, Henry, had died, partly to comfort herself and partly to provide some companionship for Lucy, her daughter, who was to die of dysentery in September 1808 in early infancy. Henry baptised Lucy but gave her the pet name of Serena, because of her gentle nature. She was also a beautiful child with a pink and white complexion which was much admired in the Indian climate. He loved to see the children when he felt stronger and would allow Serena to sit solemnly by him as he worked on his translation. Mrs. Sherwood had left her first daughter, Mary, while still a baby, behind in England in 1805 when she sailed for India. She now resolved that although her next child would be born in India she would take it to England and leave it there under the care of her sister in order that it might grow to adulthood. A heartbreaking but wise decision which many mothers in India had to make and which effectively made parents and children strangers when the parents eventually returned to England. Mrs Sherwood was only too aware of the effect of separation: *Eleven years before I had parted with my infant Mary in London. I cannot describe the effect of seeing her again. The intense interest, the strangeness of finding myself the mother of an almost grown-up girl, the close connection and the strange disunion of habits, the shyness and yet strong affection on one side, and maybe almost fear of these new-found parents —*

Mrs. M. M. Sherwood
1775 – 1851

all these things mingling, made up something more than pleasure, something too much for human nature, and I despair of describing it.

Early in 1808 she had adopted another child, Sally Pownal, whose mother had died and whose father had had her fostered. Mrs. Sherwood discovered the baby in a terrible condition: *little more than two years old, but attenuated to a degree that was fearful. The skin about the mouth was stretched until the mouth and teeth were quite prominent. The cheeks were fallen in, the eyes staring, and the whole physiognomy that of the most eager famine.* Mrs. Sherwood removed her forthwith from her foster mother. This was Sally, (who married a Mr. Thomas Bird, a glover in Worcester, in 1826).

In June, much to Henry's delight, Corrie, who also knew the Sherwoods, arrived en route from Chunar near Benares for his new post at Agra. Accompanying Corrie was his sister, Mary, who stayed with the Sherwoods while Corrie stayed with Henry. The three of them led a pleasant life, going for gentle walks along the banks of the Ganges or sitting on the moored budgerow in the cooling evening breeze and talking as Henry gradually regained his strength. Henry enjoyed the company of his old friend and also found his sister a pleasant companion. She and Henry became close but whether there was a romance between them is unclear. Certainly rumours reached Lydia which Henry denied in a letter to her dated August 14th, 1810 in which he describes their discussions and walks together.

Once Henry had recovered from the worst effects of his terrible journey, his duties as military chaplain were much the same as in Dinapore. In Cawnpore he was responsible for the moral welfare of two regiments, the Dragoons and Artillery, and found himself alone in his views on swearing: *At the General's: as usual met with a cold reception. Ever since a conversation I had with him on the wickedness of swearing, he has been reserved and distant. He has never been very cordial, and now he is likely to be less so, though it was done in the gentlest way, he did not seem to like it.* Very often at formal dinners no one paid any attention to his saying grace. He had no church so was forced to conduct his first parade service outside under the burning sun. He collapsed with fever and on recovering put in a request to have the use of the billiard room. This was refused but he was offered the use of the riding school instead.

On a happier note, he enjoyed the company of the other Europeans either stationed at the cantonment or visiting it. Although cantonments were primarily barracks and so laid out with military precision they were also enclaves where European society with a church, club and shops and houses or bungalows with their English gardens could be enjoyed. Mrs. Sherwood describes Henry's love of company as follows: *No man I ever met was more merry amongst his friends than H. Martyn; he was a most hearty and frequent laugher, a happy spirit, although his private journals are often sad.* Henry mentions a party he threw one evening at his bungalow at which the Sherwoods were guests:

> *Julio, the Italian Monk, who had been ordered to*
> *Lucknow just at the time I was sent here, arrived. Captain and*
> *Mrs Sherwood of 53rd (both believers) dined with us. It was an*
> *odd party — one English protestant clergyman, one officer, one*
> *lady, one Arabian converted Mahometan, one Catholic monk,*
> *and one Indian.*

It is the same gathering that Mrs. Sherwood also describes so vividly. She starts with a description of Henry's living quarters situated between the Sepoy Parade and the Artillery Barracks which was approached along a depressing avenue of *funereal* palm trees and aloes. At the end of the avenue lay two bungalows, one where Henry lived and the other connected to it by a long passage where Sabat and his wife lived. They were surrounded by a strange collection of huts and sheds where servants, schoolmasters and poverty stricken Indians, who relied on Henry for daily handouts of food, lived. She continues:

> *It was a burning evening in June, when after sunset I*
> *accompanied Mr Sherwood to Mr Martyn's bungalow, and saw*
> *for the first time, its avenue of palms and aloes. We were*
> *conducted to the chabootra* [a paved or plastered platform
> attached to the bungalow or in the garden] *where the company*
> *was already assembled; there was no lady but myself. This*
> *chalbootra was many feet square, and chairs were set for the guests.*

A more heterogeneous assembly surely had not often met, and seldom, I believe were more languages in requisition in so small a party. Besides Mr Martyn and ourselves, there was no one present who could speak English. But let me introduce each individual separately.

She commences with a description of Sabat:

His eyebrows were arched, black, and strongly pencilled; his eyes dark and round, and from time to time flashing with unsubdued emotion, and ready to kindle into flame on the most trifling occasion. His nose was high, his mouth wide, his teeth large, and looked white in contrast with his bronzed complexion and fierce black mustachios. He was a large and powerful man, and generally wore a skull-cap of rich shawling, or embroidered silk, with circular flaps of the same hanging over each ear. His large, tawny throat and neck had no other covering than that afforded by his beard, which was black. His attire was a kind of silk jacket, with long sleeves fastened by a girelle, or girdle, about his loins, to which was appended a jewelled dirk. He wore long trousers, and embroidered shoes turned up at the toes. In the cold season he threw over this a wrapper lined with fur, and when it was warmer the fur was changed for silk. When to this costume is added ear-rings, and sometimes a golden chain, the Arab stands before you in his complete state of Oriental dandyism. This son of the desert never sat in a chair without contriving to tuck up his legs under him on the seat, in an attitude very like a tailor on his board. The only languages which he was able to speak were Persian, Arabic and a very little bad Hindustani; but what was wanting in the words of this man was more than made up by the loudness with which he uttered them, for he had a voice like rolling thunder.

The rest of the party is equally colourful and she describes an elegant, handsome, young Italian Jesuit priest, whom Henry had met in Patna, decked out in a robe of finest purple satin, who converses with Henry partly in Italian and partly in Latin.

Mrs. Sherwood also describes Sabat's wife:

> *He was at that time married to his seventh wife; that is according to his own account.* (Sabat was well-known for boasting). *Ameena was a pretty young woman, though particularly dark for a purdah walla, or one according to Eastern custom, who is supposed always to sit behind a purdah or curtain.*

She describes visiting Ameena in her bungalow and finding her sitting on cushions with mosquito nets festooning them. She is very dismissive of Ameena's enforced boredom with nothing to relieve the monotony except gossip, having her hands and eyelids stained with henna and having her hair dressed. Mrs. Sherwood, with her stern upbringing, feels she should be reading or sewing or using the time more constructively. Ameena has remained Muslim and her marriage to the converted Christian Sabat is not a happy one from Henry's account of an anecdote told to him by Sabat. Ameena asks Sabat where Christians go after death and he replies: *To heaven and their Saviour.* She then asks where Mahometans go. Sabat replies to hell and the devil. Ameena plays her trump card: *Well then, I will continue to be a Musselman, because I should prefer hell and the devil without you, to heaven itself in your presence.*

Henry is exhausting himself with his evangelical preaching which was not falling on receptive ears. As well as preaching to the troops and their wives he was also addressing beggars who, in order to pre-empt continual interruptions for alms, he encouraged to gather outside his bungalow once a week. He would preach to them before giving them alms. Mrs. Sherwood gives a contemporary account of these gatherings of up to 500 Indian beggars on Sunday evenings in the garden:

> *They were young and old, male and female, tall and short, athletic and feeble, bloated and wizened; some clothed in abominable rags, some nearly without clothes; a temperature often rising above 92°F whilst the sun poured its burning rays upon us*

140

through a lurid haze of dust ... I still imagine that I hear the calm,
distinct and musical tones of Henry Martyn as he stood raised
above the people ... From time to time low murmurs and curses
would arise in the distance, and then roll forward till they became
so loud as to drown the voice of this pious one (Martyn), generally
concluding with hissing and fierce cries.

Henry would be left hoarse and faint from his exertions, leaving him feeling dejected at the lack of progress he was making in his missionary calling. He writes dispiritedly: *I do not perceive that any good is done among them* and adds: *Upon the whole my work, you see, is different from what I expected when I left England, less apostolic and much less romantic.*

Mrs. Sherwood admired Henry and when her second son was born in Cawnpore in 1811 she named him Henry Martyn. By then she had lost two children, named Henry and Lucy, to the vagaries of the Indian climate and disease. She published a book called *Little Henry and his bearer* in 1814 which was as popular as the later *Uncle Tom's Cabin.* The child's saintly character and his evangelical zeal to convert the heathen are based partly on the character of the real Henry Martyn who shared her evangelical belief in saving Indian souls and that of her beloved first son, Henry. To the modern reader the book reveals the attitude of Europeans to the Indian of their day which is uncharitably racist in tone and reflects a supreme confidence in white Protestant European moral and religious superiority.

In November 1809 Henry received a further blow when he learnt that his beloved younger sister Sally was dying from tuberculosis: *Consumption has seized her, as it did my mother and sister, and will carry her off as it did them, and now I am the only one left. Oh, my dear Corrie, though I know you are well prepared, how does nature bleed at the thought of a beloved sister drooping and dying.* However, it is her death which acts as the catalyst for the resumption of correspondence with Lydia: albeit on a platonic footing, that of siblings.

Henry is now pragmatic and critical of his fellow clergy (even William Carey) who are arguing about funds for translation going to other translators who are perhaps more skilled than they in the native tongues in India. However, Henry now speaks fluent Hindustani, and understands local dialects and is openly critical of clergy who have no grounding in any of the native languages. He is nearing the completion of his revised Urdu New Testament with Mirza. The translation was to receive much praise by Urdu scholars when it was received in Serampore. Henry now sees his main work as translation of the New Testament into Persian and Arabic and sees the latter as of key importance because as it will open up vast areas to evangelical teaching.

Henry remained in Cawnpore, to be the scene of a terrible massacre of women and children, during the Indian Mutiny of 1857, which would further fix the European perception of India as a country full of dangerous heathen tendencies which needed to be curbed by the spread of Christianity by a morally superior race, until September 1810, when, because of his poor health, the General gave him extended leave. Instead of taking the opportunity to travel back to Europe he decides instead to travel to Muscat, and then Shiraz in Persia in order to do further work on the Arabic and Persian translations of the New Testament. His fears over the standard of Sabat's and his translation have proved to be right.

But meanwhile what has been happening to Lydia who has been pressured by her mother to turn down Henry's proposal of marriage and to break off her correspondence with him? Her Diary is full of remorse at the hurt she has caused Henry, of whom she now hears news through Emma. She blames herself constantly for entering into a correspondence with him and allowing herself to have encouraged him *by expressing too freely my regard*. She turns more and more to her religion which, although it isolates her from her mother, brings her some comfort. By the autumn of 1809 she is setting out a Plan of Conduct by which she will live her life:

> *September 8. I wish to lay down a regular Plan of*
> *Conduct, to be observed religiously, as far as circumstances will*
> *permit, and to bend them to it, if possible, — not suffering trifles*
> *to occasion a departure from what affects my soul's peace, and the*
> *glory of my God. First then, — I will (Lord help me here) make*
> *conscience of early rising, and of employing my thoughts exclusively*
> *on God and eternal things till breakfast. — I will try the effect of*

early rising on my health; if it grows worse, then I must submit.
Resolve then, if awake, never to remain in bed after six, — not one
moment. From breakfast till eleven, I will read some book of
Divinity. From that hour to dinner I will devote to the service of
my fellow-creatures and to exercise and recreation, not pleasure.
From dinner to tea shall be spent in my dear mother's company,
— at seven I will retire for meditation and secret prayer one hour.
Mondays, letter writing; Tuesdays and Fridays, visiting the sick;
Wednesdays, the school; Thursdays, my father shall be the
particular object of my attention; Saturdays, settle all worldly
business. — Lord, help me thus to live.

Her life is so different and yet in many ways so similar to the one she would have led as Henry's wife in India with its emphasis on good works, teaching the poor and disadvantaged children in Marazion of which there were many, religious contemplation and her wish to lead a life of increasing piety. It is an interesting reminder of how important letters were to a woman of her social status that she set aside a whole day, Mondays, for letter writing. Her mother commands every day from dinner (lunch) till tea, while her father, who is declining in health, is allotted Thursdays. Her mother's continuing opposition to her professed faith is evident with the reference to *secret prayer*. On October 23rd, four days after her 34th birthday she expresses her uncertainty about resuming correspondence with Henry: *I am under some painful forebodings respecting my dear absent friend, and know not how to act. I am strongly impelled to write to him, now that he is in affliction and perhaps sickness himself, — yet I dread parting from the plain path of duty.* Her mother would no doubt object if she felt that her daughter was about to embark once again on a correspondence which had so nearly taken her away from Marazion and her family. Lydia is torn by her compassion for Henry, who is mourning the death of his sister Sally and who is himself clearly in very poor health. She realises that if she is to resume a correspondence with Henry she will need her mother's permission so that her intentions are not misconstrued.

However, Henry is petitioning for a resumption in corresponding with Lydia and writes a persuasive letter on October 10th, 1809 to her brother-in law, the Reverend Thomas Hitchins.[50] It opens on a plaintive note:

> *My Dearest Brother,*
>
> *I am again disappointed in receiving no letter from you. The last intelligence from the West of England is Lydia's letter of 8th July 1808. Colonel Sandys has long since ceased to write to me, and I have no other correspondent.*
>
> *It is very affecting to me to be thus considered as dead by almost all my natural relations and early connections; and at this time, when I am led to think of you and the family to which you are united, and have been reading all your letters over, I feel that I could dip my pen deep in melancholy; for strange as it may seem to you, I love so true, that tho' it is now the fifth year since I parted from the object of my affection, she is as dear to me as ever; yet on the other hand I find my present freedom such a privilege that I would not lose it for hardly any consideration. It is the impossibility of compassing every wish, that I suppose is the cause of any uneasiness that I feel. I know not how to express my thoughts respecting Lydia better than in Martial's words — Nec tecum possum vivere nec sine te.*

Later in the same long letter he continues:

> *You two are such bad correspondents that on this ground I prefer another petition for the renewal of Lydia's correspondence, — she need not suspect any thing now, nor her friends, that I should trouble her upon the old subject, even if I were settled in England — for O this vain world! quid habet commodi? quid non potius laboris?*

---

[50] Original held at The Courtney Library, Royal Institution of Cornwall, Truro.

But I never expect to see England more, nor do I expect
that tho' all obstacles should be removed, she would ever become
mine unless I came for her, and I now do not wonder at it, tho' I
did before. If any one of my sisters had had such a proposal made to
them, I would never have consented to their going, so you may see
the affair is ended between us. My wish is that she would be scribe
for you all, and I promise on my part to send you thro' her an
ample detail of all my proceedings; also she need not imagine that
I may form another attachment — in which case she might
suppose a correspondence with an unmarried lady might be
productive of difficulties, — for after one disappointment I am not
likely to try my chance again, and if I do I will give her the earliest
intelligence of it, with the same frankness with which I have
always dealt (with her).[51]

The reference to the propriety of Lydia corresponding with him if he found another attachment refers to Mary Corrie, Daniel Corrie's sister whose stay in Cawnpore had given rise to gossip. Henry very correctly establishes the basis on which the correspondence will be resumed with his assurance that he has no wish to try to persuade Lydia to come out to India and he regards the whole affair as finished. It would have fallen to Emma to communicate this to Lydia and her mother.

Lydia is fully aware that both Henry's sisters have now died from tuberculosis, and that he is suffering from symptoms of the same dreaded disease. Furthermore the Reverend Malachy Hitchins had died in March 1809. Sally's death affects Henry deeply. He refers to it on March 23rd, 1810 when he receives a letter from Simeon with the sad news:

... she was my dear counsellor and guide for a long time in
the Christian way, and she has finished her own journey very
happily.

---

[51] (This concluding portion of the letter had been carefully concealed by paper gummed over the original MS. It was removed by water and steam.) Footnote by Henry Martyn Jeffery: *Two Sets of Unpublished Letters*.

He realises that now he has *no relation left, to whom I feel bound by the ties of Christian fellowship; and I am resolved to form no new connection of a worldly nature, so that I may henceforward hope to live entirely as a man of another world.*

Lydia, presumably with her mother's permission, suggests in October 1809, when she writes to Henry to express her condolences over Sally's death, that they could resume corresponding on a new basis: that of brother and sister. However, she still worries that this resumption of correspondence between two unattached people may be construed by others as improper. On October 19th, her 35th birthday, having acknowledged that the past year has been a difficult one, Lydia takes as her motto or text for the year: "*I will trust and not be afraid, for the Lord Jehovah is my strength and my song; He is also my salvation.*" Four days later she is confiding her torment about writing to Henry:

> *I am under some painful forebodings respecting my dear absent friend, and know not how to act. I am strongly impelled to write to him, now that he is in affliction and perhaps sickness himself, — yet I dread departing from the plain path of duty. "O Lord, direct me" is my cry. I hope my desire is to do Thy will, and only Thy will.*

Lydia is only too painfully aware that her action may be misconstrued by her family and friends plus the fact that Samuel John is still not yet married adds to her concern about the propriety of entering into correspondence with a man who may by now have found another woman to be his wife. She continues:

> *I have given him up to Thee, — O let me do so sincerely, and trust in Thy fatherly care. I am poor and needy, — Lord think upon me for Thy mercy's sake. Heaven is my only ... ... of rest, — I will look to that blessed state more, — Lord, enable me to.*

At the beginning of 1810 her entry for January 1st reads:

Had a remembrance of those most dear to me, in prayer,
and found it very sweet to commend them to God, especially my
friend in India, — perhaps not now in India, but in Heaven. O to
join him at last in Thy blissful presence

She continues by chiding herself for the sins of *self esteem and desiring the esteem of others* as well as *indolence and pride.* Henry is very much in her thoughts and on January 20th she writes:

So lifeless is my heart that I am insensible almost now
that anxiety is awakening afresh for my absent friend. No letter
from him again tells me something is wrong, — but the Lord
orders right and I will hope.

Jeffery inserts a note that the expected letter would be to her sister Emma, not herself. While she is so preoccupied for news of Henry another piece of news arrives on January 23rd:

Heard yesterday of the marriage of Mr John, — what a
mercy to me do I feel it, — a load gone off my mind, for every evil,
I heard him committing, I feared I might have been the cause of by
my conduct ten years since, — I rejoice in this event for his sake
and my own

It must have been an enormous relief to her to feel she was now freed from any moral obligation towards her former suitor. News of Henry which she has been so anxiously waiting for arrives on February 6th, 1810 and with Samuel John seemingly happily married at last she writes to Henry: *Heard at last of the safety of my friend in India, and write to him, many fears on my mind as to its propriety.* The following month on March 5th Lydia is praying for his return to England because of his poor health: *I am sensible of a very remarkable change in the desires of my soul before God, respecting my absent friend. I with freedom and peace now pray continually that he may be restored to his friends and country; before I never dared to ask anything but that the Lord would order this as His wisdom saw fit, and thought it not a subject for prayer.*

His injured health causes me to believe that India is not the place for his labours. Not only is she worrying about Henry's health she is once again full of anxiety about Samuel John, whose marriage has proved to be very unhappy. She refers to him on April 1st: *the state of wretchedness into which the person I have injured is plunged, by marrying another.* She writes again to Henry on April 23rd. *Wrote to India.* The following month on May 29th she records the death of her father, Pascoe Grenfell: *After an illness of only five days I am deprived of my poor afflicted and too much neglected father. O the bitterness of my feelings for not acting on every occasion with more tenderness towards him, — for not attending to his wishes, and bearing with his infirmities.* He was 79. Now Lydia was faced with the prospect of caring for her widowed mother.

On March 30th, 1810 Martyn wrote the first[52] of 11 letters based on this new platonic relationship proposed by Lydia as brother and sister:

> *Since you kindly bid me, my beloved friend, to consider*
> *you in the place of my dear sister, whom it has pleased God in his*
> *wisdom to take from me, I gratefully accept the offer of a*
> *correspondence, which it has ever been the anxious wish of my*
> *heart to establish. Your kindness is the more acceptable, because it*
> *is shown in the day of affliction. Though I had heard of my dearest*
> *sister's illness, some months before I received the account of her*
> *death, and though the nature of her disorder was such as left me*
> *not a ray of hope, so that I was mercifully prepared for the event,*
> *still the certainty of it fills me with anguish.* He continues by
> expressing his sorrow at the suffering she has had to endure
> *which have been unfortunately detailed to me with too much*
> *particularity. Would that I had never heard them, or could efface*
> *them from my remembrance!*

He then dwells on the effect of a death on a family before turning to the basis of their new pen relationship:

---

[52] His response to her letter probably written on October 23rd, 1809.

I hope often to communicate with you on these subjects, and in return for your kind and consolatory letters, to send you, from time to time, accounts of myself and my proceedings. Through you, I can hear of all my friends in the West. When I first heard of the loss I was likely to suffer, and began to reflect on my own friendless situation, you were much in my thoughts, — whether you would be silent on this occasion or no? whether you would persist in your resolution? Friends indeed I have, and brethren, blessed be God! but two brothers cannot supply the place of one sister. Clearly at this time the resumption of communication with Lydia brought great comfort to Henry and once again it is Emma who had acted as intermediary:

When month after month passed away, and no letter came from you, I almost abandoned the hope of ever hearing from you again. It only remained to wait the result of my last application through Emma. You have kindly anticipated my request, and I need scarcely add, are more endeared to me than ever.

Of your illness, my dearest Lydia, I had heard nothing, and it was well for me that I did not.

He signs: *Yours most affectionately.*

The reference to her illness probably refers to the summer and autumn of 1808. Henry is delighted to be in direct contact once more with Lydia. He writes to David Brown on April 3rd concerning Sabat and the translation work and mentions *my long lost Lydia, however, consents to write to me.*

The change in Henry's tone when the correspondence is resumed in 1810 is marked and the content concerns health and family instead of heartfelt longings for Lydia and pleadings for her to join him. He writes to her again almost three weeks later on April 19th and completes the letter on

April 26th.[53] In this long letter he confides to her that his health is causing him concern.

> *I begin my correspondence with my beloved Lydia, not*
> *without a fear of its being soon to end. Shall I venture to tell you,*
> *that our family complaint has again made its appearance in me,*
> *with more unpleasant symptoms than it has ever yet done.*

He refers to being ill in 1808 after his arrival at Cawnpore and then describes his present symptoms which are *chiefly a pain in the chest, occasioned, I suppose, by over-exertion the last two Sundays, and incapacitating me at present from all public duty and even from conversation. You were mistaken in supposing that my former illness originated from study. Study never makes me ill — scarcely ever fatigues me — but my lungs! death is seated there; it is speaking that kills me. May it give others life.*

Lydia has presumably suggested that his over-zealous studies are the cause but even Henry now admits that it is the over-exertion of preaching to large numbers in the heat and dust at Cawnpore. References to ill-health and death by both Henry and Lydia become a regular topic in their letters and are a reminder how prevalent diseases like tuberculosis were and the fear they aroused. Lydia refers to her anxiety when she receives this letter:

> *December 8th 1810: Heard a few days since from India.*
> *Much alarmed to know the state of my friend's health, yet I hope,*
> *my fears were not well grounded.*

Henry continues his letter by taking Lydia up on her argument that he should be more restrained in his preaching:

> *But you know how apt we are to outstep the bounds of*
> *prudence, when there is no kind monitor at hand to warn us of the*
> *consequences.*

---

[53] Received by Lydia November 29th, 1810.

Had I been favoured with the one I wanted, I might not now have had occasion to mourn. You smile at my allusion, at least I hope so, for I am hardly in earnest. I have long since ceased to repine at the decree that keeps us so far asunder as the east is from the west, and yet am far from regretting that I ever knew you. The remembrance of you calls forth the exercise of delightful affections, and has kept me from many a snare.

He thanks God that he did not remain in England because he feels, had he done so, he too would now be dead like his two sisters. On the subject of his death he argues *Death, I think, would be a less welcome visitor to me, if he came to take me from a wife, and that wife were you.* He seems preoccupied with the meaning of death and turns to St. Paul for enlightenment yet *when I turn to commentators, I find that I have passed out of the spiritual to the material world, and have got amongst men like myself. But soon, as he says, we shall no longer see as in a glass, by reflected rays, but see as we are seen, and know as we are known.*

There is an interval of six days before he resumes the letter on April 25th announcing that his health has recovered. Now it is Sabat who is causing him problems and distress with his duplicity:

... my mind is a good deal distressed at Sabat's conduct. I forbear writing what I think, in the hope my fears may prove groundless; but indeed the children of the East are adepts in deceit. Their duplicity appears to me so disgusting at this moment, that I can only find relief from my own misanthropy by remembering HIM.

The *duplicity* is a reference to a letter he has received from a certain Syud Hosyn of Baghdad who has quarrelled with Sabat and has sent Henry an account of what Sabat is saying behind Henry's back, which is not at all to Henry's liking. Furious, he labels him a liar. Then, on a lighter note, there follows a description of a dinner party where the level of conversation and lack of literary reference disappointed Henry's keen intellect when no one has read any poetry by Cowper which Henry immediately rectifies by reading

151

some aloud to them. He refers to the gathering as: *Poor people! here a little, and there a little, is a rule to be observed in speaking to them.* A short paragraph, written on the 26th, concludes the letter in which he again refers to the pain returning in his chest: *so much so that I can hardly speak. Well! now I am taught, and will take more care in the future.*

Sadly Henry ignores his own advice.

Near Gangwaugh Colly on the River Hoogly
Thomas Daniell 1820

Chapter 11 — 'Death is seated in my Lungs'

By 1810 tuberculosis has claimed his sisters' lives and his elder step-brother, John, will die from it the following year. Henry realises that he will not escape its clutches either as his symptoms increase and he accepts that *death is seated in my lungs*. Yet in spite of his precarious health he is undeterred at the thought of undertaking a long and hazardous journey to Shiraz in Persia in order to do further work on the Persian translation with which he is dissatisfied. Before he prepares for this epic journey he receives a letter, dated February 5th, 1810 from Lydia. His reply, dated August 14th, 1810 is not received by Lydia until March 28th, 1811. He immediately makes a reference to the rumours which have reached Lydia about his marrying another woman, and reveals his sensitivity to her position if this were true.

> *With what delight do I sit down to begin a letter to my beloved Lydia! Yours of the fifth of February, which I received a few days ago, was written I perceive, in considerable embarrassment. You thought it possible it might find me married or about to be so. Let me begin, therefore, with assuring you, with more truth than Gehazi did his master, "Thy servant went no whither"* [54] *my heart has not strayed from Marazion, or Gurlyn, or wherever you are. Five long years have passed, and I am still faithful.*

---

[54] 2 Kings 5,25: Ge-ha-zi is the servant of Elisha. Elisha replies: 26. 'Went not mine heart with thee?'

Lydia had referred to Miss Corin [sic.] in her Diary, dated May 2nd, 1807, and had perhaps understandably presumed that Miss Corrie, Daniel Corrie's sister, had travelled out to marry Henry. The thought of another woman sharing Henry's love and life clearly pained her then so soon after she herself had turned down his proposal. David Brown had written to Simeon in 1808 concerning this rumour of Mary Corrie's engagement to Henry. Now some three years later Lydia brings the subject up again to ensure that their resumption of correspondence is not based upon any misunderstanding which would flout the rules of propriety. Lydia would be well aware that a woman who had rejected a proposal of marriage should not be writing, even if it was on a platonic basis, to her former suitor who was either about to be married or indeed already married. Henry dismisses her fear with an affirmation of his constancy to her and an affirmation of his faith: *Five long years have passed and I am still faithful.*

Henry continues by praising her good works but cannot resist pointing out:

> *I rejoice at the accounts you give me of your continued good health and labours of love. Though you are not so usefully employed as you might be in India, yet as that must not be, I contemplate with delight, your exertions at the other end of the world. May you be instrumental in bringing many sons and daughters to glory. What has become of St. Hilary and its fairy scenes? When I think of Malachy, and the old man, and your sister, and Josepha, &c., how some are dead, and the rest dispersed, and their place occupied by strangers, it seems all like a dream.*

Life in Cornwall must now have seemed a world away to Henry after five years in India and all the experiences he has had since leaving Lydia in her safe domestic scene. With this in mind Henry encloses some extracts from his Journal in order to give Lydia a clearer picture of the life he is leading before continuing by writing a description of a typical day with Daniel and Mary Corrie:

> *... we all live here in bungalows or thatched houses, on a piece of ground enclosed. Next to mine is the church, not yet opened for public worship; but which we make use of at night with the men of the 53rd. Corrie lives with me, and Miss Corrie with the Sherwoods. We usually rise at daybreak, and breakfast at six. Immediately after breakfast we pray together, after which I translate into Arabic with Sabat, who lives in a small bungalow on my ground. We dine at twelve, and sit recreating ourselves with talking about dear friends in England. In the afternoon I translate with Mirza Fitrut into Hindostanee, and Corrie employs himself in teaching some native Christian boys whom he is educating with great care, in the hopes of their being fit for the office of catechist. I have also a school on my premises for natives; but it is not well attended. There are not above sixteen Hindoo boys in it at present; half of them read the book of Genesis. At sunset we ride or drive, and then meet at the church, where we often raise the song of praise, with as much joy, through the grace and presence of our Lord, as you do in England. At ten we are all asleep.*

It is as if they had recreated a little England there with the newly built church as its centre. He continues by acknowledging that his work lies in translation rather than in the missionary field as he had originally hoped and recognises that Corrie's ill-health will also preclude his travelling around to spread the Gospel.

He ends this final letter from Cawnpore with a reference to his own reported death, a rumour which had been circulating in Cambridge. He assures Lydia that he is:

> *... perfectly well, though not very strong in my lungs; they do not seem affected yet, but I cannot speak long without uneasiness. From the nature of my complaint, if it deserves the name, it is evident that England is the last place I should go to. I should go home only to find a grave. How shall I therefore ever see*

157

*you more on this side of eternity? Well! be it so, since such is the
will of God: we shall meet, through grace, in the realms of bliss.*

*I am truly sorry to see my paper fail. Write as often as
possible, every three months at least. Tell me where you go, and
whom you see, and what you read.*

He resumes his letter on the 17th with an ominous reference to his health:

*I am sorry to conclude with saying, that my yesterday's
boasted health proved a mistake; I was seized with violent sickness
in the night, but to-day am better. Continue to pray for me, and
believe me to be*

Your ever affectionate,

H. Martyn.[55]

Lydia fails to respond to Henry's request that she write to him *every three
months at least.* He does not acknowledge receiving a letter from her until
July 12th, 1812, when he has sent nine letters to her. He writes somewhat
despondently on June 23rd, 1811 from Shiraz: *This is now the seventh letter I
send you, without having received an answer.* Back in Marazion Lydia is
expressing her deep concern about the state of Henry's health and during
1810 is of the opinion that he should leave India and return to England. She
now takes the pragmatic view that his cause would be better served by doing
so but at the same time accepts that the decision does not lie with Henry but
is in the Lord's hands. To add to her anxiety Samuel John's marriage, which
took place in January, is already proving to be unhappy by April of the same
year and she blames herself for John's unhappiness. Lydia expresses her
anxieties about Henry on January 20th, 1810: *No letter from him again tells
me something is wrong, — but the Lord orders right and I will hope.* (Lydia is

---

[55] Henry's letter dated August 14th, completed on August 17th, 1810 and received by Lydia on March
28th, 1811.

here referring to expected letters from Henry to her sister Emma.) However, four days later her concerns for Henry's welfare are displaced by news of Samuel John's marriage. By now John was 35 and on January 23rd, had married a much younger woman of 22, Mary Grylls of Helston, who came from a respectable family: *Heard yesterday of the marriage of Mr John, — what a mercy do I feel it, — a load gone off my mind, for every evil I heard of his committing, I feared I might be the cause of by my conduct ten years since, — I rejoice in this event for his sake and my own.*

However, there was little time for rejoicing for on April 1st of the same year John's young wife gave birth to a daughter but the child was not his. Christopher Wallis reports in his Journal: *Mr John cannot reconcile this birth, as his begotten, as she and he both allow that he had no connection with her before his marriage — a Captain Bowen living at Halvose is the reputed father. She says so, but he doubted it, bringing in proof many other men who had knowledge of the lady.* Not an auspicious start to their marriage and they would later separate.

Once again Lydia becomes depressed and repeatedly berates herself for being the cause of all this suffering:

> *April 1: My soul has been cast down and disquieted within me greatly, yet will I remember Thee Lord, and what I have experienced in seasons of trial before. I have been made to possess (?)[56] the sins of my youth and my transgressions, with its guilt and misery, from the state of wretchedness into which the person I have injured is plunged by marrying another. The darkness of soul has been great, and I seemed scarcely to know Jesus received sinners and has power to forgive sins, — condemnation in my own conscience, — and at the final bar God seemed the same. It yet appears strange, that having been the cause of so much sin and misery to another, I can possibly escape.*

---

[56] Question mark inserted by Jeffery.

Mercifully Lydia was spared the further and far greater trauma of the financial scandal concerning Samuel John which broke in September 1829. The following is an extract from the *Royal Cornwall Gazette* dated September 19th: ... *no doubt you will have heard of the shocking and villainous conduct of Samuel John. He has quitted the kingdom, after having robbed this neighbourhood of about £30,000 or £40,000.*[57] The outrage and the gossip of the good people of Penzance and Marazion engendered by this scandal can be imagined! In the same issue of the *Gazette* Uriah Tonkin wrote: *He had such an appearance of open frankness, of honest upright conduct, with affability and cheerfulness of demeanour and disposition upon all occasions, that his delinquency is really astonishing, at the same time shocking and deplorable.* It was assumed that John had absconded to America but instead he took refuge in Paris, where he later died. When the news of this latest misdemeanour of her former fiancé broke Lydia was already dying and it may well have been kept from her as she died on September 18th — the day before the above article in the *Gazette* was published.

But in 1810 Lydia is tortured by guilt and grief over her past actions regarding John and she is still wrestling with her conscience over the outcome at the beginning of May when she goes to stay with friends in Penzance. This unhappy frame of mind is further compounded by the death of her father, at the end of May, whom she feels she has neglected, and Emma's illness from which she doesn't recover until August. She turns to her youngest brother, George, for comfort: *How shall I thank God for such a brother.* Part of her suffering lies in her concern for her good name and reputation which she feels have been further damaged by John's unhappy marriage and the perception of others of her treatment of Henry. She is aware that she is endeavouring to put people on the right road to salvation and yet has herself transgressed, and on November 13th she wrote:

> *Jesus! Master! Have mercy on me! O my need of mercy*
> *was never greater, for I feel myself vile, — vile in turning*
> *ungratefully from the Lord, and seeking my own glory, my own*

---

[57] Quoted in *Henry Martyn's Dulcinea*: Penny Watts-Russell; *The Cornish Banner*, November 1992.

pleasure and credit. Lord, I have prayed to know myself! O what a knowledge I have gained! I am in danger of resting satisfied that I know more of my own depravity.

When Lydia receives Henry's letter written on April 19th from Cawnpore she is very alarmed by the state of his health and prepares herself for news of his death. Henry's state of health was now giving serious cause for concern not only to his friends in England but also to those around him both in Cawnpore and in Calcutta. It became obvious that he must leave Cawnpore which was having such a detrimental effect on his health. Henry was concerned about the Arabic and Persian translations of the New Testament which Sabat and he had been working on. It is clear from his comments that his confidence in Sabat's ability as a translator had been shaken. He writes to David Brown in August 1810 asking him to establish how feasible it would be for him to sail to Mocha[58] in Yemen where he could do more work on the Arabic translation. The importance of the translation to him is reflected in this comment to Brown:

> *Will the government let me go away for three years before the time of my furlough arrives? If not, I must quit the service, and I cannot devote my life to a more important work than that of preparing the Arabic Bible.*

His fears about the Persian translation were proved right when he received news from Calcutta that the printed version of Sabat's and his Persian version of the first two Gospels needed many amendments before publication. In his reply to the Reverend Brown he takes it upon himself to *share so deeply in Sabat's disgrace* and *when we come to Calcutta let him be confronted by his accusers, and let us hear his defence. It is just possible that things may not be so bad; but I have little hope.*

John Sargent summarises the criticism of the translation: *By those, however, who were considered competent judges at Calcutta, it was still deemed unfit for*

---

[58] Now Al Mukha in Yemen.

general circulation, inasmuch as it was thought to abound with Arabic idioms, and to be written in a style, pleasing indeed to the learned, but not sufficiently level to the capacities of the mass of modern readers.

The other alternative would have been to return to England where he could visit Cambridge and give a first hand account of his work in Bengal to Simeon. He would also be able to see Lydia once more. However, even Henry has realised that this is not feasible. In his last letter to Lydia from Cawnpore, dated August 14th, 1810 and quoted above he remarks: *From the nature of my complaint, if it deserves the name, it is evident that England is the last place I should go to. I should only go home to find a grave.*

He began making preparations to leave Cawnpore in October and to travel down to Calcutta where he would be granted indefinite sick leave. Lydia is clearly still much in his thoughts and increasingly he refers to his times with her in Cornwall. He records a dream he has had of happier personal times in his Journal:

> *September 22: Was walking with L —, both much affected, and, speaking on the things dearest to us both. I awoke, and behold, it was a dream! My mind remained very solemn and pensive; I shed tears. The clock struck three, and the moon was riding near her highest noon; all was silence and solemnity; and I thought with pain of the sixteen thousand miles between us. But good is the will of the Lord, even if I see her no more.*

Brown decided that Henry should travel to Arabia first and then on to Persia in order to revise his translations although he recognises in a letter to Henry that in his delicate state of health *Your flame may last as long, and perhaps longer, in Arabia, than in India.* Any hopes of Lydia and Henry seeing each other again were over. Instead they would continue their correspondence with each others' image frozen in the summer of 1805.

On September 30th the new church, which Henry had founded, opened in Cawnpore and Henry, fittingly, gave the first sermon there and Daniel Corrie read the prayers. The congregation were fully aware of Henry's weakened state and the fact that they would never see him again. The same evening, undeterred by his weakness and having almost fainted, he insisted on addressing the unruly crowd of Indian beggars for the last time in the garden.

The following day, October 1st, 1810, he said goodbye. All his friends at Cawnpore were concerned about his health, especially Daniel Corrie, who had taken over Henry's duties as chaplain and with whom he was persuaded to leave all his documents under seal until his return. Mrs. Sherwood describes them all as feeling *very, very low* as they watched him depart in his budgerow with Sabat for David Brown's home at Aldeen near Calcutta at the start of his journey to Arabia and Persia. He was now 29 years old.

His journey, first down the Ganges and then down the Hooghli River to Aldeen was mercifully uneventful. He arrived on the last day of October. In a letter dated October 6th[59] from the Ganges he writes to Lydia:

> *My Dearest Lydia,*
>
> *Though I have had no letter from you very lately, nor have anything particular to say, yet having been days on the water without a person to speak to, tired also of reading and thinking, I mean to indulge myself with a little of what is always agreeable to me: for, as my affection for you has something sacred in it, being founded on, or at least cemented by, an union of spirit in the Lord Jesus; so my separation also from you, produces a deadness to the world, at least for a time, which leaves a solemn impression as often as I think of it. Add to this, that I must not indulge the hope of ever seeing you again in this world, I cannot think of you without thinking also of that world where we shall meet. You mention in one of your letters my coming to England, as that which may eventually prove a duty. You ought to have added, that in case I do come, you will consider it a duty not to let me come away without you. But I am not likely to put you to the trial. Useless as I am here, I often think I should be still more so at home. Though my voice fails me, I can still translate and converse. At*

---

[59] Started October 6th, 1810 en route to Calcutta and finished on November 5th from Calcutta. Received by Lydia March 28th, 1811.

*home I should be nothing without being able to lift up my voice on
high. I have just left my station, Cawnpore, in order to be silent six
months. I have no cough, nor any sign of consumption, except that
reading prayers, or preaching, or a slight cold, brings on pain in
the chest. I am advised, therefore, to recruit my strength by rest. So
I am come forth, with my face towards Calcutta, with an ulterior
view to the sea.*

*I think of having my portrait taken in Calcutta, as I
promised Mr Simeon five years ago. Sabat's picture would also be a
curiosity.*

He describes Sabat: *Sabat's countenance is indeed
terrible; noble when he is pleased, but with the look of an assassin
when he is out of humour. I have had more opportunities for
knowing Sabat than any other man has had.* He continues:
*Affection I do feel for him, but admiration, if I did once feel it, I
am not conscious of it at present. I tremble for everything our dear
friends publish about our doings in India, lest shame come to us
and them.*

This is a reference to the standard of the Arabic and Persian translations
which is weighing heavily on Henry's mind, whereas the completed Urdu
version is receiving wide approbation. Henry has no plans to take Sabat with
him on the next stage of his adventures and a somewhat disgruntled Sabat left
Calcutta as a trader for Penang. He was later imprisoned and met a cruel
death by being tied up in a sack and thrown into the sea.

Henry ends this letter on November 5th, four days after arriving at
Calcutta, by explaining that part of the letter has gone missing and that
because of *constant conversation with dear friends here* the pains in his chest
have returned once more preventing him from preaching. Finally he tells her
of his plans to leave within three weeks for the Persian Gulf *where if I live, I
shall solace myself in my hours of solitude with writing to you.* These references
to his poor state of health were to further alarm Lydia when she received the
letter the following year.

When he arrives at Aldeen his old friend, Brown, is shocked by his appearance: *He is much altered, is thin and sallow, but has the same loving heart.* Henry stayed in Calcutta while he made arrangements and gained permission from Lord Minto, the Governor General and General Hewett, Commander in Chief for his proposal to travel to Persia and his extended furlough. This he received on January 1st, 1811. Undeterred by his failing health he first planned to sail to Muscat in Arabia Felix before crossing the Persian Gulf to Bushire, the major port in Persia, and then travel inland across hazardous terrain to Shiraz where he planned to stay for six months working on his translation. He would then continue to Isfahan and finally to Kermanshah in Persia before travelling to Baghdad, then a province of the Ottoman Empire, to do further work on the Arabic translation. He hoped to discover en route ancient copies of the Gospel which he believed were hidden in the mountains near Kermanshah. In Calcutta he renewed his friendship with Thomas Thomason, who had known him from their days as curates to Simeon. In a letter he wrote to Simeon, Thomason expresses his concern about Henry's planned journey to Arabia:

> *This bright and lovely jewel first gratified our eyes on Saturday last. He is on his way to Arabia, where he is going in pursuit of health and knowledge. You know his genius, and what gigantic strides he takes in everything. He has some great plan in his mind, of which I am no competent judge; but as far as I do understand it, the object is far too grand for one short life, and much beyond his feeble and exhausted frame. Feeble it is, indeed, how fallen and changed! His complaint lies in his lungs, and appears to be incipient consumption. But let us hope that the sea-air may revive him; and that change of place and pursuit may do him essential service, and continue his life many years. In all other respects, he is exactly the same as he was. He shines in all the dignity of love, and seems to carry about him such a heavenly majesty, as impresses the mind beyond description. But if he talks too much, though in a low voice, he sinks, and you are reminded of his being 'dust and ashes.'*

Henry may have been able to play down his poor health in letters to Lydia but it was a cause for concern to friends in Calcutta, who now saw for themselves how ill he had become. Their concern was still further increased by his apparent disregard for it with his plan to travel to Persia. His changed image in his portrait,[60] painted for Simeon while he was in Calcutta, shocked Simeon so deeply when he saw it at India House in 1812 that he turned away from it in anguish and wept.

---

[60] The portrait is now kept at Holy Trinity Church in Cambridge. A copy hangs on the dining hall staircase in his old college, St John's.

Chapter 12 — 'Everything bore the appearance of contentment'

I now pass from India to Arabia, not knowing the things that shall befal me there, but assured that an ever-faithful God and Saviour will be with me in all places whithersoever I go. May He guide and protect me, and, after prospering me in the thing whereunto I go, bring me back again to my delightful work in India! I am perhaps leaving it to see it no more;— but the will of God be done; my times are in his hand, and He will cut them as short as shall be most for my good: and with this assurance, I feel that nothing need interrupt my work or my peace.

On January 7th, 1811 Henry left Calcutta for Bombay. He had been refused passage to Bombay by one captain who was worried that Henry would try to convert the Arab crew and cause a mutiny. At the mouth of the Hooghli he boarded the *Ahmoody*, an Arab coaster which was taking the Honourable Mountstuart Elphinstone,[61] who had led the first diplomatic mission to Afghanistan in 1809 at the age of thirty, en route to Bombay to his posting as Company Resident in Poona. Elphinstone liked Henry and was delighted by his company. He writes:

We have in Mr Martyn an excellent scholar and one of the mildest, cheerfulest and most pleasant men I ever saw ... He is

---

[61] Elphinstone published: *History of India* in 1839.

extremely religious and disputes with the Abyssinian about the
faith, but he talks on all subjects and makes others laugh as
heartily as he could do if he were an infidel ... He is a man of good
sense and taste, simple in his manners and character and cheerful
in his conversation.

The voyage to Bombay took almost six weeks and, although Henry suffered from his customary seasickness, the enforced idleness was beneficial to his health. He writes a long letter to Lydia which he starts on February 4th and finishes on February 18th when he has arrived in Bombay. Giving his address as '*At sea, Coast of Malabar*,' he starts:

> *The last letter I wrote to you, my dearest Lydia, was dated*
> *November, 1810. I continued in Calcutta to the end of the year,*
> *preaching once a week, and reading the Word in some happy little*
> *companies, with whom I enjoyed that sweet communion, which all*
> *in this vale of tears have reason to be thankful for, but especially*
> *those whose lot is cast in a heathen land.*

He describes preaching to the Bible Society before describing his strategy for pre-empting the pain of saying farewell to his friends and colleagues:

> *Leaving Calcutta was so much like leaving England, that*
> *I went on board my boat without giving them notice, and so*
> *escaped the pain of bidding them farewell. ... One of my fellow*
> *passengers is Mr Elphinstone, who was lately Ambassador at the*
> *Court of the King of Cabul, and is now going to be Resident at*
> *Poonah, the capital of the Mahratta Empire. So the group is*
> *rather interesting, and I am happy to say not averse to religious*
> *instruction, — I mean the Europeans. As for the Asiatics, they are*
> *in language, customs, and religion, as far removed from us as if*
> *they were inhabitants of another planet. Among the mixed crew*
> *are Abyssinians and Arabs: I speak a little Arabic sometimes to the*
> *sailors, but their contempt of the Gospel, and attachment to their*
> *own superstitions, make their conversion appear impossible.*

Did Lydia realise that the Marathas were warriors? They would put Elphinstone's life in some considerable danger while he was in Poona. Henry refers to being tormented by seasickness which continued *all down the Bay of Bengal*. From Colombo, in Ceylon, their first port of call, Henry sent a piece of cinnamon bark to Lydia which he collected during a welcome interlude ashore:

> *The captain having proposed to his passengers they should go ashore and refresh themselves with a walk in the cinnamon-gardens, Mr E. and myself availed ourselves of the offer, and went off to inhale the cinnamon breeze. The walk was delightful. The huts of the natives, who are (in that neighbourhood at least) most of them Protestants, are built in thick groves of cocoa-nut-tree, with openings here and there, discovering the sea. Everything bore the appearance of contentment. I contemplated them with delight, and was almost glad that I could not speak with them lest further acquaintance should have dissipated the pleasing ideas their appearance gave birth to. In the gardens I cut off a piece of bark for you. It will not be so fragrant as that which is properly prepared; but it will not have lost its fine smell, I hope, when it reaches you.*

For Henry Ceylon seems to represent a Garden of Eden and his attitude to the natives, who he notes are mostly Protestant, is markedly different to the *Asiatics* earlier in the letter.

Refreshed by this welcome interlude ashore in Ceylon they set sail again and, once Cape Comorin is sighted, *the great promontory of India* at its southernmost point, Henry is reminded of the south coast of Cornwall and of the idyllic time he spent with Lydia before leaving England:

> *At a distance green waves seem to wash the foot of the mountain but on nearer approach little churches were seen, apparently on the beach, with a row of huts on either side. Was it these maritime situations that recalled to my mind Perran church and town in the way to Gurlyn; or that my thoughts wander too*

often on the beach to the east of Lamorran? You do not tell me
whether you ever walk there and imagine the billows that break at
your feet to have made their way from India. But why should I
wish to know? Had I observed silence on that day I should have
spared you much trouble and myself much pain. Yet I am far from
regretting that I spoke; since I am persuaded that all things will
work together for good.

These memories of Cornwall, in particular the references to Lamorran, near where his elder sister, Laura, lived; Perran en route to Gurlyn near St. Hilary, and Lydia's home at Marazion appear now to give him the context to reconcile his sadness at Lydia's refusal to come out to India with their mutual love and trust in the Lord. He has accepted his continuing celibacy:

As for what we should be together, I judge of it from our
friends. Are they quite beyond the vexations of common life? I
think not — still I do not say whether they gained or lost by
marrying. Their affections will live when ours (I should say rather
mine) are dead. Perhaps it may not be the effect of celibacy; but I
certainly begin to feel a wonderful sense of indifference to all but
myself. From so seldom seeing a creature that cares for me, and
never one that depends at all upon me, I begin to look upon men
with reciprocal apathy.

He himself realises he has changed and comments on Mr. Brown's remark on seeing his portrait painted for Simeon in Calcutta:

... a striking likeness, that it was not Martyn that arrived
in India, but Martyn the recluse.

He resumes this letter four days later on the 10th with an affirmation of his faith in Christ before describing Goa, which he had visited on the 7th. Goa was Portuguese at that time, and he expresses his frustration at not speaking the language. The group is taken on a Thomas Cook type tour round the various buildings among which is a monastery in which is the tomb of Francis

Xavier, the Apostle of India. Henry is appalled when they later visit a convent to find the nuns were discontented and apathetic. Much to his disappointment the Archbishop refuses to meet him, possibly because of English and Portugese officers accompanying him. Nor is he admitted to the Hall of Examination which was used by the Inquisition to cross examine prisoners: ... *we were told that when the officers of the Inquisition touch an individual, and beckon him away, he dares not resist; if he does not come out again, no one must ask about him, if he does, he must not tell what was done to him.* A chilling reminder of the power of the Catholic Church at that time.

On February 18th, his thirtieth birthday, he writes that they have reached Bombay:

> *Thus far I am brought in safety. On this day I complete my 30th year. "Here I raise my Ebenezer; Hither by thy help I'm come.*[62]

He ends this fascinating letter:

> *In a few days I expect to sail for the Gulf of Persia in one of the Company's sloops of war.*[63]

The next day he writes to the Reverend Thomas Hitchins[64] and comments on the vagaries of the postal system: *I find that among others, two letters to my sister Emma were lost in the spring of 1809 — for I find in a memorandum of their having been written & it appears from yours of 5th Feb. 1810 that they have not been received.* This would explain Henry's delight on receiving the letter from Lydia setting up the resumption of their correspondence after his sister Sally's death. In his reply from Cawnpore on March 30th, 1810 he refers to his own efforts to regain his direct contact with Lydia with *my last*

---

[62] Reference to memorial stone erected by Samuel after the victory of Mizpeh: 1 Sam. 7:12: from Hebrew: 'eben-ha- 'ezer meaning stone of help: often applied to Wesleyan chapel buildings in Cornwall.

[63] There is no reference in Lydia's Diary to receiving a letter from India in 1811 after March 28th of that year. The next reference is February 1st, 1812.

[64] Letter dated February 19th, 1811 to Rev. Thomas Hitchins: Oriental and India Office Library now part of British Library: ref: Mss.Eur A.87.

application through Emma. You have kindly anticipated my request. In his letter to Thomas Hitchins he refers to this: *From what I said in my first letter to Lydia, the first since my renewal of our correspondence, you will have ceased to expect a letter from me. In the fullness of my satisfaction at that happy turn of my affairs, I said she should have all I could send to Europe — but tho I do not repent my promise nor retract it for my letters to her contain almost the whole of my journal, together with what is written only upon my heart, I cannot resign the pleasure of seeing your handwriting, & that of the dear partner of your joys & cares — especially as the number of my friends is diminishing fast.* Although he is once more corresponding with Lydia and the role of Emma as intermediary is no longer necessary she and her husband symbolise the familial link with Cornwall. Henry dismisses any fears as to his health with *appearances of a pulmonary complaint no longer exist* before describing all the problems which have beset the translation work. He vents his outrage at the conduct of the chaplains at the Presidency: one of them *has been suspended from his functions for his profligate conduct, & the other is superannuated* and then describes how *There was to have been a great horse race on Sunday morning, but having received notice of it I informed the Governor (at whose house I am staying) & he forbad it.* He must have made himself very unpopular with the pleasure seeking population of Bombay.

He is fully cognisant with the dangers which the next leg of his journey will bring when he sets off from Bombay for the Persian Gulf in a Company sloop of war *sent to cruise against the Arab pirates. Not less than 25 armed ships of these miscreant Arabs are out, taking all they meet with, & as usual murdering every Christian.* At the end of the letter he refers to a touching detail: *I hope you named me godfather to my little namesake. I have never yet been a sponsor except to a little Lydia, L. Martyn Brown.*

Henry was to remain in Bombay, derived from Portuguese Bom Bahia, meaning beautiful bay, for almost five weeks, staying at Government House and although the climate was regarded as extremely unhealthy, those fortunate enough could escape to the Malabar Hills. While in Bombay Henry made some very useful contacts one of whom was Sir John Malcolm, who espoused British supremacy in India and was to retire to England in 1822 a wealthy man. He knew Persia well, spoke fluent Persian and had some influence among the local Governors just having returned from his second trade mission to Persia. Malcolm was skilled in the art of flattery which he had used with some success in 1800. He was sent on a mission to win the friendship of the Shah and so block French ambitions in Persia. He arrived at the Shah's court bearing gifts of guns, pistols, telescopes and jewelled watches as gifts for the Shah and his senior officials. He left Persia in 1801 having secured two treaties: one political and the other commercial. However, in 1808 when he arrived on a second mission the Shah refused to see him — he had been won over by the French and Russians — and Malcolm had to retreat. The Shah was persuaded by a gift of a large diamond from George III to change sides once more and Malcolm returned to Persia in 1810 to secure terms for a new treaty which would enable the British to monitor how easy it would be for Russia and France to invade. This story about Malcolm and the Shah is quoted in George Smith, *Henry Martyn* (1892):

> *'What induced you to hasten away from Shiraz without seeing my son?'*
>
> *'How could I,' replied the Colonel with his ever ready tact, 'after having been warmed by the sunshine of your Majesty's favour, be satisfied with the mere reflection of that refulgence in the person of your son?'*

The art of diplomacy was to prove a closed book to Henry in his dealings with the mullahs and the Shah's Vizier in Persia.

Malcolm supplied Henry with valuable letters of introduction, which would be very necessary to ease the way on his journey, *to great men at Bushire, Shiraz and Ispahan* [sic.] to carry with him. Henry expects to have to wait at least a month in Bushire before he can receive *the ambassador's permission to enter Persia*. Sir Harford Jones, who had preceded Sir Gore Ouseley as Ambassador to the Shah of Persia, wrote in his letter of introduction: *His intention is to go by Shiraz, Isfahan and Kermanshah to Baghdad and to endeavour to discover some ancient copies of the Gospel ...His knowledge of Arabic is superior to that of any Englishman in India. He is altogether a very learned and cheerful man, but a great enthusiast in his holy*

175

calling. He adds that Henry has assured him that he will not enter into any religious controversies. A promise that Henry found himself unable to keep when confronted by the learned mullahs in Persia who were well-skilled in religious debate! He paints a pleasing character portrait of him with: *I am satisfied that if ever you see him, you will be pleased with him...He will give you grace before and after dinner, and admonish such of your party as take the Lord's name in vain; but his good sense and great learning will delight you, whilst his constant cheerfulness will add to the hilarity of the party*[65]. Everyone who comes into contact with Henry recognises his extreme piety yet he is a valued and delightful companion and welcome dinner guest because of his easy social skills.

On March 25th, 1811 he sailed for Muscat in Arabia, sharing a cabin with the captain, aboard the *Benares*, a ship of the East India Company: *who in company with the Prince of Wales (a warship) was ordered to cruise in the Persian Gulf against Arab pirates,* is Henry's comment in his Journal. The Company's navy which was based in Bombay was designed to protect shipping against the marauding Marathas and other pirates. The Joasmi pirates were Arabs and had terrorised the traffic in the Persian Gulf for over 100 years. They had been conquered by the fanatical Wahabee branch of Islam. Their presence in the Gulf had been tolerated by the East India Company until 1797 when a British vessel had been seized. Since then a policy of trying to clear them from the coast had been pursued. However, although by the time Henry sailed in 1811 the Bombay Government had captured their stronghold, the Sultan of Muscat was fighting the Wahabees for his kingdom, a feudatory of Britain.

Henry anchors at Muscat on April 21st and writes to Lydia the same day:

> *My dearest Lydia,*
>
> *I am now in Arabia Felix; to judge from the aspect of the country, it has few pretensions to the name, unless burning barren rocks convey an idea of felicity.*

---

[65] Giles Hunt: *Mehitabel Canning—A Redoubtable Woman* p. 257.

Henry was still a Cornishman at heart and much preferred a lusher landscape as found at Lamorran or Gurlyn. He describes the final leg of this journey:

> *... and expect to proceed up the Gulf to Bushire, as soon as we have taken in our water.* He continues laconically: *You will be happy to learn that the murderous pirates against whom we were sent, having received notice of our approach, have all got out of the way; so that I am no longer liable to be shot in a battle, or decapitated after it, ...*

adding that he has greatly enjoyed this voyage, partly because he has been able to pursue his studies with less interruption. No doubt the sea air and enforced rest had benefited his health. He is in good spirits especially as there are two Armenians on one of the other ships *who do nothing but read the Testament.* Henry hopes that one of them will travel onward with him to Shiraz after they arrive at Bushire.

Henry shows his disappointment at not yet having received a letter from Lydia. There is no reference in her Diary between April 23rd in 1810 and February 1st, 1812 of writing to Henry although she makes references to receiving letters from him in 1810. The agreed new relationship based on correspondence is proving to be very one-sided especially as it was she who had proposed it after his younger sister Sally died. He asks her plaintively:

> *When will our correspondence be established? I have been trying to effect it these six years, and it is only yet in train. Why there was no letter among those dated June and July, 1810, I cannot conjecture, except that you had not received any of mine, and would write no more. But I am not yet without hope that a letter in the beloved hand will yet overtake me somewhere.*

The reason for this lack of correspondence on Lydia's part may be that she is suffering from renewed guilt over Samuel John and is going through terrible torment as she tries repeatedly to make progress in strengthening her faith which has isolated her from some members of her family. She acknowledges receiving letters from Henry and from his accounts of his health is half-expecting to receive news of his death. She writes on November 30th, 1810:

> *Heard yesterday, and again today from India. The illness*
> *of my friend fills me with apprehension on his account and I*
> *seemed called on to prepare for hearing of his removal. I wish to*
> *place before my eyes the blessedness of the change to him, and,*
> *though agitated and sad, I can bear to think of our never more*
> *beholding each other in this world. This indeed has long been my*
> *expectation, and that he should have left the toils of mortality for*
> *the joys of heaven should, on his account, fill me with praise, — yet*
> *my heart cannot rise with thankfulness. I am stupefied, insensible*
> *to any feelings but that of anxiety to hear again and know the*
> *truth, and that my heart could joy in God at all times; but alas!*
> *all is cold there! Oh return blessed Spirit of life and peace.*

On December 8th she refers to receiving another letter from Henry which only re-confirms her anxieties about his health. She appears even more resigned to the fact that he is dying and accepts that they will probably never meet again except in heaven. This may have led her not to write to Henry until she received this much more optimistic letter in which there is no mention of health problems.

In the closing paragraph of his letter from aboard ship Henry refers to his planned return to England:

> *As it may be a year or more before I shall be back, you*
> *may direct one letter after receiving this, if it be of a very old date*
> *to Bombay; all after to Bengal, as usual. Believe me to be ever, my*
> *dearest Lydia,*
>
> *Your most affectionate*
>
> *H. Martyn.*[66]

---

[66] Received by Lydia on February 1st, 1812. Her reply was received by Henry on July 12th, 1812 in Tabriz.

The improvement in his health brought about by the sea voyage has led an optimistic Henry to contemplate returning to England after completing his translation work. The contrast between Henry's mental state and Lydia's in the early part of 1811 is marked: He is full of plans for the next stage in his translation work in Persia and, although condemning non-Christians for their lack of faith, his faith remains undiminished.

On April 23rd Henry went ashore with the Captain to act as interpreter at a Council of State with the Wazeer. In a letter to Corrie Henry explains its purpose which was: *to discuss the relations between the Government of Bombay and these mighty chieftains.* In spite of understanding Hindi, Farsi and Arabic Henry was over-optimistic in hoping to understand the local dialect and reports sadly that: *The Wazeer uttered something in Arabic, not one word of which could I understand* so it fell to the East India Company's agent, who Henry describes as *an old man in whom pride and stupidity seem to contend for empire,* to translate. Although originally from India, he had forgotten most of his Hindi so he translated what the Wazeer said into Persian which Henry then translated into English for the Captain. Henry describes them all as being impatient to leave Muscat which was a dangerous place to linger with the minatory Wahabees only some 30 miles away.

Chapter 13 — Gool and Bulbul, roses and nightingales

At night on April 25th Henry set sail for Bushire, in Persia, to the west in the Persian Gulf, where he landed on May 22nd. During this voyage, which was rough with strong north-westerly winds blowing most of the time, Henry is once again racked with sea sickness but is working on a new arrangement of Hebrew roots and re-reading Lydia's letters.

Henry remained for ten days in Bushire, a pleasant port which had close trading ties with Muscat and a prosperous Arab quarter with narrow winding alleyways and mud brick houses which traditionally had two knockers on their doors: one for women which gave a lighter knock and a heavier one for the use of male visitors: a female servant would open the door to the lighter knock and a male one to the heavier knock. Since 1759, when the East India Company moved its base there, Bushire had become not only the main port for the province of Fars but for all Persia. While waiting for the permission to travel inland on to Shiraz, the party prepared itself for the long and gruelling journey which lay ahead of some 200 miles. This would involve crossing successive ranges of the Zagros mountains where peaks rise to 10,000 feet, before reaching Shiraz which lies on the plateau at 5,000 feet. In June the heat would be intense, 50° centigrade and over 90% humidity on the coast which would make the journey exhausting and dangerous for Henry.

In Bushire he stayed with an English merchant and his Armenian wife and sister *who spoke nothing but Persian at table; the servants and children the same.* He describes when calling on the Governor, a Persian Khan, the Persian etiquette in welcoming a visitor:

... he was very particular in his attentions, seated me in his own seat, and then sat by my side. After the usual salutations and enquiries, the calean (or hookah) was introduced; then coffee in china cups placed within silver ones, then calean, then some rose water syrup, then calean.

In trying to find a subject to converse about Henry admires the stained glass windows, and, wishing to compliment his host, adds that European stained glass work is inferior. He is taken aback when the Governor expresses his surprise *that Europeans, who were so skilful in making watches, should fail in any handicraft work.* Henry takes this remark as a slur on European art and hastily changes the subject to admiring the decoration on the Governor's calean which *had several little paintings of the Virgin and Child.* Henry asks if it is unlawful to have such things to which *he answered very coolly, 'Yes;' as much as to say 'What then?'*

There was an Armenian Orthodox community and church which he visits. The Armenian priest, who has sent for him to come to his church, douses him in incense four times, in his enthusiasm to show his respect. Henry comments in a letter to Corrie: *But though his civility was well meant, I could hardly prevail upon myself to thank him for it.* A new, Armenian Church, built in 1819 by members of the substantial British community, reflects the later British missionary activity with the graves in the small cemetery bearing witness to their faith.

Henry enjoyed the welcome cooling breeze blowing off the Persian Gulf as he walked along the seashore in the evenings, talking with his host. He decided to adopt Persian dress as being more comfortable for the forthcoming journey and describes his colourful attire it in a letter to Daniel Corrie:

On the 30th of May, our Persian dresses were ready, and we set out for Shiraz. The Persian dress consists of, first stockings and shoes in one; next a pair of large blue trousers, or else a pair of huge red boots; then the shirt; then the tunic; and above it the coat, both of chintz, and a great coat. I have here described my

own dress, most of which I have on at this moment. On the head is
worn an enormous cone, made of the skin of the black Tartar
sheep, with the wool on. If to this description of my dress I add that
my beard and moustaches have been suffered to vegetate
undisturbed ever since I left India, — and that I am sitting on a
Persian carpet, in a room without tables or chairs, — and that I
bury my hand in the pillau, without waiting for spoon or plate,
you will give me credit for being already an accomplished Oriental.

Henry, with his Armenian servant, Zecharia, who was from Isfahan, set off for Shiraz at ten o'clock on a moonlit night in a caravan of about 30 mules and horses, some laden with things for the British Ambassador. The party planned to travel by night to avoid the intense heat of the day which Henry records at one point as being 126°f (60°C). The first part of the journey lay across the burning heat of salt flats which stretch endlessly away, then turn into desert before the relief of an oasis of date palms and orange trees is reached. As night approaches one of the muleteers sings this song which Henry transcribes in Persian, with a translation, for Corrie:

Think not that e'er my heart could dwell
Contented far from thee:
How can the fresh-caught nightingale
Enjoy tranquillity.

O then forsake thy friend for naught
That slandreous tongues can say;
The heart that fixeth where it ought,
No power can rend away.

The next day Henry suffered intensely from the heat while trying to rest under a tree:

At first the heat was not greater than we had felt in
India; but it soon became so intense as to be quite alarming. When
the thermometer was above 112°, fever heat, I began to lose my
strength fast; at last it became quite intolerable. I wrapped myself

183

up in a blanket and all the warm covering I could get, to defend myself from the external air; by which means the moisture was kept a little longer upon the body, and not so speedily evaporated as when the skin was exposed ... in this state I composed myself, and concluded that, though I might hold out a day or two, death was inevitable.

The following day Henry improves his cooling system:

I got a tattie[67] made of the branches of the date tree, and a Persian peasant to water it; by this means the thermometer did not rise above 114°. But what completely secured me from the heat was a large wet towel, which I wrapped round my head and body, muffling up the lower part in clothes.

About 60 miles from Bushire, at Dalaki, the steep, rocky sand-coloured mountains rear up like a wall from the edge of the plain. Now the caravan was starting the long and exhausting climb up successive gorges through the towering ranges of the Zagros. Henry gives this description of the danger:

This night, for the first time, we began to ascend the mountains. The road often passed so close to the edge of tremendous precipices, that one false step of the horse would have plunged his rider into inevitable destruction.

The caravan also faced the threat of being attacked by bandits and robbed so where possible they stopped at a fortified caravanserai which offered safety to traders, pilgrims and travellers. These were built on all trade routes and were sited approximately 15 to 20 miles apart, a system which had already been in place for over 2,000 years. At one pass they meet a man *with a load of ice, which he willingly disposed to us,* no doubt a most welcome additional cooling aid! In another valley one of the muleteers fears he has sighted robbers but it

---

[67] Tatty or Tattie: Hind. tatti; a screen or mat, made of the roots of fragrant grass and hung over windows and doors and kept wet so that hot winds blow on them and cool the house: a system which Henry knew from India.

turns out to be a false alarm although Henry notes that the terrain *was fitted to be a retreat for robbers, there being, on each side, caves and fastnesses from which they might have killed every man of us.*

The exhausting journey with its steep ascents through narrow passes to higher plateaux coupled with the lack of sleep and extreme temperatures, further debilitated Henry and by the time the caravan reached Carzeroon (Kazerun) he was suffering from a high fever. To make matters worse, although it was the second city of Fars, the group *could get nothing but bread, milk and eggs, and those with difficulty.* Furthermore, the Governor ignored their arrival in spite of being *under great obligations to the English.* Fortunately the next part of the journey proved easier apart from the nuisance and discomfort of mosquitoes. On June 7th Henry describes reaching the lush Dustarjan valley which reminds him of England. They pitch their tents *near a crystal stream, on the banks of which we observed the clover and golden cup: the whole valley was one green field, in which large herds of cattle were browsing. The temperature was about that of spring in England.* Henry is able to get some rest and catch up on his sleep. The next day they travel three parasangs (about ten miles) and stop for the day at a caravanserai before setting off at night for Shiraz where they arrive on the morning of June 9th. Henry is exhausted.

Encamped on the plain outside the walled city is Sir Gore Ouseley,[68] the British Ambassador, who was later to play a vital role in helping save Henry's life. Henry ate dinner with him before entering one of the gates of the famed beautiful city of poetry, nightingales, wine and gardens — Shiraz. In a letter to the Reverend David Brown dated June 24th he writes:

Behold me therefore in the Athens of Fars, the haunt of the Persian man. Beneath are the ashes of Hafiz and Sadi;[69]

---

[68] 1770 – 1844, diplomat. Ambassador to the Court in Shiraz and by November 1811 Ambassador to the Court in Tehran. Arranged peace terms between Russia and Persia, signed in 1813. Received by Alexander I in St Petersburg, 1814. Returned to England 1815. Orientalist: Persian, Arabic and Urdu. Henry baptised his daughter in Shiraz - died in infancy.

[69] Sa'dí, (1189 – 1290) travelled in Iraq and Syria; captured by the Crusaders: *Bustân (The Orchard), Golestân (The Rose garden):* Hafez 1325? –1389: undisputed master of the *ghazal* a difficult poetic form with single rhyme and complexity of metre: *Divân.*

above, green gardens and running waters, roses and nightingales
... One thing is good here, the fruit; we have apples and apricots,
plumbs, [sic.] *nectarines, greengages and cherries, all of which are*
served up with ice and snow.

It must have seemed a veritable paradise after the rigours of his journey although he was perhaps disappointed to find that all song birds in Persia may be referred to as nightingales.

The following morning he presents his letter of introduction from Malcolm to Jaffier Ali Khan, who would be his host in Shiraz. Jaffier offers breakfast after the usual ceremony of caleans and coffee, *curry, pilaws, various sweets cooled with snow, and perfumed with rosewater, were served in great profusion in china plates and basins, a few wooden spoons being beautifully carved.* After this sumptuous breakfast his host takes him to a summer house in the garden where he introduces him to his brother-in-law, Mirza Seid Ali, who would guide Henry with the Persian translation of the New Testament. Much work was needed to be done on it and the translation was not to be finally finished until February 24th, 1812. Henry forgets his promise not to get involved in religious debate and as the three of them sit in the garden amidst the cooling sound of water and the welcome shade of the trees he is drawn into a debate on Sufism, a branch of Islam, of which his host was a passionate admirer. Jaffier and Henry continue to debate on religion throughout his stay.

On June 23rd he writes the first of three letters from Shiraz to Lydia.

My dearest Lydia,

How continually I think of you, and indeed converse with you, it is impossible to say. But on the Lord's-day in particular, I find you much in my thoughts, because it is on that day that I look abroad, and take a view of the universal church, of which I observe that the saints in England form the most conspicuous part. On that day too, I indulge myself with a view of the past, and look over again those happy days, when in company with those I loved, I went up to the house of God with a voice of praise. How then shall

I fail to remember her, who of all that are dear to me, is the dearest? It is true that I cannot look back on many days, nor even many hours spent with you; — would they had been more! — but we have insensibly become more acquainted with each other, so that, on my part at least, it may be said that separation has brought us nearer to one another. It was a momentary interview but the love is lasting, everlasting. Whether we ever meet again or not, I am sure you that will continue to feel an interest in all that befalls me.

He then refers to the death of his sister Sally and how:

you bid me consider that I had one sister left while you remained; and you cannot imagine how consolatory to my mind this assurance is. To know that there is one who is willing to think of me, and has leisure to do so, is soothing to a degree which none can know but those who have, like me, lost all their relations.

Could Lydia, living with her now widowed mother, have imagined how distant and isolated Henry must have felt from friends in England now that he was in Persia or how important and welcome letters were? He continues the letter by hoping that she has received his letter from Muscat, his only letter from there to Europe. He assures her that:

I am in perfect health; of my spirits I cannot say much; I fancy they would be better were 'the beloved Persis' by my side. This name, which I once gave you, occurs to me at this moment I suppose because I am in Persia, intrenched in one of its valleys, separated from Indian friends by chains of mountains and a roaring sea, among a people depraved beyond all belief, in the power of a tyrant guilty of every species of atrocity. Imagine a pale person seated on a Persian carpet, in a room without table or chair, with a pair of formidable mustachios, and habited as a Persian, and you see me.

187

He adds to the letter on the 26th saying that he expects to be in Shiraz for six months:

> *The reason is this: I found on my arrival here that our attempts at Persian translation in India were good for nothing; at the same time they proposed, with my assistance, to make a new translation. It was an offer I could not refuse, as they speak the purest dialect of Persian.*

His worst fears over the translation have been proved correct and Henry must have regretted all those hours spent working on the translation with the difficult and demanding Sabat which have now proved to be wasted. He continues by describing the enforced seclusion of women which he feels makes for dull company before turning his attention to religion and his unflattering opinion of Islam:

> *I am visited by all the great and the learned; the former come out of respect to my country, the latter to my profession. The conversation with the latter is always upon religion, and it would be strange indeed, if with the armour of truth on the right hand and on the left, I were not able to combat with success, the upholders of such a system of absurdity and sin. As the Persians are a far more unprejudiced and inquisitive people than the Indians, and do not stand quite so much in awe of an Englishman as the timid natives of Hindoostan, I hope they will learn something from me.*

He reports that some are of the opinion that he has come to Persia to convert to Islam whereas others are suspicious that he plans to bring *from India some more, under the pretence of making them Mussulmans, but in reality to seize the place. They do not seem to have thought of my wish, to have them converted to my religion; they have been so long accustomed to remain without proselytes to their own.*

188

He adds to this letter on July 2nd and July 3rd commenting on the number of visitors who interrupt his translation work in order to debate different religious views with him:

> *I have more and more reason to rejoice at my being sent*
> *here; there is such an extraordinary stir about religion throughout*
> *the city, that some good must come of it.*

Henry missed no opportunity to engage in debate with the Islamic scholars in Shiraz. His tenacity is to be admired but in fact he made little headway with the mullahs. He expresses admiration for their eloquence, wishing he had the same eloquence with which to make converts of them.

He ends this letter on a practical note by telling Lydia that letters can now reach him much more quickly if she sends them: *care of Sir Gore Ouseley, Bart., Ambassador at Tehran, care of J. Morier, Esq., Constantinople, care of G. Moon, Esq., Malta,* adding that he has seen *newspapers of only four months' date, so that I am delightfully near you.* He closes the letter, somewhat plaintively, with: *This is now the seventh letter I send you, without having received an answer.*[70]

Life in Shiraz, with its pleasant climate and intellectual stimulation is suiting Henry's health, which has improved, whereas Lydia continues to battle with her conscience berating herself for vanity and entertaining worldly thoughts. There is an increased melancholy about her Diary entries, a resignation about her daily life and the passage of time as she enters her 36th year. Her first entry for 1811 on January 1st reflects a loss of self-esteem:

> *I enter on a new year with very painful feelings of my own*
> *weakness in grace, and every natural gift also. O Lord be pleased to*
> *have mercy on me, and as nature decays, so let grace be*
> *strengthened. I am conscious of decay in spiritual things, and am*
> *low in every sense, unable to do aught worthy of that God whom I*

---

[70] Received by Lydia on January 31st, 1812, which she replied to on February 1st and Henry received at Tabriz July 12th, 1812 but refers to the date as February 14th.

would serve. All I can do is to hope in Thee still, and to believe for
Thy mercy's sake, O Lord, Thou will not forsake me.

On February 9th her entry reveals she is depressed by her lack of progress in her faith when she looks back over the preceding ten years:

> *Above ten years have I professedly engaged myself to be the*
> *Lord's, and during that long space what progress might have been*
> *expected? But I have nothing to glory in when I look back on it, —*
> *nothing now to rejoice in of my own.*

Is she thinking of Henry and her lost opportunity to feel truly loved by him and valued for her spiritual and practical aid in India? This sense of recrimination about the past continues:

> *March 19th. Still with my face Zionward O bless the*
> *Lord, my soul, and all within me, for were it not by his help this*
> *could not be. I have walked very carelessly, and at a distance from*
> *God, — yet to return unto Him with my whole heart is my desire.*

She receives a letter from Henry, begun on August 14th, 1810, from Cawnpore, which is full of news and ends with a request: *Write as often as possible, every three months at least. Tell me where you go, and whom you see, and what you read.* Yet she does not write to him until February 1st the following year which is explained by these entries in which her frustration with her own life and loss of faith are obsessing her causing her to become depressed. She refers to receiving this letter:

> *March 28. Heard from my dearest friend in India. Rose*
> *early. Found my spirits engaged in prayer, but was far ... otherwise*
> *in reading. Such dullness and inattention, as ought deeply to abase*
> *me, vanity and a desire to appear of importance in the school, beset*
> *me. I am in everything discovering my sins. Lord let me not lose*
> *sight of Thee, or I do despair and perish.*

The problems in her own life during 1811 seem to preclude any correspondence with the faithful Henry who in his isolation longs for a letter from his beloved Lydia. By May she is still berating herself:

> *May 24. I have to lament, and do lament, the dreadful disorder of my mind, occupied by trifles, and neglecting to watch or pray, but just at stated times, and in them most negligently and with little feeling. True, I find sorrow stirring within me for the loss of Thy presence, my God, and pride seems to have its share in this distress to find myself so worthless, so ungrateful, to know and prove that my nature is inconstant and so little spiritual.*

This introspection and self-analysis continue:

> *June 7. Convinced how far I am from enjoying the real presence and favour of God. I desire to return to this, the record of my heart. I have here said much in a vain-glorious spirit, I fear, yet it was some help to circumspection when I regularly set down the state of my mind. Lord in a deeper sense of the real vileness of my nature, and with lower views of myself, I now again pray to be able to continue this exercise, and O for a single eye to Thy glory in it.*

In her entry for December 3rd she refers to hearing of a neighbour's being insane:

> *who had the gift of a strong intellect, which I have been lamenting too often the deficiency of. O Lord, I felt reproved for my want of thankfulness. O that I could humbly endeavour to use my poor measure of abilities to Thy glory, and be satisfied, so that I am engaged in the service of God, according to the means He has vouchsafed to give me.*

She belittles her own intellect. Her entries reveal an intelligent and deeply sensitive woman who has to bear the frustration of being trapped at home with an ageing and strong-willed mother. Henry fell in love with Lydia and clearly admired her for her mind and piety. John Sargent regarded her *as worthy* of Henry and when Simeon, who had initially argued for Henry to continue a life of celibacy, finally met her he obviously sent good reports of her to the Reverend David Brown at Aldeen and was prepared to intercede for Henry when she turned down his proposal.

Mullahs in Isfahan, October 2000

Chapter 14 — 'It is the custom here, to think much and speak little'

Henry is required to present himself at the court of Prince Abbas Mirza, the heir to Futteh Ali Shah, who had succeeded his uncle, Aga Mohammed Khan, the founder of the Kajar dynasty, in 1798. The Shah controlled great wealth and power and was being wooed by the European powers of France, Russia and Britain. Henry records the meeting in the presence of the British Ambassador with Prince Abbas Mirza on July 6th, 1811. It provides a fascinating glimpse into court life:

> *Early this morning I went with the Ambassador and his suite to court, wearing, agreeably to costume, a pair of red cloth stockings, with green high-heeled shoes. When we entered the great court of the palace, a hundred fountains began to play. The prince appeared at the opposite side, in his talar, or hall of audience, seated on the ground. Here our first bow was made. When we came in sight of him, we bowed a second time, and entered the room. He did not rise, nor take any notice of any but the Ambassador, with whom he conversed at the distance of the breadth of the room. Two of his ministers stood in front of the hall, outside; the Ambassador's Mihmander, and the Master of the Ceremonies, within at the door. We sat down in order, in a line with the Ambassador, with our hats on. I never saw a more sweet and engaging countenance than the Prince's; there was such an appearance of good nature and humility in his demeanour, that I*

could scarcely bring myself to believe that he would be guilty of
anything cruel or tyrannical.

Henry's meeting with the Shah's Vizier would be a very different experience.

Henry is now isolated from contact with other Christians and is dejected at not having received any letters either from England or India. In letters to Corrie, who is still Chaplain at Cawnpore, he expresses his dislike of Persia and the Persians, particularly their laziness which irks him as it is making the translation work progress more slowly than he had hoped. He compares Persia unfavourably to India which now holds happy memories and associations for him. Much of Henry's time while in Shiraz was taken up with debates on differences between Islam and Christianity with the Sufis and Shia Muslims. Henry could hold his own in debate not only with his host, Jaffir Ali Khan, but also with Mirza Ibrahim, the most influential and powerful mullah in Shiraz, who prepared and published a defence of Islam in answer to arguments which Henry had raised against it. It was published in Arabic for Henry's benefit. Henry responded by producing three tracts defending the Christian position and attacking Islam. He clearly respected Sufis whom he describes in a letter to Corrie as *quite the methodists of the East* and, in particular, the Mullah Aga Mahommed Hasan, a disciple of a Sufi sage, Abulcasim. However, it is on the subject of the Divinity that there is no possible meeting point or compromise possible for either camp. Henry's sense of outrage at their beliefs was presumably matched by similar outrage on their part. It is to their credit that they did allow Henry to enter freely into formal debates with them. In his Journal the following description of his meeting with Abulcasim shows the gulf between the two cultures when it came to religious debate:

> *In the evening we went to pay a long-promised visit to*
> *Mirza Abulcasim, one of the most renowned Soofies in all Persia.*
> *We found several persons sitting in an open court, in which a few*
> *greens and flowers were placed; the master was in the corner. He*
> *was a very fresh-looking old man, with a silver beard. I was*
> *surprised to observe the downcast and sorrowfull looks of the*

assembly, and still more at the silence which reigned. After sitting
some time in expectation, and being not at all disposed to waste my
time in sitting there, I said softly to Seid Ali, 'What is this?' He
said, 'It is the custom here, to think much and speak little.'

However, when he was physically threatened by local boys throwing stones and shouting 'foreigner' as he rode by on his horse, Henry felt his life could be in danger after a particularly large stone had hit him:

> *They continued throwing stones at me every day, till*
> *happening one day to tell Jaffier Ali Khan, my host, how one as big*
> *as my fist had struck me in the back, he wrote to the Governor,*
> *who sent an order to all the gates, that if anyone insulted me, he*
> *should be bastinadoed, and the next day came himself in state to*
> *pay me a visit. These measures have had the desired effect; they*
> *now call me the Feringee Nabob, and very civilly offer me the*
> *Calean.*

On September 8th he writes his second letter from Shiraz to Lydia, six months after leaving India, and his eighth letter without receiving any reply. It starts on a dejected note:

> *A courier on his way to the capital, affords me the*
> *unexpected pleasure of addressing my most beloved friend. It is*
> *now six months since I left India, and in all that time I have not*
> *heard from thence. The dear friends there, happy in each other's*
> *society, do not enough call to mind my forlorn condition. Here I*
> *am still, beset by cavilling infidels, and making very little progress*
> *in my translation, and half disposed to give it up, and come away.*
> *My kind host, to relieve the tedium of being always within a*
> *walled town, pitched a tent for me in a garden a little distance,*
> *and there I lived amidst a cluster of grapes, by the side of a clear*
> *stream.*

The beautiful gardens of Shiraz were famous with their formal man-made canals and fountains and the welcome shade offered by their trees and orchards, an enchanting oasis in the otherwise barren landscape of the plateau. He continues his letter with a description of his debates involving Islam and Christianity:

> *... but frigid reasoning with men of perverse minds, seldom brings men to Christ. However, as they require it, I reason, and accordingly challenged them to prove the Divine mission of their prophet.*

Henry has seemingly forgotten his undertaking not to try to convert non-believers. He continues with a description to Lydia of the response from the mullahs:

> *In consequence of this, a learned Arabic Treatise was written, by one who was considered the most able man, and put it into my hands; copies of it were also given to the college and the learned. The writer said that if I could give a satisfactory answer to it, he would become a Christian, and at all events, would make my reply as public as I pleased. I did answer it, and after some faint efforts on his part to defend himself, he acknowledged the force of my arguments, but was afraid to let them be generally known.*

Henry shows no fear when it comes to defending his faith.

In this letter to Lydia Henry explains an enforced change of plan:

> *A few days ago I was on the eve of my departure for Ispahan, [sic.] as I thought, and my translator had consented to accompany me as far as Bagdad; but just as we were setting out, news came that the Persians and Turks were fighting thereabouts, and that the road was in consequence impassable.*

References such as this in his letters to Lydia bring a reminder of how dangerous the countries Henry lived and worked in could be as the Ottoman Empire disintegrated and Napoleon challenged Britain and Russia. Henry had planned to travel to Baghdad to work on the Arabic version of the New Testament but with this news of fighting between the Persians and Turks he has to accept a changed route. Henry asks Lydia to send any letters to Constantinople instead of Tehran as previously arranged. He then turns to reporting the improvement in his health brought about partly by the climate of Shiraz, which at 5,000 feet was very different to Cawnpore and partly by the fact that he is not travelling vast distances on horseback under the cruel sun.

Finally he turns to the subject of this silence from Lydia:

> *I read your letters incessantly, and try to find out something new, as I usually do, but look with pain at the distant date of the last. I cannot tell what to think, but I cast all my care upon Him who hath already done wonders for me, and am sure that, come what will, it shall be good, it shall be best.* [71]

Lydia is proving to be a less regular correspondent than Henry would have wished. She finally writes to Henry on February 1st the following year.

Life continues for Henry in Shiraz until the end of October. In his final letter to Lydia from Shiraz, dated October 21st, 1811 he starts by bemoaning the Persian work ethic:

> *This state of inactivity is becoming very irksome to me. I cannot get these Persians to work, and while they are idle I am sitting here to no purpose. Sabat's laziness used to provoke me excessively, but Persians, I find, are as torpid as Arabs, when their salary does not depend on their exertions, and both very inferior to*

---

[71] Lydia does not record receiving any letters between January 31st, 1812 and December 12th, 1812. The latter was his penultimate one, dated July 12th from Tabriz. She refers writing to Henry from Perran during the week of July 18th, 1812.

199

*the feeble Indian, whom they affect to despise. My translator comes
about sunrise, corrects a little, and is off, and I see no more of him
for the day.*

To pass his time Henry is reading the Psalms in Hebrew and finding much to
interest him. He refers to his enjoyment of study: *I write with the ardour of a
student, communicating his discoveries, and describing his difficulties to a fellow
student.* With his linguistic ability and love of learning perhaps Cambridge
would have provided the right context to fully realise these talents but Henry
was also driven by a missionary zeal to convert the infidel and he was now in a
country which he felt was ready for converts to Christianity.

Again he expresses his feeling of loneliness at this isolation from other
Europeans and turns to his comforting memories of being with Lydia:

> *I think of you incessantly; too much I fear, sometimes: yet
> the recollection of you is generally attended with an exercise of
> resignation to His will. In prayer I often feel what you described
> five years ago as having felt, — a particular pleasure in viewing
> you as with me before the Lord, and entreating our common
> Father to bless both His children. When I sit and muse, my spirit
> flies away to you, and attends you at Gurlyn, Penzance, Plymouth
> Dock, and sometimes with your brother in London. If you
> acknowledge a kindred feeling still, we are not separated, our
> spirits have met and blended. I still continue without intelligence
> from India; since last January I have heard nothing of any one
> person whom I love.*

The reference to Lydia's being in London with her brother, presumably
Pascoe, her eldest brother, or possibly George, reveals that Lydia did go there
occasionally to see her relatives. Yet, in spite of being cut off from news of
friends and family in India and England for almost nine months, Henry's zeal
for converting the Muslims in Persia is undimmed as he describes his
optimism for winning converts:

Persia is, in many respects, a field ripe for the harvest.
Vast numbers secretly hate and despise the superstition imposed on
them, and as many of them have heard the Gospel, approve it; but
they dare not hazard their lives for the name of the Lord Jesus. I
am sometimes asked whether the external appearance of
Mohammedanism might not be retained with Christianity; and
whether I could not baptize them without their believing in the
divinity of Christ? I tell them, No.

He continues by rejoicing that the translation of the New Testament into Persian will bring so many new converts to Christianity. From this letter he appears full of optimism for the future and adds a postscript to the letter explaining a change in route plans for his journey to Baghdad:

It is now determined that we leave Shiraz in a week; and
as the road through Persia is impassable through the commotions
which are always disturbing some part or other of this unhappy
country, I must go back to Bushire.

However, there are more delays with the translation and due to the general political unrest Henry decides to remain in Shiraz for the winter. He has an unexpected reunion with Abdul Masih (Abdool Massee'h), who had been born in Delhi and given the name Sheikh Saleh. He had been a such a zealous Muslim that he had persuaded his Hindu servant to be circumcised. Saleh, who worked as a Persian and Arabic translator, when en route back to Lucknow broke his journey to stay with his father at Cawnpore and heard Henry preach. Instead of jeering at Henry's message of salvation he had been moved by his preaching and in 1810 moved there to work for Sabat bookbinding and copying Persian manuscripts. He accompanied Henry to Calcutta where on Whit Sunday in 1811 he had been baptised Abdool Massee'h (servant of Christ) by David Brown in Calcutta. At their meeting in Shiraz Henry presents him with a copy of his Persian New Testament in which he had written: *There is joy in Heaven over one sinner that repenteth* and signed it. Later the same year Abdul Masih joined Corrie in Agra as an evangelist. Simeon was later to have Masih's portrait hanging in his rooms in King's College.

When Henry does finally leaves Shiraz on May 12th, 1812, having finally completed the Persian New Testament on February 24th, he takes a route via Isfahan because he wishes to present two copies of the newly translated New Testament to the Shah of Persia and his heir, Prince Abbas Mirza. Henry's next letter to Lydia is almost nine months later and much has happened in the interim.

'he breaks his journey at the delightful garden of the Shah at Kashan'

Chapter 15 — 'Heard from Tebriz from Mr. M.'

Lydia had spent most of 1811 wrestling with her loss of faith and depression but the New Year finds her in a more optimistic frame of mind:

> *January 3 1812: Let me with humble fear, begin the year*
> *by acknowledging what heaven and earth might be astonished at,*
> *— that my hope in God revives after a long night of dark distress*
> *and want of every spiritual feeling. O Lord, Thou art to be*
> *praised. Could I do it more effectually, O how happy should I be,*
> *but must rejoice with trembling. Rejoice in the Lord, and tremble*
> *at the iniquity within, the base ingratitude.*

On February 1st she records receiving a letter from Henry and writing to India. His subsequent letter dated June 23rd, 1811 from Shiraz had instructed her to send letters by the quicker route which took only four months via Malta, Constantinople and Tehran. This would suggest that Henry's letter is the one written from Muscat on April 22nd, 1811 in which he writes confidently:

> *As it may be a year or more before I shall be back* [in
> India]*, you may direct one letter after receiving this, if it be not of*
> *a very old date, to Bombay; all after to Bengal, as usual.*

In the same entry for February 1st, 1812 it is evident that she is once again battling with depression and loss of faith:

My conviction of being declining in spiritual life is deeper
and deeper. I would stop and pause at what is before me. It is no
particular outward sin, but an inward loss I mourn. O yes, cold
and insensible as my heart is, I do mourn and long for it to be as in
days past. Can I not return? I have seasons of relief, but still I have
not attained to the state I once enjoyed. In prayer I am straitened,
and in reading have neither feeling or apprehension of what I
read. O let me seek more earnestly the help of the Divine spirit,
and an application of redeeming blood to my soul. I come to Thee,
O compassionate Saviour, as I am, the most unworthy and the
meanest of all. This I feel and know to be the case, — if Thou wilt
save me it must be wholly from Thy own mere grace. Whatever
faith I exercise, it must be on Thy power to save. It is difficult for
one so ungrateful as I am to hope in Divine mercy and grace, —
but its being Divine encourages me.

However, by March, her mental state is very different, as she has found a
sense of fulfilment and social usefulness when she is happily absorbed in
setting up a School of Industry in Marazion where religion would be taught
alongside the more practical subjects to children:

March 1: I experience a wonderful change from clouds
and darkness to warm sunshine, — resting on the arm of Jehovah
I am strengthened. I feel sweetly disposed to trust God for wisdom,
strength, and all I want in the new concern, which has occupied
my attention, — the establishment of a School of Industry. O may
more be taught and learnt in it than to use the fingers or the
tongue. O may the hearts of the children be affected, and the truths
of God impress their minds early, — Lord I beg Thee to keep me in
this work, free from anxiety of mind as to its success, to leave it
entirely and confidently in Thy hands, — Amen. The prospect of
the meetings being removed where the gospel may be preached at
all times without interruption, has produced a happy effect on my
mind, — Lord, I thank thee for this deliverance.

206

The customary long delays of several months between letters being sent and being received are reflected in Henry's letter to Daniel Corrie from Shiraz on December 12th, 1811.

> *Dearest Brother,*
>
> *Your letters of January 28 and April 22 have just reached me. After being a whole year without any tidings of you, you may conceive how much they have tended to revive my spirits.*

He continues by urging Corrie to avoid over-exertion during the hot season in Cawnpore and goes on to explain his own new philosophy of living:

> *I am endeavouring to learn the true use of time in a new place, by placing myself in idea twenty or thirty years in advance, and then considering how I ought to have managed twenty or thirty years ago. — In racing violently for a year or two, and then breaking down? In this way I have reasoned myself into contentment, about staying so long at Shiraz.*

He has resolved to take enough time to finish the New Testament translation:

> *... even if I had been detained there on that account for three or six years? What work of equal importance can ever come from me? So that now I am resolved to wait here till the New Testament is finished, though I incur the displeasure of Government, or even dismissed the service. I have been many times on the eve of my departure, as my translator promised to accompany me to Bagdad; but that city being in great confusion, he is afraid to trust himself there; so I resolved to go westward through the north of Persia, but found it impossible, on account of the snow which blocks up the roads in winter, to proceed till spring.*

Henry finally leaves Shiraz as part of a caravan, which included the Reverend William Canning, the new chaplain to Sir Gore Ouseley, travelling north on the evening of May 12th, 1812:

> *A little before sunset I left the city and at ten at night the cafila started. Here ended my stay at Shiraz. No year of my life was ever spent more usefully, though such a long separation from my friends was often a severe trial.*

He took the two uncorrected copies of the New Testament, doing corrections en route, hoping to present them to Fateh Ali Shah Kajar, and his heir, Prince Abbas Mirza, personally. In order to do this he would need a letter of introduction from the British Ambassador, Sir Gore Ouseley, who had his residence in Tabriz, in the north of Persia near the border with Turkey. The party reached the plain of Persepolis after ten hours riding in spite of Henry sustaining a fall from his horse. Henry had visited the ruins of the once great city while staying in Shiraz and records feeling *a little disappointed.* Ever Eurocentric he is disparaging about its majestic architecture describing it as like *their clumsy neighbours the Indians.* He makes no reference to the exquisite bas-relief work depicting scenes of homage to Darius but instead regards it as a staging post for Alexander and his troops who sacked it, reducing this once great city to heaps of masonry and rubble. Perhaps his early classical education blinkered his view! The next part of the journey lay through barren country between two mountain ridges where they encountered increasingly stormy weather. During their ascent to a higher plateau, the weather gets bitterly cold as they cross the highest land between the Persian Gulf and the Caspian Sea. Henry records seeing the black tents of nomads and passing through desperately poor villages which are suffering from the effects of drought.

On May 22nd, soon after sunrise, the party arrived in the beautiful city of Isfahan. It had enjoyed its full glory during the reign of Shah Abbas the Great who had made it his capital in 1598, built palaces and laid out a town plan with wide avenues and gardens. He created the vast Royal Square in which polo matches could be watched from the balcony of one of his palaces.

It has some of the most exquisitely tiled mosques in Iran so it is no surprise to learn that in Safavid times when its glory was at its height it was referred to as *Isfahan is half the world*. Henry is accommodated in one of the King's palaces and, much to his delight, he meets up with his Shiraz scribe. Together they complete corrections for the Prince's copy of the New Testament.

Linked by the Bridge of Thirty Arches (Si-o-Se pol) over the Zâyandeh-rud is the Armenian Christian suburb of Jolfa, which was created by Shah Abbas 1. It lay on the route of all caravans arriving from the south which passed through it as they made their way to the centre of Isfahan. It enjoyed prosperity and at one time there had been 20 bishops, 100 clergy and 24 churches. There were still about 500 houses and 12 parish churches and 24 clergy when Henry visited but he is surprised to discover that the bishops can speak little Persian.

Henry resumes his long journey at the end of the month when he sets out for Tehran. After some difficulty in gaining entry he breaks his journey at the delightful gardens of the Shah at Kashan, situated on the edge of the harsh Great Salt Desert, where the running water cascading over turquoise-coloured tiles along the man-made channels, fish ponds and the shade of the trees from the fierce sun beating down entranced Henry. He comments frequently on the gardens he encounters in Persia which were such a source of delight with their landscaping in which water played such a dominant role both visually and aurally in their design based on earlier Mughal influence. Next he passed through one of the holiest cities of Persia, Qom. Perhaps it was fortunate that Henry was unsuccessful here in gaining an audience with the chief mullah of Persia who pleaded age and infirmity as an excuse for not receiving him, for it would no doubt have led to a heated religious debate. Soon after sunset he set off again across the desert, arriving in Tehran three days later on June 8th.

Henry now faced another delay, a logistic one. There were no muleteers to be found who would do the journey further north to Tabriz. Henry decided to go alone to the Shah's summer camp at Karaj where he hoped to find the British Ambassador and the Shah. Much to his disappointment neither was there but in spite of lacking a necessary letter of introduction from the Ambassador he decided to present himself to the Shah's Vizier.

Although he had a letter of introduction from Jaffier Ali Khan, his wealthy host in Shiraz, he was rebuffed. After spending three days waiting he was summoned to the Vizier's levée and found that he had been invited to justify his beliefs. He was irritated by constant interruptions and when the Vizier called upon him to avow: *God is God, and Mohammed is the prophet of God*, Henry proclaimed instead: *God is God, and Jesus is the Son of God*. As can be imagined there was uproar and Henry's copy for presentation to the Shah was almost trampled under foot. Henry had no option but to hurriedly rescue his precious copy, wrap it up in a towel and retreat, riled by the contempt that they showed only too openly for him. It was a disastrous encounter. Diplomatic skills were clearly not Henry's forte! The Vizier wasted no time in sending a message telling him that he would need either to be presented by the British Ambassador or present a letter of introduction from him. Henry, who was now joined once again by his companion William Canning, travelled towards Tabriz, first to Sultaniyeh where he hoped to find the Ambassador and then to Zanjan, an important trading centre about 150 miles from Tabriz. It was here that Henry and many in the party fell sick, including Canning, who describes their terrible ordeal in some detail, revealing his dislike of Persia and its people, in a long a letter to his sister, Bess Barnett.[72]

At a village three stages from Tabriz, I thought Martyn and the servants so unwell that I sent off an express to Sir Gore Ouseley to inform him of our situation hoping that he might send us some medical assistance or at any rate be prepared for our reception. In the evening the messenger returned with a letter from Sir G.O. informing us that he had sent a surgeon to [?] Seidabad two stages from hence to meet us. We started that night and arrived at Enjan early next morning. This was merely a place for keeping cattle in and with great difficulty we persuaded the people to receive us and clean out a cowhouse, that we might spread our beds and take some rest during the day. The pitiless villagers, however, beheld the servants fainting under the heat of the sun and yet they had not the feeling to offer them any shelter. But this is truly Persian. Wretches! I

---

[72] Transcription of letter from William Canning to his sister, Tabriz, 2 September 1812: MAR 10/1 Henry Martyn Centre, Cambridge. Quoted in *Mehitable Canning – A Redoubtable Woman*: ed. Giles Hunt (Royston,2001)See pgs. 258 – 261.

never thought it possible for me to feel a detestation and abhorrence of a whole nation but I really do of this. Execrable race! I cannot bear to think that our country should have the slightest intercourse with them. Somehow the weakened party and the acutely ill Henry struggled on to Seidabad where the doctor treated Henry and Canning himself became ill. Henry finally arrived, eight weeks after leaving Shiraz, at the main gate of Tabriz: *Some of the people seemed to feel compassion for me and asked if I was not very ill. At last I reached the gate and asked a man to show me the way to the ambassador's house.* Canning, in his letter to his sister paints the alarming scene when he burst in on the Ouseleys:

Before daybreak I mounted a Horse with my foot in a sling instead of stirrup and only one shoe on. Thus equipped with my Pantaloons ripped from top to bottom to give ease to my swollen legs, a beard of about a week's growth, long Mustachios, an Arab Abha to cover my rugged dirty clothes, looking very pale and wild I entered the Breakfast Parlour of Sir G.O. I believe I alarmed Lady O. a good deal, but I really was not quite in my right mind at the time or I should not have done so.

Henry was nursed devotedly by Lady Ouseley (according to Canning she hated Persia) for two months at the British Ambassador's residence. In a letter to Simeon, dated August 8th he describes his terrible illness:

My Dearest Brother and Friend,

Ever since I wrote, about a month, I believe, I have been lying upon the bed of sickness for twenty days or more; the fever raged with great violence, and for a long time every species of medicine was tried in vain. After I had given up hope of recovery, it pleased God to abate the fever; but incessant headaches succeeded, which allowed me no rest day or night. I was reduced still lower, and am now a mere skeleton; but as they are now less frequent, I suppose it to be the will of God that I should be raised up to life again. I am now sitting in my chair, and wrote the will with a strong hand; but as you see I cannot write so now. Kindest

*love to Mr John Thornton[73], for whose temporal and spiritual
prosperity I daily pray.*

Your ever affectionate friend and brother.

It was from here that he wrote to Lydia on July 12th, having received a letter
from her at last, dated, poignantly, February 14th; she refers to writing this
letter to Henry on February 1st in her Diary — the first for 18 months. His
Journal entry for July 9th reads: *Made an extraordinary effort, and, as a
Tartar was going off instantly to Constantinople, wrote letters to Mr Grant, for
permission to come to England, and to Mr Simeon and Lydia, informing them
of it.* He begins the letter by acknowledging receipt of hers and then describes
his terrible illness from which he is still barely recovering:

> *My Dearest Lydia,*
>
> *I have only time to say that I have received your letter of
> February 14. Shall I pain your heart by adding, that I am in such
> a state of sickness and pain, that I can hardly write to you.*

He then explains that he has applied for leave of furlough to come to
England:

> *I ought to inform you that, in consequence of the state to
> which I am reduced by travelling so far overland, without having
> accomplished my journey, and the consequent impossibility of
> returning to India the same way, I have applied for leave to come
> on furlough to England.*

It is a relatively short letter, its tone is pessimistic reflecting the outlook of a
still seriously ill man especially when he continues:

---

[73] John Thornton was joint executor of his will with John Sargent.

212

Perhaps you will be gratified by this intelligence; but oh, my dear Lydia, the probability of my reaching England alive is but small; and this I say, that your expectations of seeing me again may be moderate, as mine are of seeing you. Why have you not written more about yourself? However, I am thankful for knowing that you are alive and well.

Henry now recognises that his health may not bear up to undertaking another long journey. He suggests that she write to Alexandria in Egypt or to Constantinople where *though I shall not go there, I hope Mr Morier will be kept informed of my movements.*

Kindest love to all the saints you usually mention.

Yours, ever most faithfully and affectionately.

His terrible fever continued raging until July 21st. Henry writes how bark and other tonics were administered to relieve it but views himself *as too far gone* to benefit.

The resumption in their correspondence after Henry has written nine letters without receiving a reply comes too late to offer much comfort or solace to him. Lydia records writing to him on July 18th, August 30th and September 30th in 1812. When this letter arrives with news of his terrible illness it alarms Lydia. She notes in her Diary on December 12th, 1812:

Heard from Tebriz from Mr M., with an account of his dangerous state of health and his intention of his returning to England if his life was spared. This intelligence affected me variously. The probability of his death, the certainty of his extreme sufferings, and distance from every friend pressed heavily upon my spirits; I was enabled to pray, and felt relieved. Of his return no very sanguine expectations can be entertained. Darkness and distress of mind have followed this information.

It was to be his penultimate letter to his beloved Lydia.

Henry was forced by his tuberculosis and his increasing debility to relinquish his dream of presenting the translation to the Shah personally or to his son Prince Abbas, even though the Prince was in residence in Tabriz, as he was too ill. Sir Gore Ouseley did present it later and the Shah publicly expressed his approval at the translation:

> *In the Name of the Almighty God, whose glory is most excellent.*

> *It is our august command that the dignified and excellent our trusty, faithful, and loyal well-wisher, Sir Gore Ouseley, Baronet, His Britannic Majesty's Ambassador Extraordinary (after being honoured and exalted with the expressions of our highest regard and consideration), should know that the copy of the Gospel, which was translated into Persian by the learned exertions of the late Rev. Henry Martyn, and which has been presented to us by your Excellency on the part of the high, dignifiede, learned and enlightened Society of Christians, united for the purpose of spreading abroad the Holy Books of the religion of Jesus (upon whom, and upon all prophets, be peace and blessings!), has reached us and has proved highly acceptable to our august mind.*

> *In truth, through the learned and unremitted exertions of the Rev. Henry Martyn, it has been translated in a style most befitting sacred books, that is, in an easy and simple diction. Formerly, the four Evangelists, Mathew, Mark, Luke and John, were known in Persia; but now the whole of the New Testament is completed in a most excellent manner: and this circumstance has been an additional source of pleasure to our enlightened and august mind. Even the four Evangelists which were known in this country had never been before explained in so clear and luminous manner. We, therefore, have been particularly delighted with this copious and complete translation. If it please the most merciful God, we shall command the Select Servants, who are admitted to*

our presence, to read[74] to us the above mentioned book from the beginning to the end, that we may, in the most minute manner, hear and comprehend its contents.

Your Excellency will be pleased to rejoice the hearts of the above-mentioned dignified, learned and enlightened Society with assurances of our highest regard and approbation; and to inform those excellent individuals who are so virtuously engaged in disseminating and making known the true meaning and intent of the Holy Gospel, and other points in sacred books, that they are deservedly honoured with our royal favour. Your Excellency must consider yourself as bound to fulfill this royal request.
Given in Rebialavil, 1229.
(Sealed)   Fateh Ali Shah Kajar.[75]

Praise indeed and generous recognition for all Henry's care in making sure that the translation was both correct and easily accessible in style and language. In a letter to Lord Teignmouth, President of the British and Foreign Bible Society, dated September 20th, 1814,[76] Ouseley reveals that before presenting the copy to the Shah he had paved the way for a sympathetic response by having had copies made and then distributed to Sufis who were close to the Shah. He felt they would be more inclined to give it a fair reading and be therefore better able to discuss it sympathetically and knowledgeably with him. It was also Gore Ouseley who took the original manuscript to St. Petersburg where in 1815 the first edition of 5000 copies was published by the Russian Bible Society.

---

[74] *'I beg leave to remark that the word 'Tilawat,' which the translator has rendered 'read' is an honourable signification of that act, almost exclusively applied to the perusing or reciting the Koran. The making use, therefore, of this term or expression shows the degree of respect and estimation in which the Shah holds the New Testament. — Note by Sir Gore Ouseley.'* Footnote from George Smith: *Henry Martyn Saint and Scholar* p 487.

[75] Quoted in George Smith: *Henry Martyn, Saint and Scholar* pp 486 –487.

[76] Quoted in George Smith: *Henry Martyn, Saint and Scholar* pp 484 from the *Eleventh Report of the British and Foreign Bible Society*, 1815, Appendix, No. 51.

When Henry writes his last letter to Lydia on August 28th, 1812 he is still far from well but is optimistically planning the return route to England on the basis of Sir Gore Ouseley's advice and help. It is a much longer letter than the previous one and dwells in the first part on his illness and the humbling effect it has had on him:

> *I wrote to you last, my dear Lydia, in great disorder. My fever had approached nearly to delirium, and my debility was so great, that it seemed impossible I could withstand the power of disease many days. Yet it has pleased God to restore me to life and health again; not that I have recovered my former strength yet, but consider myself sufficiently restored to prosecute my journey. My daily prayer is, that my late chastisement may have its intended effect, and make me all the rest of my days more humble and less self-confident. Self-confidence has often let me down fearful lengths, and would, without God's gracious interference, prove my endless perdition.*

Does he perhaps refer to his disastrous handling of his meeting with the Shah's Vizier and regret that he had not been more diplomatic in his response in defence of Christianity? He then refers to seeing her again *to give an account of all my discussions with these mystic philosophers, must be reserved to the time of our meeting.*

> *Do I dream? that I venture to think and write of such an event as that! Is it possible that we shall ever meet again below? Though it is possible, I dare not indulge such a pleasing hope yet. I am still at a tremendous distance; and the countries I have to pass through, are many of them dangerous to the traveller, from the hordes of banditti, whom a feeble government cannot chastise.*

He then describes the dangers that face him and explains that Sir Gore Ouseley has advised him to go first to Constantinople and from there to Syria:

In favour of this route, he urges, that by writing to two or three Turkish governors on the frontiers, he can secure me a safe passage at least half-way, and the latter half is probably not much infested. In three days, therefore, I intend setting my horse's head towards Constantinople, distant about thirteen hundred miles.

A long and difficult journey for a man who is only just recovering from a serious and debilitating illness. He appears to have forgotten his letter to Corrie and his resolution to manage his time and health better. Henry was fully aware of the dangers that lay ahead and adds:

Nothing, I think, will occasion any further detention here, if I can procure servants who know both Persian and Turkish; but should I be taken ill on the road, my case would be pitiable indeed.

A prescient comment. Next he refers to the kindness of Lady Ouseley during his illness and his great disappointment at not being able to present Prince Abbas Mirza personally with the copy of the Persian New Testament but takes comfort in the Ambassador presenting it at some time in the future. He also feels that he has achieved some success in Persia in an awakening of interest in the Gospels, especially in Shiraz and looks confidently to the Persians starting a march to enlightenment: *As they are ripe for revolution in religion as well as politics.* Henry responds to Lydia's enquiry in her letter about Sabat by admitting that he has no information about him apart from one letter from him from Calcutta complaining that since Henry left no one was interested in him. He comments:

He is to be sure the most tormenting creature I ever yet chanced to deal with — peevish, proud, suspicious, greedy; he used to give daily more and more distressing proofs of his never having received the saving grace of God. But of this you will say nothing; while his interesting story is yet fresh in the memory of people, his failings had better not be mentioned.

A damning summary of poor Sabat whose Persian translation had proved to be such a disaster. He ends the letter:

> *My course from Constantinople is so uncertain that I hardly know where to desire you to direct me; I believe Malta is the only place, for there I must stop in my way home. Soon we shall have occasion for pen and ink no more; but I trust I shall shortly see thee face to face. Love to all the saints.*
> *Believe me to be yours, ever*
>
> *Most faithfully and affectionately*
>
> *H. Martyn.*

Henry was never to see or hear from his beloved Persis again.

Chapter 16 — 'Living or dying, remember me!'

Henry set out on horseback at sunset, with two baggage horses, on September 2nd, 1812 on a long and hazardous journey when he was still not fully recovered from his near fatal illness. Accompanying him was his faithful Armenian servant Sergius, who spoke a little Persian and, most importantly – Turkish, which Henry did not, together with a groom, Antoine, baggage horses and a guard. Sergius was to travel with him to Constantinople where Henry would present letters to the British Ambassador. This pale European was a cause of much interest as he passed on his way or stopped in villages to rest. Their route, first across the plain of Tabriz with its vast views *towards the west and south-west, stretches away to an immense distance, and is bounded in these directions by mountains so remote, as to appear from their soft blue, to blend with the skies.* They followed the ancient Persian Royal Road which took them first near to Mount Ararat and then on to Yerivan, a fortress town. Here he calls on the Governor, on September 11th, who at first totally ignores him and goes through several displays to impress his visitor:

> *After a compliment or two he resumed his devotions. The next ceremony was to exchange a rich shawl dress for a still richer pelisse, on pretence of its being cold. The next display was to call for his physician, who, after respectfully feeling his pulse, stood to one side; this was to show that he had a domestic physician.*

The ever important letter of introduction from Ouseley lay unread during all this but finally after a translator has read it to him his attitude to Henry is kind and solicitous. Henry is summoned again in the afternoon and this time there is no ceremony. Henry describes the beguiling scene:

> *A fountain, in a basin of white marble, was playing before him, and in it water-grapes and melons were cooling; two time pieces were before him, to show the approach of the time of lawful repast; below the window, at a great depth ran a broad and rapid stream, over rocks and stones, under a bridge of two arches, producing an agreeable murmur; on the side of the river were gardens, and a rich plain; and directly in front, Ararat.*

The Governor is now extremely helpful and orders a guard and four horses to accompany Henry for the ongoing journey but, because they were not ready the following day, Henry decides to ride alone to the monastery at Ech Miazin, or Three Churches, where there were about 100 monks. This was the site of the chief see of the Armenian Church:

> *Within the entrance, I found a large court with monks, cowled and gowned, moving about. On seeing my Armenian letters, they brought me to the patriarch's lodge, where I found two bishops, one of whom was Nestus, at breakfast on pilaws, kubebs, wine, arrack, &c, and Serafino with them.*

After showing Henry to his room, Serafino tells Henry his story. Born to Armenian Roman Catholic parents, he is Armenian and his birth name is Serope. When his father died in Erzerum while he was still a boy his mother placed him in the care of missionaries and he was taken to Rome where he spent eight years being educated. He spoke English, French and Italian and *became perfectly Europeanised*, according to Henry. However, after his ordination he decided to join the Armenian Church and returned to his home town, Erzerum, before joining the monastery. He is planning to make reforms and is in charge of educating the young Armenians training for the ministry. Henry enjoys the monks' kind hospitality and finds their company so interesting that he informs Nestus *that I was so happy in being here, that, did duty permit, I could almost be willing to become a monk with them.* A rather alarmed Nestus responds that they had quite enough monks! Henry spends five days here and on September 15th reports that with Serope's help he has been preparing *for the mode of travelling in Turkey.*

> *All my heavy and expensive preparations at Tebriz prove to be incumbrances which must be left behind: my trunks were exchanged for bags; and my portable table and chair, several books, large supplies of sugar, &c, were condemned to be left behind. My humble equipments were considered as too mean for an English gentleman; so Serope gave me an English bridle and saddle. The roads in Turkey being much more infested with robbers than those of Persia, a sword was brought for me.*

Another guard, Melcom, *a brave and trusty man of the monastery,* who has his own arms and will carry Henry's money, joins the group, but speaks only Turkish.

On September 17th Henry sets off across the plain of Ararat. He decides to stop for a bathe in the Araxes while his guard Melcom stands by. As they are riding to catch the party up again they are overtaken by a hunter who fortunately turns out to be friendly but almost injures Henry when he spots partridges and fires a pistol at them causing his horse to jump with fright at the noise so that his lance which is balanced across his saddle almost pierces Henry or his horse. By September 19th they have taken on three extra guards as they are entering an even more dangerous area. They cross and recross the Araxes and then start ascending mountains, which Henry describes as a long and difficult route, before emerging on a plateau from where they can see Russia, Persia and Turkey. They finally arrive at their first stop in Turkey, a small village called Fiwick. It has been a long and arduous day and Henry records: *I was rather uncomfortably lodged, my room being a thoroughfare for horses, cows, buffaloes, and sheep. Almost all the village came to look at me.* Before they reach the next town, Kars, they have to traverse a dangerous area but decide to take the shortest route in spite of the threat of being attacked by a tribal chief. At Kars, with its huge burial ground and its fort, and its reassuring European appearance, Henry is taken to an Armenian house where he enjoys some welcome peace and privacy. On September 22nd the party leaves Kars with a new guard, a Turk by the name of Hassan who shows increasing intolerance over Henry's weak state of health by riding at high speed during the burning heat of the day. Soon the fever and sweating return with Henry growing increasingly weaker by the day. Sergius was alarmed and tried his best to find resting places for Henry where he could be quiet and recover a little of his strength but it was not easy with the unsympathetic and intolerant Hassan constantly harrying him. Henry records travelling for eleven and a half hours on September 24th, which, although they had a pleasant bathe in a hot spring en route where Hassan smokes his calean while up to the neck in water, much to Henry's amusement, is a long day's riding. The following day they reach Erzerum with its bustling streets and shops. Henry's outfit of Persian and European mix causes comment and some hostility. Henry in turn comments on the Turkish dress of Turkish fez, turbans and the opulent materials used for the clothes, which he compares to pictures he has seen.

It is after leaving Erzerum on September 29th that Henry's health begins to decline alarmingly. He starts reporting attacks of fever, headaches and extreme loss of appetite. On October 1st he records travelling from seven in the morning till eight at night over mountainous tracks. That evening, while sitting by a fire *near fainting from sickness,* he learns that plague is raging in Constantinople and thousands are dying. The town of Tokat, which was close on their route, was also beset by plague. Henry records: *Thus am I passing inevitably into danger. O Lord, thy will be done. Living or dying remember me!* The entry in his Journal on October 5th records his failing health and exhaustion:

> *I was tolerably well till after sunset, when the ague came on with a violence I had never before experienced. I felt as if in a palsy, my teeth chattering and my whole frame shaking violently ... Aga Hosyn and another Persian on their way here from Constantinople, going to Abbas Mirza,[77] whom I had just before*

---

[77] Prince Abbas Mirza, son of the Shah of Persia.

224

been visiting, came hastily to render me assistance if they could.
The Persians appear quite brotherly after the Turks. While they
pitied me, Hassan sat in perfect indifference, ruminating on the
further delay this was likely to occasion. The cold fit, after
continuing two or three hours, was followed by a fever, which
lasted the whole night, and prevented sleep.

October 6, 1812: No horses being to be had, I had an
unexpected repose. I sat in the orchard, and thought, with sweet
comfort and peace, of my God; in solitude my company, my friend
and comforter. Oh, when shall time give place to eternity! When
shall appear that new heaven and new earth wherein dwelleth
righteousness! There, there shall in nowise enter in anything that
defileth: none of that wickedness which has made men worse than
wild beasts, — none of those corruptions which add still more to
the miseries of mortality, shall be seen or heard of any more.

This was the last entry in Henry's Journal. He died ten days later on October 16th, 1812 aged 31 in the very circumstances he had feared in his letter to Lydia. It was the faithful Armenian servant, Sergius, who brought the sad news and a bundle of personal effects including letters and his Journal, or *A Narrative*, as Henry termed his account of his time in Persia and his final tragic journey as far as Tokat, to Isaac Morier, who was the father of Sir Gore Ouseley's secretary, in Constantinople, a further 600 miles' ride away. Henry was buried without a coffin in the Armenian cemetery of the Church of Karasoon Manoog at Tokat with the honours usually given only to an Armenian Archbishop. An Armenian Archbishop officiated at the ceremony.

Charles Simeon had written to Charles Grant on August 1st informing him that the portrait of Henry had just arrived and making arrangements to stand the cost of framing it. He reports the sad news that the Reverend David Brown is dying and Corrie is ill but Thomason is *labouring away*. In the final paragraph he turns to the subject of Henry and writes confidently:

My letters from Mr Martyn are most interesting. I shall
hope to shew you one or two. I suppose he left Shiraz in the Spring;

*& is gone through Armenia to Mesopotamia & Syria, on account
of the extreme danger of going as he intended from Bussorah to
Bagdad.*

> *I trust that so distinguished a servant of the Company has
> found no difficulty in having his furlough extended to two years.*[78]

Simeon writes more sombrely from King's College to Charles Grant on
December 9th:

My Dear Sir,

*You have heard of Mr Brown's death. You have heard also of Mr Martyn's
dangerous illness—He writes me word that he has written to you a letter to lay
before the Directors to desire a Furlough to come to England for his recovery. If
you have not received his letter, pray send me word by Return of Post that I may
send you mine. But I fear that he will be no more, before any letter can reach him
— He is at Tebritz —*

*I think Tebritz is between Busheer & Shiraz; if you answer this pray tell me
if I am right —*[79]

On December 26th, unaware that events have finally overtaken his
protégé he writes to Grant:

My Dear Sir,

*A thousand thanks to you for your kind [?] compliance with my wishes. My
object was to supply my dear Brother with all that he may want to pay
Physicians, & to secure the best accommodations on board of ship for anytime
that it may be needful. With that view I could earnestly wish that ~~the~~ every
different Consul might be empowered to assist him to the full extent of his
necessities, providing only that the amount altogether shall not exceed 1000£.
And this might be done by each Consul being empowered & requested to inform
him that there are letters of Credit lodged for him in such & such different
places, to the amount of one thousand pounds in all — I have this day rec. a*

---

[78] Letter dated August 1st, 1812 from Charles Simeon to Charles Grant: Henry Martyn Centre,
Westminster College, Cambridge: MAR 1/17.

[79] Letter dated December 9th, 1812 from Charles Simeon to Charles Grant: Henry Martyn Centre,
Westminster College, Cambridge: MAR 1/17.

letter which says, that he expects Alexandria in Egypt ~~to be~~ or Constantinople to be the place where he shall reach the Mediterranean.

It is desirable too that the Consuls be authorized to inform him that the money is a present, & not a loan; for then he will have no anxiety about the repayment of it.

I think I shall write a few lines to <u>him</u> at each place, & forward it to you, to be counter-signed or inclosed in another of your own to the consul.

Did I not know that your heart is in perfect unison with mine in this matter, I should make ten thousand apologies for the liberty I am taking: but I believe you will account nothing a trouble which you can do for such an honoured Servant of the Lord — I therefore without apology, but not without lively gratitude: subscribe myself,

My Dear Sir
Most affectionately Yours
C. Simeon.[80]

K.C. Camb
Dec 26. 1812

Two days before Henry's death Simeon had visited India House in London and saw the portrait which Henry had had painted as a gift before he left Calcutta in 1810. It would hang over Simeon's fireplace in his rooms at King's. He writes on October 14th, 1812 to Thomason:

> *I opened, and put up the picture of my ever dear and honoured brother, Mr Martyn. I had indeed, after it was opened at the India House, gone to see it there, and notwithstanding all that you had said respecting it to prepare my mind, I was so overpowered by the sight, that I could not bear to look upon it but turned away and went at a distance, covering my face, and, in spite of every effort to the contrary, crying aloud with anguish; E. was with me; and all the bystanders said to her, 'That I suppose is his father.' And I think it probable, that if I had been his father, or his mother either, I should not have felt more than I did on that*

---

[80] Letter dated December 26th, 1812 from Charles Simeon to Charles Grant: Henry Martyn Centre, Westminster College, Cambridge; MAR 2/19.

occasion. Shall I attempt to describe the veneration and love with which I look at it? No words that I can write will convey any adequate idea; nothing but your own tender mind can exactly conceive what I feel ... in looking on that image of my beloved friend. In seeing how much he is worn I am constrained to call to my relief the thought, in whose service he has worn himself so much.

Henry looked a shadow of the man who had set out with such faith seven years earlier. A few months later Simeon learnt of his death and wrote to Charles Grant, Chairman of the East India Company on February 11th, 1813:

> *My Dear Sir,*
>
> *Grieved I am to communicate to you the most distressing intelligence of Mr. Martyn's death at Tokat in Asia Minor on his way either to Constantinople or to Aleppo. From the account being given by Mr. Isaac Morier, I apprehend Constantinople was the place to which he was proceeding. His papers and property are secured. He had set out from Tabriz on the first of September (much too soon for the state in which he had been) and died about 16th of October; but whether from the heat and fatigue of travelling, or from the plague, which was raging there, is uncertain. Just what words can express the loss which India, and the whole world has sustained! [81]*

On May 19th, 1815, he wrote from King's College to Thomason *Mr Martyn's papers are all safe. We have his Journals till within a few days of his death. What a glorious life will his be.* Thomason died in 1829 but Simeon, unlike so many of his young protégés who died relatively young, lived till the

---

[81] Quoted by Graham Kings in *Foundations for Mission and the Study of World Christianity: The Legacy of Henry Martyn.* Henry Martyn Centre.

age of 78. He caught a chill after visiting Ely Cathedral to pay his respects to the Bishop and was buried in the Fellows' Vault at King's.

Chapter 17 — 'The Intelligence Affected me Variously'

The poignancy of the correspondence is captured in Lydia's Diary entries from July 18th, 1812 with references to letters she is writing to Henry which he will never receive; news of his death, which she receives on February 14th, 1813; and finally in the arrival on April 21st of his last letter from Tabriz written on August 28th, 1812.

Lydia notes on July 18th, 1812: *At Perran. Wrote, during the week, and thought much of —.* Perran was associated by both her and Henry with happy times in their courtship. During the summer Lydia continues to be more optimistic about life and in particular her faith. This is reflected by a happy entry on August 2nd when she is staying with her brother, George, and his family, at Perran:

> *Had one delightful hour with my blessed brother, longed to sanctify the meeting by prayer, but he shrinks from the exercise, and I could only mentally pray. Lord teach him better in this respect, and enable him to join in prayer and praise on all fit occasions. How sweet is Thy word to my taste, O Lord, — "sweeter than the honey or honeycomb" said David, and I trust I can say the same. I must not boast, — I have nothing in myself to glory or confide in, but it seems to me that at this moment, when every earthly comfort I could possibly desire is mine, in the society of a brother so dear, and all circumstances so congenial to my taste attend our place of meeting, that though I do prize these things, still, my God, to hear of Thee, to be alone with Thee is truly my chief happiness, and I could leave my friends most loved to come to*

Thee, — for Thou art unmixed delight, — Thou art perfect
beauty and excellence, glorious, blessed, and only worthy my
supreme love.

She records writing to Henry on August 30th and again on September 30th. She continues in this positive and optimistic frame of mind brought about by hours set aside for solitude which she describes in her entry for October 4th:

At Perran, alone. Very happy in my soul for several days
past. The Lord has afforded me what I so much wanted and
desired, — a season of retirement, — and the effect proves to me
that in future I must observe more strictly certain hours for it in
the day, whatever I neglect or whatever I break through.

She continues this entry by describing how she has attended church with George which has delighted her. She remarks how favourable everything seems but then refers to her illness:

I am free of bodily pain, and merely and mercifully
confined from weakness and the fear of a return of my complaint. I
have a room to myself, — a thing the more prized because for some
time deprived of it.

The latter is a reminder that a spinster of 37 often had little choice in family arrangements and often had to accept with good grace what was allotted to her by parents or brothers. Her reference to her 'complaint' may be the first indication of the disease which would later kill and which she feared so much–cancer. The following day she is upbraiding herself for levity, censoriousness and satire, fearing that her *spirit is altogether light and trifling.* Instead she prays for a return *to tumult, storm, and all the conflicts of an enraged world, rather than a dangerous calm.*

At the end of the year on December 12th she writes:

Heard from Tebriz from Mr M., with an account of his
dangerous state of health and intention of returning to England if

*his life was spared. The intelligence affected me variously. The
probability of his death, the certainty of his extreme sufferings, and
his distance from every friend pressed heavily on my spirits; I was
enabled to pray, and felt relieved. Of his return no very sanguine
expectations can be entertained. Darkness and distress of mind
have followed this information. I cannot collect my thoughts to
write, or apply as I ought to anything. O let me consider this as a
call to prayer, and watchfulness, and self examination. Lord assist
me.*

She had received the penultimate letter which Henry wrote on July 12th,
1812, when recovering from the journey to Tabriz, which so very nearly killed
him. Four days later on December 16th she is beset by anxiety:

> *A season of great temptation, darkness and distress. At no
> period of my life have I stood more in need of Divine help, and O
> may I earnestly seek it. Lord, I would pray, give me a right
> understanding, and enable me seriously to consider and weigh in
> the balance of the sanctuary all I do, — yea let my thoughts be
> watched. Sleep has fled from mine eyes, and a fearful looking for of
> trial and affliction, however this affair ends, possess my mind.*

On Boxing Day she is anxiously thinking of Henry's journey:

> *Thought much today of my dear friend. I cannot think of
> him as having gained the heavenly crown, but as struggling with
> dangers and difficulties. Secure in them all of Thy favour, and
> defended by Thy power, he is safe, and pass but a few years or days,
> and he will enter into the rest of God. Let me, too, follow after him
> as he follows Christ.*

Lydia's pessimism over Henry appears again on New Year's Eve: *This trial of
my dear friend calls me to think of eternity, and warns me to be conversant with
death.* By January 4th, 1813 Lydia is depressed and anxious about Henry,

who she now refers to as *my beloved friend*, but she is also in the throes of an inner crisis which manifests itself as a loss of faith again which obsesses her:

> *After a night and day spent in great conflict and agony of mind I, this evening, enjoy a respite from distressing apprehensions. I was reduced to the lowest, as to animal spirits and spiritual life, when it occurred to me I would go to the Meeting, where I found a sweet, O may it be a lasting relief from my cares ... The state of my beloved friend less occupies my mind than I sometimes think is reconcilable with a true affection for him, but the truth is the concerns of my soul are more pressing.*

She describes her mental torment in vivid Wesleyan imagery on January 8th:

> *Tempest-tossed, almost a wreck, I have no resource but that the Lord will send from above, and deliver me out of the strange waters. I am as one on a boisterous sea, without light, without a pilot, or compass, or any strength to guide the shattered bark. I have no happiness in God, and am left to myself; I cannot believe, I can't pray, but in words, and have no life or power.*

However, by February she is regaining her mental strength, teaching at the Sunday School and taking pleasure in listening to good sermons. There is no entry between February 8th and February 20th when she records the expected but saddening news of Henry's death.

Poignantly the news reaches her on February 14th, St. Valentine's Day, just four days before Henry would have been 32 years old. The entry is written in large, scrawled handwriting reflecting her grief at the news:

> *Heard on the 14th of the removal of my most tender, faithful, and beloved friend to the joys of Heaven. O I could not wish his absence from them prolonged. What I only wished was, and now I am reconciled to that too, — I wished to have been honoured by God so far as to have been near him, or that some*

*friend had been. Lord, if this was wrong, forgive me. — I will
endeavour, yea, I am enabled to say this too, "Thy will be done."*

Although the thought of his dying alone far from her or friends distresses her
she accepts it as God's will and draws comfort from the fact that with his
death she can feel close to his spirit and is released from her earthly vanity of
wishing to live up to his example. Quoted in an article entitled *Henry Martyn*
in the Church Quarterly Review dated October 1881 is the following
account of the news of Henry's death and its effect on Lydia. It is written by a
niece in an unpublished letter.[82]

> *I lived near her until her death, and perfectly recollect the
> event of Henry Martyn's unexpected loss. The remembrance of her
> agonized countenance when first she entered my father's house
> after that calamity, is impressed on my memory... the
> circumstances of his affecting death, and my aunt's **intense** sorrow
> produced an ineffaceable remembrance on my mind. I can never
> forget the "Upper Chamber" in which she took refuge from daily
> cares and interruptions, and the kind welcome which there
> awaited those who sought her advice and sympathy — its view of
> lovely Mount's Bay across a group of fruit trees and whispering
> white coelibes — its perfect neatness, though with few ornaments.
> On the principal wall hung a large print of the Crucifixion of our
> Lord, usually shaded by a curtain, and at its foot (where he would
> have chosen to be) a portrait of Henry Martyn.*

The reference to 'Henry Martyn's unexpected loss' perhaps reflects a lack of
understanding on the part of the niece. Lydia writes on February 28th, 1813:
I felt this afternoon as if he were present, as I sat alone in the garden. She
examines their relationship giving valuable insight into it on March 2nd:

> *O how shall I, with wonder and praise, listen in eternity
> to the relation of his last days! The excess of affection now, and the*

---

[82] *Church Quarterly Review, October 1881: Henry Martyn.*

unwillingness I feel that he should have suffered, make it amongst
my mercies, that a veil is drawn over that period of his life ... I
have been thinking how necessary for me it was that we are thus
separated; for during his life, I felt such a desire to please and to be
worthy of the regard he entertained for me, that it was my bane,
and caused me to forget God as the first object I was to think of
and please. I accept the punishment sent for this offence, — may it
prove an effectual cure of this evil in my heart.

Was this perhaps an unspoken reason for her refusing Henry that she realised that he had found his true religious mission in life and she realised subconsciously she couldn't fulfil Henry's expectations of her as a wife and fellow missionary in India? This sense of being unworthy of his love is a theme she returns to again when Sargent's biography of Henry is published and her relationship with Henry becomes more public.

With Henry's death Lydia entertains the constant hope that they may be united in heaven:

When I get to Heaven, — delightful thought! — that
when I shall again meet my dearest friend, there will be no
possibility of our loving each other inordinately, but that we shall
be happy, because we supremely love God.

Lydia continued to love Henry until the end of her life. Now he has become a paradigm for all that is saintly yet she feels she is unable to emulate this which leads to bouts of depression:

Brought low again. O may this temptation make me
lowly, humble, broken-hearted, and at last produce entire
dependence on God. I have endeavoured to discover the cause of my
depression, and see how it arises from a vain and evil desire to be
something, to bestow, communicate what is good to others, in short
it is dissatisfaction with what God has made me as to natural
abilities ... I am tormented with fears that even in eternity I shall

236

never be capable of enjoying the same happiness my departed
friend does, and it seems as if no other would satisfy me.

This expression of dissatisfaction with herself is written on April 24th, three days after receiving Henry's final letter from Tabriz. Throughout this period she is suffering from depression and a real fear that she will never achieve the salvation and happiness which she feels Henry deservedly has. On June 3rd she refers to him as a saint:

I think more of a departed saint, than of the King of
Saints. It is strange that now I should be more in danger of loving
too well a creature passed into the skies, than when he lived on
earth. But so it is, continually my thoughts revert to him.

Ten days later she is still struggling with her conscience and has turned to her sister Emma for counsel:

A letter from my dearest Emma containing wholesome,
though at first unwelcome counsel, has been of singular use to me.
The snare is seen, if not broken. Yes, I have lost my hold of
everything that used, and ought, to support me by allowing,
without restraint, the remembrance of my dear friend, to fill my
mind. My almost constant thoughts were of him, and pride at the
preference he showed me was fed as well as affection. Now I have a
painful, difficult part to act. A sacrifice I must offer of what has
become so much my happiness, as to interfere with my enjoyment
of God. I must fly from the recollection of an earthly object, loved
too well, viewed too much, — let me follow his faith, and consider
the end of his conversation, — Jesus Christ, the same for ever.

Emma has offered sound advice. However, from her entries in her Diary these fears and depression about her own worth and salvation continue to trouble and obsess her. She seeks solace in carrying out her good works and prayer. She notes the deaths of family members, visiting the sick and of trying to bring comfort to the dying through prayer, yet she remains self-critical. There is a continuing tension between mother and daughter still evident with this entry for November 30th, 1813:

> *Disappointed this evening of going to Meeting — felt very sinfully displeased at it. Self-will took the garb of zeal for God, and I was very wrong in resisting my mother's will, and pleading my right to act in this respect as I saw best ... No grace in this frame of mind, and want of submission to a parent.* And on December 3rd she writes: *I am sensible of a proneness to impatience and self-will towards my dear mother, not yielding cheerfully as I ought, to her wishes, contending my right to judge and act for myself. Now this is contrary to my duty as a child, and especially as a Christian.*

Lydia continued to live quietly with her ageing widowed mother at Marazion, devoting herself to a life of increasing piety.

In 1819 Sargent was to publish his biography of Henry. Simeon approached Lydia to obtain her consent *that under the veil of anonymeity her own intimacy with the subject of the Memoir might be announced to the Christian public*[83] and at the end of 1815 Lydia refers to the forthcoming book:

> *Wrote this day to Mr Simeon. I have reason to search into my heart and watch the risings of pride there, both respecting the notice of this blessed saint, and the avowal to be expected of my being the object of so much regard from another still more eminent in the Church of Christ. I have ever stood amazed at this, and now that in the providence of God it seems certain that my being so favored is likely to be made known, vanity besets me. I sought concealment, and lo! all is made known to many, and much will be even known to the world. It is strange for me to credit this, and strange that, with my natural reserve and the peculiar reasons that exist for my wishing to have this buried in silence, I am nevertheless composed about it.*

---

[83] Henry Martyn Jeffery: *Introductory Preface to Extracts from the Religious Diary of Miss L. Grenfell.*

By 1817 the tone of her Diary is much happier. She reports visits of members of the Church Missionary Society and finds great comfort at first in the new minister, Mr. Lyte, who wrote hymns including *Abide with me* and *Praise my Soul the King of Heaven*. The Reverend Henry Francis Lyte was by all accounts a man of great personal charm and possessed of good looks. He records in his Diary in 1827 in his *Journey to Geneva and Back* having to repel the advances of a *young and handsome Bernoise*. He made his escape after having given her *two tracts and a lecture which abashed her*. He also knew John Sargent and visited him at his home, Lavington Hall near Chichester, in the same year.

Lyte came to Marazion in 1817 as a bachelor of 24 and after his marriage in 1818 he records his ministry there as being happy: *I was married at Bath on the 21ˢᵗ of January and immediately brought my dear wife down here, to my little residence at the end of the world where we have continued to live in happy retirement ever since, every day I believe, mutually better pleased with our choice.* They lived on Fore Street, the main street in Marazion and would have been close neighbours of Lydia. Lyte records: *The inhabitants are a quiet ordinary kind of people, chiefly tradesmen, whom a little money saved in the till and a sprinkling of hair powder over their heads and the copes of their coats, have transformed into gentlemen. We all live very comfortably together, and I believe that they are, in general well pleased with their parson.*[84]

But by September of the following year Lydia writes: *Many circumstances conspire to render the removal of our present minister desirable* having remarked of his *un-chrisian conduct* and goes so far to attribute his unsettled and inconsistent behaviour to mental derangement in November 1817. Lyte left Marazion for Brixham in 1819 but his wife, Anne was unhappy there. Lyte was invited to apply for the living in Penzance in 1831.

In January, 1819 Lydia receives a copy of Sargent's *Memoir* and remarks:

> *... reading only a few pages has convinced me that,*
> *without a greater resemblance in the spirit of our friend, I can*
> *never partake of that blessedness now enjoyed by the happy subject*

---

[84] W. Maxwell-Lyte, *British Weekly*, 3.4. 1947: quoted in Henry Frances Lyte: *Brixham's Poet and Priest;* B.G. Skinner (1974).

of it, in the presence of his Saviour. It is chiefly in humility,
meekness, and love I see the sad, the total difference.

She continues to read the *Memoir* but *not on the Sabbath*. On June 30th she goes to Torquay for a short break and returns in a more sanguine state of mind. Jeffery comments on her changed appearance:

> *When the book appeared, Miss Grenfell was perceptibly*
> *altered; she was no longer young and buoyant. Although she had*
> *experienced no hardship, and lived in a tranquil round of simple*
> *duties and occasional visits (the furthest being Torquay), weak*
> *health, the losses of friends and relations, and her own anxieties*
> *and sorrows had weakened her energies, and induced languor and*
> *lassitude, which she herself attributed to sloth.*

On October 3rd just before she is 45 she announces that:

> *The worship of God will begin to-day in the chapel after*
> *being discontinued for one year. I feel great joy at the prospect.*

But just over two weeks later on her birthday, October 19th, 1819, she writes:

> *Entered my 45th year; ... Found on the 16th joyful*
> *thoughts of the blessedness of him, who on that day rested from his*
> *labours, and reached the repose of Heaven. Let me follow his faith,*
> *and consider the end of his conversation, the blissful enjoyment of*
> *God. — Felt today a peculiar sort of pain in my breast — thought*
> *of cancer.*

There is then a gap of four months in her Diary until February 27th, 1820.

She reports *an attack of illness* on June 4th and seems depressed on June 25th:

> *Gladly would I part from this dull clod of earth and come*
> *to Thee, and reach the pure pleasure of the spiritual state. There,*

there dwells the blessed Martyn, who bows before the throne of a glorious company of blessed saints, washed with him and clothed in spotless robes. O (that) I may be brought to them.

In 1820 she is in good health and still living with her mother although she expresses her guilt at neglecting her:

> *November 25: Passed the day chiefly with my dear mother. I quit her more than I ought, and therefore, more than I need. I feel the bad effects of too much engagement of mind about the state of others; my health and spirits are mercifully great. I am now in the society of persons of amiable, cultivated minds, who are active and excellent in conduct, but not far advanced in spiritual-mindedness, or eminent for faith, simple faith in Christ. This too, is dangerous.*

She notes each anniversary of Henry's death: *October 16th, 1820: I have now survived my beloved friend eight years.*

On April 15th, 1821 comes shattering news when she writes:

> *A memorable period in my life; may it prove one in my experience. Threatened with cancer in my breast. At first I could not write the word, or hear or think of it, so terrible the disease, or the usual remedy for it, appear.*

On May 9th she learns that it is indeed cancerous and she charts its progress in her Diary:

> *Learnt yesterday that the disorder was cancerous from a physician, Dr Fox, and from Mr Moyle. The intelligence I felt more from having indulged so freely in hope the last few days. O that the Lord may strengthen me, not suffer me to sink mentally or spiritually! The body is of less consequence, but my spirits are so fluctuating, and such a terror seizes me of the possible operation necessary, as empties my mind of everything else at times. O that I*

could trust more, then I should not be afraid. O that I could lie
passive and exalt in this certainty, that the will of God is done by
whatever I am called to endure.

She receives some comfort from her anxiety when she is reassured a week later that *contrary to the opinion of my physician, there seems ground to hope the complaint may be removed without extraction.* During this time she retreats to the privacy of her room and spends her time in rigid self-examination, prayer and the contemplation of her own death. Her prayers seem to have been heard when she writes more optimistically on June 17th: *My complaint mercifully kept under if not removed.*

While she is coping with her cancer she receives a visit from Charles Simeon and John Sargent[85] on September 27th, which instead of bringing some comfort to her in her distress over the diagnosis, re-awakens all her guilt at the way she treated Henry on the last meeting: *So many things crowded on my mind, that the utmost confusion followed.* On November 25th she reports:

> *I have been affected with a slight return of pain and*
> *complaint in my breast. Lord, I beseech Thee to arm my soul with*
> *resolution, and strengthen it by faith in Thee, and I shall fear*
> *nothing.*

Her sister, Emma, who had played such a vital role as confidante to both Lydia and Henry, was herself ill by January, 1822, and it is Lydia who nurses her devotedly. She makes reference to this when she responds on February 9th to a request to write something for the Christian Remembrance: *but affliction in my Family, & under our own roof compelled me to this this* [sic.] *delay.*[86] It is a stressful time for Lydia for not only is she coping with her

---

[85] In a footnote Henry Martyn Jeffery suggests Simeon was in Cornwall *'preaching in* [sic.] *behalf of the Jews.'*

[86] Letter dated February 9th, 1822 found attached to Martyn's letter dated February 19th, 1811 written to Rev. Thomas Hitchins from Bombay: Oriental and India Office Library, now part of British Library: ref Mss. Eur A. 87.

mother and Emma's ill-health, as well as her own problems, her brothers are warring.[87]

However, her devotion to Henry Martyn's memory remains. She reports on January 11th the following year: *Placed in my room yesterday the print of dear Martyn*. Her mother, the redoubtable Mrs. Grenfell, was still alive in 1823 although *bending under the weight of years and increasing infirmities, — O may she be prepared for approaching death*. Lydia is leading a quiet life which she describes on October 2nd, 1823:

> *I wish to make a resolution of speaking less in company*
> *and thinking more, of writing less in private and reading more, of*
> *attending less to the trifles of life and praying more. I purpose*
> *passing the hour after breakfast in reading and prayer, and from*
> *reading time to dinner devoting to my dear mother and anything*
> *needful to be done in the family.*

So Lydia's last few years were spent in declining health, tending to her ailing mother, coping with various problems within the family as well as pursuing good works and praising her Lord. She reports on her cancer again in February 1824:

> *I am visited again with that local disease, which is so*
> *formidable, and which, though once removed, may now be fixed.*
> *Unexpected was the discovery to me three days since, and my*
> *nature shrank from it as before for a few moments.*

The prospect of the disease terrifies her but she places her faith in God for removing it:

> *My health is improved, although the local complaint*
> *continues, as it did once before for eight months, and yet was*
> *removed by the mercy and power of God.*

---

[87] See Chapter 1 — Marazion, Cornwall: above.

On June 24th she had attended a lecture in Penzance by Professor Farish[88] who had spent time with Henry at Cambridge in 1805 before he left for India. John Sargent, who held Lydia in high esteem according to Jeffery's *Preface*, visited Lydia on June 26th, 1824 which brings her great comfort and peace of mind. As her cancer advances Lydia turns inward to her faith to find solace from pain and fear. Her mother, who was largely responsible for standing in the way of her daughter's happiness by claiming that she needed Lydia to remain at home with her, died in 1826, just three years before Lydia, and was buried on December 7th at the Marazion Quaker Burial Ground aged 92, although it is noted on the burial transcript: NOT A MEMBER.

Lydia's Diary ends on June 18th, 1826 with a prayer:

> *Jesus, the Son of Righteousness, O let Thy light shine and love penetrate again my dark, hard heart. To save is Thy work, to show mercy Thy glory displayed. O let thy holy Spirit enter and fill my soul. Away life's vanities, and be all ready for the presence of the Lord, who dwells by faith in the heart. What have I obtained, whilst I have given up to seek Thee, O Lord? Only distress and disatisfaction. My friends gone to heaven, seem to reproach me, that I aim not to follow them, as they follow Christ. The beloved Martyn, the seraphic Louisa Hoare, and my dear Georgina's[89] spirit are employed in perpetually beholding that God, whom I neglect and remain unconcerned, when I do not delight in, or serve (Him.) O let me be joined to them in the sweet work of adoration and praise to Him, who hath loved us, to Jesus, our one Lord and Saviour. Amen.*

---

[88] *Rev. W. Farish: Professor of Chemistry and afterwards Jacksonion Professor. Also itinerant advocate for the Church Missionary Society:* Footnote by Henry Martyn Jeffery.

[89] Two footnotes by Jeffery: *An authoress, and member of the Gurney family, who died in 1816 and, her niece, the only child of Major Thomas and Phillis Hill, who died June 23, 1823.* Jeffery implies this is Louisa Gurney, Elizabeth Fry's sister. She is not. Georgina was in fact the only daughter of the Hills' but there were 3 sons also of the marriage. George gave a silver pap boat to Georgina, inscribed on the base: G.G. to Georgina as a christening gift which is now in the Royal Cornwall Museum.

The cancer was to kill her three years after her final Diary entry. There is an addendum by E.H. (Emma Hitchins) Lydia's loving and supportive sister throughout all her trials and tribulations: *This prayer was answered on the 21st September, 1829*. Underneath are two lines which read:

And now they range the heavenly plains
And sing in sweet heartmelting strains.

The handwriting is close to Lydia's but they may have been added by another hand.

In his *Introductory Preface to Extracts from the Religious Diary of Miss L. Grenfell*, Jeffery suggests: *It may well be that we have the latest record of her thoughts on June 18, 1826, by reason of her mental affliction.* He also notes on his MS transcript of her Diary: *During the interval of 1826 – 1829, or part of it, she was in retreat, under care, about 1827 — 28.* If Jeffery's surmise is correct as to her mental illness, it is a tragic ending to her life. He also adds that there had been revision to the Diary before it came into his hands so it is quite possible that Emma and subsequent relations had excised parts of it, if indeed she had suffered a further mental breakdown, perhaps suspecting that after her death it might become public because of her connection with Henry Martyn, thereby protecting her.

Lydia Grenfell spent her last days at the vicarage at Breage, a small village between Helston and Marazion, where her sister Mary lived. She died from breast cancer just a month before her 55th birthday. Two brief notices appeared: one in *The West Briton and Cornwall Advertiser* and the other in the *Royal Cornwall Gazette* . The first reads:

On Monday evening last, at Breage Vicarage, in the 54th
year of her age, Miss Lydia Grenfell, late of Marazion.

The latter reads:

At Breage Vicarage in the 54th year of her age Miss Lydia
Grenfell, late of Marazion.

She was buried in Breage churchyard on September 22nd, 1829 with her faith undiminished and confident in the hope that she would in death be reunited with the man she loved and admired so deeply, Henry Martyn. Jeffery describes her headstone on which there was a cartouche where her name and the year of her death and the following were inscribed: *For a small moment have I forsaken thee, but with great mercies will I gather thee.* Her sister, Mary, the wife of the Reverend Humphrey Willyams, the Vicar of Breage, died the following year and was buried near her. Sadly no trace of either headstone remains. Her will, drawn up on January 15th, 1827 is simple:

> *I give and bequeath to my beloved Anna Maria Maynard all my household furniture of whatever description, likewise plate, linen, china, wines and other liquor and all goods and chattels I may die possessed of, likewise whatever sum or sums of money I may leave after the discharge of my just debts. And I hereby nominate and appoint the Rev. Humphrey Willyams and Mr William Maynard executors in trust to this my will and last testament, hoping that they will take care that these my last bequests may be fully and duly executed.*
>
> *Signed, sealed and delivered*
>
> *Lydia Grenfell*
>
> *In the presence of Mary Willyams, Hester Millett*
>
> *Dated the 15th day of January 1827.*

Lydia and Henry's love story is a tragic one of a relationship which foundered, partly due to the vast distance separating them and the concomitant difficulty of conducting a correspondence with the long delays between sending each other a letter and receiving the reply. Because Lydia's letters have not survived there is no way of knowing whether she was guilty of encouraging Henry to believe that her feelings of affection for him matched his love for her. Certainly his expectation that she would join him in India, which he so confidently expected her to, was shattered by her refusal. Why Lydia refused to enter into a formal engagement, when she felt so strongly attracted to him, seems to have been caused by several reasons. From reading her Diary the following piece together. Lydia's prior engagement to Samuel John, which she broke off on June 23rd, 1800, the same year as her conversion, haunted her conscience. When the Diary opens in 1801 she expresses her remorse and guilt over her action with her phrase *hoped for pardon for broken vows to men.* Although she never expects to see John again she still harbours deep feelings for him when she writes on February 24th, 1802:

I have suffered this week in mind from the illness of him, from whom I am separated on earth, perhaps for ever, yet to whom my heart is more closely united than to any earthly object. God knows the truth of all I say, and alone is acquainted with the feelings of my heart.

She continued to hold herself responsible for John's happiness until he married. It is at the beginning of 1804 that she records that John is soon to marry in London, but for some reason he did not marry until 1810. When she first mentions Henry in her Diary on August 29th, 1804 there is no suggestion that she is attracted to this young man apart from his preaching, although he learns from Emma Hitchins that *his attachment is not altogether unreturned.* When Henry returns to Cornwall in July, 1805 Lydia enters into a much closer relationship and from her entries appears to be in love with Henry but when he presses her to enter a formal engagement she retreats from committing herself with *we had better go quite free.*

Henry acknowledges in a letter to Emma, dated August 28th, 1805, from Madeira, that until the problem of S.J. is resolved he will not pursue the subject of marriage with Lydia and respects her for her decision. When Lydia writes a letter on November 16th, 1805 *perhaps for the last time* to Henry it seems that she has decided that their relationship must be ended. But Henry never receives this letter because it is captured at sea. Lydia then writes five unsolicited letters to Henry in which her language towards him appears to have been affectionate. She receives no letters from him, between December 1805 and March 2nd, 1807 when she receives his proposal, dated July 30th, 1806. In her Diary entries after she has written her refusal on March 5th, she refers to *I wrote what duty required me* and feels that *The state of my mind lately has led me to fill too much of my Diary with expressions of regard for an earthly object, and now I am convinced of the evil of indulging this affection.* She refers to her continuing sense of moral obligation to Samuel John on June 20th with:

> *My chief concern now is lest I should have given too much*
> *reason for my dear friend's hoping I might be prevailed on to*
> *attend to his request, and I feel the restraint stronger than ever,*
> *that having before promised, I am not free to marry ...* and a little
> further on in the same entry she writes *that first when I regarded*
> *him otherwise than as a Christian brother, I believed myself free to*
> *do so, imagining him I first loved to be united to another.*

So it would seem that if Samuel John had married in 1804 then Lydia would have quite possibly agreed to an engagement to Henry before he left Cornwall in 1805 or accepted his proposal which she received in 1807. However, there was another obstacle in the way of their happiness.

When Henry receives her refusal, his reply, dated October 24th, 1807, although well reasoned, shows how shattered he is, yet he is generous in his response hoping to persuade her to change her mind. It is from reading this letter that the real obstacle to their marriage is revealed: Mrs. Grenfell — by then she was 73. In it Henry eloquently attempts to justify himself to Mrs. Grenfell. He accepts that Lydia's filial duty is important but argues that her duty to God is greater and may be fully realised by service to the Church in India. From his reference to his *means* it is probable that Mrs. Grenfell felt that Henry was not financially secure enough and, coming from a good family herself, the Tremenheeres, she was related to leading families of West Cornwall. Furthermore having married into a family with strong commercial interests — her husband Pascoe, having been Mayor of Marazion in the 1770's, in which he was replaced in 1778 by a Robert King because he was *absent beyond the seas in Holland*,[90] and having enjoyed the lucrative post of

---

[90] Quoted on page 3 in *The Charter Town of Marazion.*

commissary to the States of Holland — she clearly thought Henry was not of their class and so unworthy of her youngest daughter. A telling comment from a niece would seem to corroborate this view:

> *Her mother was aged and had no other unmarried*
> *daughter; and besides the connexion with the Martyns was*
> *distasteful to her. I should say that my aunt's ideas of parental*
> *authority, up to middle life even, were extreme, as I well remember*
> *her expressing them on later occasions.*[91]

Simeon's notes on his meeting with Lydia at Colonel Sandys house at Lanarth on April 25th, 1807 certainly record *the consent of her mother was indispensable* and that this obstacle is *insurmountable* whereas the other three obstacles Lydia put forward of her health, the indelicacy of her travelling out to India alone and her former engagement to Samuel John can all be resolved. But for Lydia, the last unmarried daughter at home, her duty was clear. She must obey her mother's wishes however selfish or misinformed they might appear to Henry. Yet there is another factor which may have governed Mrs. Grenfell's opposition to Lydia travelling half way round the world to join Henry – Lydia's mental health.

Lydia was prone to severe bouts of depression and became mentally unstable at times. Jeffery, in his *Introductory Preface* to *Extracts from the Religious Diary of Miss L. Grenfell* writes:

> *It is painful to be told that this gifted and highly favoured*
> *lady was placed for a year under care for mental derangement, but*
> *she recovered and retained her faculties to the close of her life.*

There are references in her *Diary* to a mental illness in 1800 when she broke off her engagement. Her mother would be well aware of Lydia's mental instability and may have had her mental welfare at heart when she stood in the way of her second chance of marriage. She would also have been well aware of the dangers involved in the voyage out to India from her nephew,

---

[91] Quoted in *Church Quarterly Review, October 1881: Henry Martyn.*

Henry Pendarves Tremenheere. By refusing to let Lydia leave their home in Marazion she may have sought to protect her youngest daughter's delicate mental equilibrium.

Lydia wrote a second letter in March 1807 bidding Henry a final farewell, which he received on November 25th, 1807. His letter acknowledging it has been lost but it arrived in Marazion on August 29th, 1808. He then decided that it was fruitless to pursue the subject any further and stopped writing. However, Lydia, in her anxiety that no further misunderstanding could take place, had written on May 9th, 1808 in answer to his letter of October 24th, 1807 and again wrote on July 8th, 1808 on the advice of Colonel Sandys. Henry refers to this letter as containing *more last words*. Their correspondence concerning love and marriage is at an end. On November 30th Lydia writes:

> *Thought of my dear friend tonight with tenderness, but entire resignation to Thy will, O our God, in never seeing or hearing from him again; to meet him above is my desire.*

A month later on December 30th she writes:

> *I reckon among my mercies the Lord's having enabled me to choose a single life, and that my friend in India has been so well reconciled to my determination.*

She continues by acknowledging she feels relief at the ending of the relationship, not least because of her *perturbed state of mind*.

From July 8th, 1808 until October 23rd, 1809, some 16 months, Lydia remains resolute in her determination not to contact Henry. But when his sister, Sally, dies she resumes writing to him on a platonic basis although with some initial embarrassment in case Henry is engaged or indeed married. Henry is delighted as he has been petitioning Emma for a resumption in their correspondence. Yet after writing two further letters, dated February 6th and April 23rd, 1810, Lydia does not respond to Henry until February 14th, 1812, when he is recovering in Tabriz. Meanwhile Henry has written nine letters without receiving a reply. Why she stopped writing during the latter part of 1810 and throughout 1811 is not explained unless Samuel John's marital problems made her feel responsible for him once again and she could not take on the added anxiety of Henry's ill-health when she was experiencing deep depressions and a loss of faith. When she does resume writing Henry receives only her letter written in February, 1812, as her letters written in July, August and September would arrive after his death in October. She receives his final letter on April 21st, 1813.

Whether they would have married had Henry managed to get back to England on extended furlough remains debateable: their faith would certainly still have remained a bond but much had happened in his six year absence. The tragic fact remains that Lydia decided that she could not travel out to India and marry the man who she so clearly loved and who loved her and expressed his love so eloquently. They accepted that their union would be in love before God's throne: as Lydia wrote in her Diary on March 31st, 1813:

> *When I get to heaven — delightful thought! — that*
> *when I shall again meet my dearest friend, there will be no*
> *possibility of our loving each other inordinately, but that we shall*
> *be happy, because we supremely love God.*

Henry Martyn is a major figure in the evangelical missionary movement of the 19th century, had he not been then this love affair would have remained private. The letters which Lydia wrote to Henry have not been traced so we only have Henry's part of the correspondence from which to piece together the progress and then the ending of this affair. Without the existence of these letters, in which he expresses so eloquently and poignantly his love and longing for Lydia to join him in his evangelical calling to India, the part which Lydia played in his life, which is now consigned so often to a footnote, might have been lost for ever.

REV. HENRY MARTYN, M.A.
CHAPLAIN OF THE HON. EAST INDIA COMPANY,
BORN AT TRURO, ENGLAND, FEBRUARY 18, 1781,
DIED AT TOKAT, OCTOBER 16, 1812.
HE LABOURED FOR MANY YEARS IN THE EAST, STRIVING TO
BENEFIT MANKIND BOTH IN THIS WORLD AND THAT TO COME
HE TRANSLATED THE HOLY SCRIPTURES INTO HINDOSTANEE
AND PERSIAN,
AND PREACHED THE GOD AND SAVIOUR OF WHOM THEY TESTIFY.
HE WILL LONG BE REMEMBERED IN THE EAST, WHERE HE WAS
KNOWN AS A MAN OF GOD

Chapter 18 — 'He was known as a Man of God'

"My mind is in chaos about him," said Charles Kingsley, speaking one day of H.M., "sometimes one feels inclined to take him at his own word, and believe him as he says, a mere hypochondriac, then the next moment he seems a saint. I cannot fathom it. Of this, however, I am certain, he was a much better man than I am."[92]

Henry Martyn's legacy has remained and he has been publicly honoured and remembered. The faithful Sergius took Henry's papers from Tokat to Constantinople and handed them to Isaac Morier from where they were returned to England. In a letter to Thomason in Calcutta, dated February 12th, 1813 Simeon records receiving news of Henry's death from Morier. The papers and Journal which Henry had left with Corrie were sent in 1814 to Henry's executors, Charles Simeon and John Thornton. They were used, together with his final Journal which Henry termed *A Narrative*, by John Sargent for his 1819 biography and by Samuel Wilberforce in 1837 for his two volume edition of *Journals and Letters*. George Smith in *Henry Martyn: Saint and Scholar*, published in 1892 does not refer to the original Journal and his quotations are based on Sargent's and Samuel Wilberforce's references. Sadly all the Journals have since been lost.

---

[92] Quoted in Preface of Jesse Page: *Henry Martyn of India and Persia.*

Henry Martyn's legacy was linguistic: his translations of the New Testament into Urdu and Persian and his supervision of its translation into Arabic. The Urdu version, sent off to the press at Serampore in 1811, was delayed in printing there until 1814 due to a fire's destroying the type face in 1812. The copy of the Persian translation was finally presented to the Shah by the British Ambassador, Sir Gore Ouseley, as promised. It was Ouseley who played an important part in drawing up the peace terms between Persia and Russia, which both countries signed in 1813. He was received by Alexander I in St. Petersburg the following year. The first Persian edition was printed in Russia in 1815 and later editions were printed in London. The following year, in 1816, the Arabic edition which Henry and Sabat had worked on was published in India.

A Mr. James Cornelius Rich, British Resident at Baghdad, had a slab placed over the grave at Tokat with an inscription in Latin. Unfortunately Henry's Christian name was incorrectly inscribed. Later the East India Company made a grant for the erection of a more suitable monument. Henry Martyn's remains were removed to the Mission burying ground at Tokat and an obelisk was placed on the new grave[93] with the inscription engraved in English, Armenian, Persian and Turkish on the four faces of the plinth. It is a fitting inscription to a talented linguist and missionary.

There are more tangible reminders of Henry's work. He is commemorated in India where there is the Henry Martyn Institute of Islamic Studies in Hyderabad (originally established in Lahore in 1930) and the Henry Martyn Divinity College in Cossipur. In Cambridge he is commemorated by the Henry Martyn Hall, dedicated on October 18th, 1887, which is the official Cambridge University inter-collegiate Christian Union headquarters and bears the following inscription over the door: *To the Inspiring Memory of Henry Martyn, Scholar, Evangelist, Confessor and Man of God, A later Generation of His own Cambridge Dedicated this home of Christian Converse and Counsel.*

Henry Martyn Hall stands next to Holy Trinity Church where as a student and then as a curate Henry would listen to Charles Simeon preach

---

[93] Recent research by B V Henry suggests that the obelisk is now in the local museum at Tokat.

and would struggle to emulate his powerful sermons for two years at the outset of his evangelical mission. Here on the south side of the chancel there is a tablet which marks his academic achievement, his work as an evangelist and his work as a translator of the New Testament. It is next to similar tablets to his great friend in India, Daniel Corrie, and his religious mentor, Charles Simeon, and his fellow curate Thomas Thomason. The Henry Martyn Centre, which includes the Henry Martyn Library, is now at Westminster College in Cambridge where there is a miniature of Henry Martyn, probably the one he had painted for Sally, his younger sister, before he left England. On the back of the miniature is a beautifully plaited lock of blond hair.

The picture, painted by Thomas Hickey,[94] that so upset Simeon was bequeathed by him to the Chancellor and scholars of the University of Cambridge. This is now in the vestry of Holy Trinity Church in Cambridge. A copy hangs in his old college, St. John's, on the Hall stairs. In St. John's College Chapel his figure is painted on the ceiling as one of the *illustriores* of the 19th century. He is in the distinguished company of William Wilberforce, Wordsworth and Whytehead, who was a missionary to New Zealand.

At Truro Cathedral in his home town he is remembered each year with the collect appointed in the New Common Worship Calendar on the Feast of Henry Martyn, Translator of the Scriptures, Missionary in India and Persia, when on October 19th the Eucharist is celebrated in the Chapel of St. Sampson next to the Baptistry. The prayer reads:

> *Almighty God,*
>
> *who by your Holy Spirit gave Henry Martyn*
>
> *a longing to tell the good news of Christ*
>
> *and skill to translate the Scriptures:*
>
> *by the same Spirit give us grace to offer you our gifts,*
>
> *wherever you may lead, at whatever the cost;*

---

[94] Portrait painter in London, Dublin and India; brother of John Hickey, an Irish sculptor.

through Jesus Christ your Son our Lord,

who is alive and reigns with you,

in the unity of the Holy Spirit,

one God, now and for ever. Amen.

It is somewhat ironic that it should be celebrated on Lydia's birthday although it might be thought entirely fitting that they are united in this celebration. In the Baptistry are eight stained glass windows, each under one of four early missionary saints to Cornwall: St. Pol de Leon, St. Cubi, St. Constantine and St. Winnow. Each set of two windows depicts scenes from Henry's life and mission in India: starting with schooldays under Dr. Cardew; setting forth from Falmouth dock; first sight of heathenism; preaching at Cawnpore; translating the New Testament with the turbanned figure of Sabat beside him; arguing with Moslem antagonists in Tehran; and finally, his burial at Tokat with full Armenian rites.[95] It is sad that in none of these numerous memorials is Lydia mentioned nor depicted. History has tried to airbrush out his muse who was such a central figure in his short life but literature has not; although Lydia's vanity, about which she berates herself so constantly, might not be flattered.

---

[95] The stained glass windows are the work of John Clayton and Alfred Bell: assistants in Gilbert Scott's office. The Baptistry was completed in March 1887.

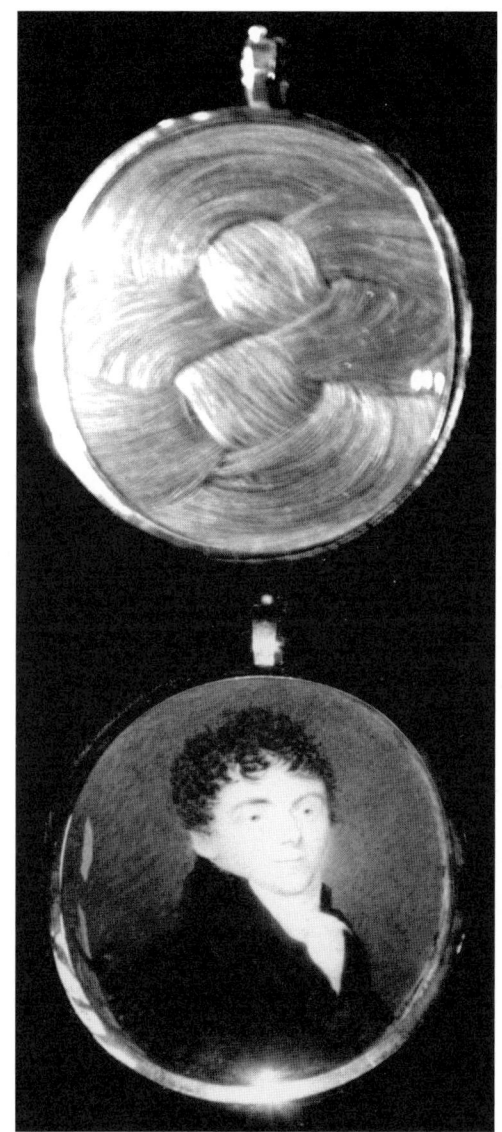

Miniature of Henry Martyn
with a lock of hair

A Vision of Saints : Lewis Morris [96]

Then came another of priestly garb and mien,
A young man still wanting the years of Christ,
But long since with the saints...
A poet with the contemplative gaze
And listening ear, but quick of force and eye,
Who fought the wrong without, the wrong within,
And, being a pure saint, like those of old,
Abased himself and all the precious gifts
God gave him, flinging all before the feet
Of Him whose name he bore — a fragile form
Upon whose hectic cheek there burned a flush
That was not health; who lived as Xavier lived,
And died like him upon the burning sands,
Untended, yet whose creed was far from his
As pole from pole; whom grateful England still
Loves.
            The awakened gaze
Turned wholly from the earth, on things of heaven
He dwelt both day and night. The thought of God
Filled him with infinite joy; his craving soul
Dwelt on Him as a feast; as did the soul
Of rapt Francesco in his holy cell
In blest Assisi; and he knew the pain,

---

[96] Scanned from George Smith: *Henry Martyn, Saint and Scholar*, The Religious Tract Society, London 1892.

The deep despondence of the saint, the doubt,
The consciousness of dark offence, the joy
Of full assurance last, when heaven itself
Stands open to the ecstasy of faith.
                        The relentless lie
Of Islam ... he chose to bear, who knew
How swift the night should fall on him, and burned
To save one soul alive while yet 'twas day.
This filled his thoughts, this only, and for this
On the pure altar of his soul he heaped
A costlier sacrifice, this youth in years,
For whom Love called, and loving hands, and hope
Of childish lives around him, offering these,
Like all the rest, to God.
                        Yet when his hour
Was come to leave his England, was it strange
His weakling life pined for the parting kiss
Of love and kindred, whom his prescient soul
Knew he should see no more?
                        The woman of his love
Feared to leave all and give her life to his,
And both to God; his sisters passed away
To heaven, nor saw him more. There seemed on earth
Nothing for which to live, except the Faith,
Only the Faith, the Faith! until his soul
Wore thin her prison bars, and he was fain
To rest awhile, or work no more the work
For which alone he lived.

Part Two — Seventeen of Henry's

Letters to Lydia

Scanned as published in John Sargent: *Life and Letters of The Rev. Henry Martyn, B.D.* 1862.

Letter 1 — Aboard *Union* at Falmouth — 27 July 1805

Union, Falmouth, July 27, 1805.

    ... As I was coming on board this morning, and reading Mr. Serle's Hymn you wrote out for me, a sudden gust of wind blew it into the sea. I made the boatmen immediately heave to, and recovered it, happily without any injury, except what it had received from the sea. I should have told you that the Morning Hymn, which I always kept carefully in my pocket-book, was one day stolen, with it and other valuable letters, from my rooms in College. It would be extremely gratifying to me to possess another copy of it, as it always reminded me most forcibly of the happy day on which we visited the aged saint. The fleet, it is said, will not sail for three weeks, but if you are willing to employ any of your time in providing me with this or any other MS. hymns, the sooner you write them the more certain I shall be of receiving them. Pardon me for thus intruding on your time; you will in no wise lose your reward. The encouragement conveyed in little compositions of this sort is more refreshing than a cup of cold water. The Lord of the harvest, who is sending forth me, who am most truly less than the least of all saints, will reward you for being willing to help forward even the meanest of His servants. The love which you bear to the cause of Christ, as well as motives of private friendship, will, I trust, induce you to commend me to God, and to the word of His grace, at those sacred moments when you approach the throne of our covenant God. To His gracious care I commend you. May you long live happy and holy, daily growing more meet for the inheritance of the saints in light.

    I remain, with affectionate regard,
    Yours most truly,
    H. MARTYN

Letter 2 — Aboard *Union* at Falmouth — 10 August 1805

Union, Falmouth, August 10, 1805.

My Dear Miss LYDIA,

It will, perhaps, be some satisfaction to yourself and your mother, to know that I was in time. Our ship was entangled in the chain, and was, by that means, the only one not under weigh when I arrived. It seems that most of the people on board had given me up, and did not mean to wait for me. I cannot but feel sensibly this instance of Divine mercy in thus preserving me from the great trouble that would have attended the loss of my passage. Mount's Bay will soon be in sight, and recal you all once more to my affectionate remembrance...

I bid you a long farewell. God ever bless you, and help you sometimes to intercede for me.

H. MARTYN.

Letter 3 — Serampore —30 July 1806

Serampore, July 30, 1806.

> *MY DEAREST LYDIA,*
> *On a subject so intimately connected with my happiness and future ministry, as that on which I am now about to address you, I wish to assure you that I am not acting with precipitancy, or without much consideration and prayer, while I at last sit down to request you to come out to me to India.*

> *May the Lord graciously direct His blind and erring creature, and not suffer the natural bias of his mind to lead him astray. You are acquainted with much of the conflict I have undergone on your account. It has been greater than you or Emma have imagined, and yet not so painful as I deserve to have found it, for having suffered my affections to fasten so inordinately on an earthly object.*

> *Soon, however, after my final departure from Europe, God in great mercy gave me deliverance, and favoured me throughout the voyage with peace of mind, indifference about all worldly connections, and devotedness to no object upon earth but the work of Christ. I gave you up entirely — not the smallest expectation remained in my mind of ever seeing you again till we should meet in heaven: and the thought of this separation was the less painful from the consolatory persuasion that our own Father had so ordered it for our mutual good. I continued from that time to remember you in my prayers only as a Christian sister, though one very dear to me. On my arrival in this country I saw no reason at first for supposing that marriage was advisable for a missionary or rather the subject did not offer itself to my mind. The Baptist missionaries indeed recommended it, and Mr. Brown; but not knowing any proper person in this country, they were not very pressing upon the subject, and I accordingly gave no attention to it. After a very short experience and inquiry afterwards, my own opinions began to change, and when a few weeks ago we received*

your welcome letter, and others from Mr. Simeon and Colonel Sandys, both of whom spoke of you in reference to me, I considered it even as a call from God to satisfy myself fully concerning his will. From the account which Mr. Simeon received of you from Mr. Thomason, he seemed in his letter to me to regret that he had so strongly dissuaded me from thinking about you at the time of my leaving England. Colonel Sandys spoke in such terms of you, and of the advantages to result from your presence in this country, that Mr. B. became very earnest for me to endeavour to prevail upon you. Your letter to me perfectly delighted him and induced him to say that you would be the greatest aid to the Mission I could possibly meet with. I knew my own heart too well not to be distrustful of it, especially as my affections were again awakened, and accordingly all my labour and prayer have been directed to check their influence, that I might see clearly the path of duty.

Though I dare not say that I am under no bias, yet from every view of the subject I have been able to take, after balancing the advantages and disadvantages that may ensue to the cause in which I am engaged, always in prayer for God's direction, my reason is fully convinced of the expediency, I had almost said the necessity of having you with me. It is possible that my reason may still be obscured by passion; let it suffice however to say that now, with a safe conscience and the enjoyment of the Divine presence, I calmly and deliberately make the proposal to you—and blessed be God if it be not His will to permit it; still this step is not advancing beyond the limits of duty, because there is a variety of ways by which God can prevent it, without suffering any dishonour to his cause. If He shall forbid it, I think, that by his grace, I shall even then be contented, and rejoice in the pleasure of corresponding with you. Your letter dated December, 1805, was the first I received, and I found it so animating that I could not but reflect on the blessedness of having so dear a counsellor always near me. I can truly say, and God is my witness, that my principal desire in this affair is, that you may promote the kingdom of God in my own heart, and be the means of extending it to the heathen. My own earthly comfort and happiness are not worth a moment's notice. I would not, my dearest Lydia, influence you by any artifices or false representations. I can only say that if you have a desire of being instrumental in establishing the blessed Redeemer's kingdom among these poor people, and will condescend to do it by supporting the spirits and animating the zeal of a weak messenger of the Lord who is apt to grow very dispirited and languid, 'Come, and the Lord be with you!' It can be nothing but a sacrifice on your part, to leave your valuable friends to come to one who is utterly unworthy of you or any other of God's precious gifts — but you will have your reward, and I ask it not of you or of God for the sake of my own happiness, but only on account of the Gospel. If it be not calculated to promote it, may God in his mercy withhold it. For the satisfaction of your friends, I should say, that you will meet with no hardships. The voyage is very agreeable, and with the people and country of India I think you will be much pleased. The climate is very fine — the so much-dreaded heat is really nothing to those who will employ their minds in useful pursuits. Idleness will make people complain of everything. The natives are the most harmless and timid creatures I ever met with. The whole country is the land of plenty and peace. Were I a missionary among the Esquimaux or Boschemen I should never dream of introducing a female into such a scene of danger or hardship, especially one whose happiness is dearer to me than my own, — but here there is universal tranquillity, — though the multitudes are so great, that a missionary needs not go three miles from his house to find a congregation of many thousands. You would not be left in solitude if I were to make any distant excursion; because no chaplain is stationed where there is not a large English society. My salary is abundantly sufficient for the support of a married man; the house and number of people kept by each Company's servant being such as to need no increase for a family establishment. As I must make the supposition of your coming, though it may be perhaps a premature liberty, I should give you some directions. This letter will reach you about the latter end of the year, — it would be very desirable if you could be ready for the February fleet, because the voyage will be performed in far less time than at any other season. George will find out the best ship; one in which there is a lady of high rank in the service would be preferable. You are to be considered as coming as a visitor to Mr. Brown, who will write to you or to Colonel Sandys, who is best qualified to give you directions about the voyage. Should I be up the country on your arrival in Bengal, Mr. Brown will be at hand to receive you, and you will find yourself immediately at home. As it will highly expedite some of the plans which we have in agitation that you should know the language as soon as possible, take Gilchrist's Indian Stranger's Guide, and occasionally on the voyage learn some of the words.

If I had room I might enlarge on much that would be interesting to you. In my conversations with Marshman, the Baptist missionary, our hearts sometimes expand with delight and joy at the prospect of seeing all these nations of the East receive the doctrine of the Cross. He is a happy labourer: and I only wait, I trust, to know the language to open my mouth boldly and make known the mystery of the Gospel. My romantic notions are for the first time almost realized, — for in addition to the beauties of sylvan scenery may be seen the more delightful object of multitudes of simple people sitting in the shade, listening to the words of eternal life. Much as yet is not done; but I have seen many discover by their looks while Marshman was preaching, that their hearts were tenderly affected. My post is not yet determined; we expect however it will be Patna, a civil station, where I shall not be under military command. As you are so kindly anxious about my health, I am happy to say, that through mercy my health is far better than it ever was in England.

Letter 3 — Serampore —30 July 1806

The people of Calcutta are very desirous of keeping me at the Mission Church, and offer to any Evangelical clergyman a chaplain's salary and a house besides. I am of course deaf to such a proposal; but it is strange that no one in England is tempted by such an inviting situation. I am actually going to mention it to cousin T. H. and Emma: — not, as you may suppose, with much hope of success; but I think that possibly the chapel at Dock may be too much for him, and he will have here a sphere of still greater importance. As this will be sent by the Overland Despatch, there is some danger of its not reaching, you; — you will therefore receive a duplicate, and perhaps a triplicate, by the ships that will arrive in England a month or two after. I cannot write now to any of my friends. I will therefore trouble you, if you have opportunity, to say that I have received no letters since I left England, except one from each of these — cousin T. and Emma, Simeon, Sargent, Bates — of my own family I have heard nothing. Assure any of them whom you may see, of the continuance of my affectionate regard — especially dear Emma. I did not know that it was permitted me to write to you — or I fear she would not have found me so faithful a correspondent on the voyage. As I have heretofore addressed you through her, it is probable that I may be now disposed to address her through you — or what will be best of all, that we both of us address her in one letter from India. However you shall decide, my dearest Lydia, I must approve your determination, because with that spirit of simple looking to the Lord, which we both endeavour to maintain, we must not doubt that you will be divinely directed. Till I receive an answer to this, my prayers, you may be assured, will be constantly put up for you, that in this affair you may be under an especial guidance, and that in all your ways God may be abundantly glorified by you through Jesus Christ. You say in your letter that frequently every day you remember my worthless name before the throne of grace. This instance of extraordinary and undeserved kindness draws my heart toward you with a tenderness which I cannot describe. Dearest Lydia, in the sweet and fond expectation of your being given to me by God, and of the happiness which I humbly hope you yourself might enjoy here, I find a pleasure in breathing out my assurance of ardent love. I have now long loved you most affectionately, and my attachment is more strong, more pure, more heavenly, because I see in you the image of Jesus Christ. I unwillingly conclude, by bidding my beloved Lydia adieu.

H. MARTYN.

Letter 4 — Serampore — 1 September 1806

Serampore, Sept. 1, 1806.

> MY DEAREST LYDIA,
>
> *With this you will receive the duplicate of the letter I sent you a month ago by the Overland Despatch. May it find you prepared to come! All the thoughts and views which I have had of the subject since first addressing you, add tenfold confirmation to my first opinion; and I trust that the blessed God will graciously make it appear that I have been acting under a right direction, by giving the precious gift to me and to the Church in India. I sometimes regret that I had not obtained a promise from you of following me, at the time of our last parting at Gurlyn as I am occasionally apt to be excessively impatient at the long delay. Many, many months must elapse before I can see you, or even hear how you shall determine. The instant your mind is made up, you will send a letter by the Overland Despatch. George will let you know how it is to be prepared, as the Company have given some printed directions. It is a consolation to me during this long suspense, that had I engaged with you before my departure I should not have had such a satisfactory conviction of it being the will of God. The Commander-in-Chief is in doubt to which of the three following stations he shall appoint me, — Benares, Patna, or Moorshedabad; it will be the last most probably; this is only two days' journey from Calcutta; I shall take my departure in about six weeks. In the hour that remains, I must endeavour to write to my dear sister Emma, and to Sally. By the fleet which will sail hence in about two months, they will receive longer letters. You will then, I hope, have left England. I am very happy here in preparing for my delightful work; but I should be happier still if I were sufficiently fluent in the language to be actually employed; and happiest of all if my beloved Lydia were at my right hand, counselling and animating me. I am not very willing to end my letter to you; it is difficult not to prolong the enjoyment of speaking, as it were, to one who occupies so much of my sleeping*

and waking hours; but here, alas! I am aware of danger; and my dear Lydia will, I hope, pray that her unworthy friend may love no creature inordinately.

It will be base in me to depart in heart from a God of such love as I find him to be. Oh, that I could make some returns for the riches of his love! Swiftly fly the hours of life away, and then we shall be admitted to behold his glory. The ages of darkness are rolling fast away, and shall soon usher in the gospel period, when the whole world shall be filled with his glory. Oh, my beloved sister and friend, dear to me on every account, but dearest of all for having one heart and one soul with me in the cause of Jesus and the love of God, let us pray and rejoice, and rejoice and pray, that God may be glorified, and the dying Saviour see of the travail of his soul. May the God of hope fill us with all joy and peace in believing, that we may both of us abound in hope through the power of the Holy Ghost. Now, my dearest Lydia, I cannot say what I feel — I cannot pour out my soul — I could not if you were here; but I pray that you may love me, if it be the will of God; and I pray that God may make you more and more his child, and give me more and more love for all that is Godlike and holy.

I remain, with fervent affection,
Yours, in eternal bonds,
H. MARTYN.

Letter 5 — Serampore —15 September 1806

Serampore, Sept 15 1806.

How earnestly do I long for the arrival of my dearest Lydia! Though it may prove at last no more than a waking dream that I ever expected to receive you in India, the hope is too pleasing not to be cherished till I am forbidden any longer to hope. Till I am assured of the contrary, I shall find a pleasure in addressing you as my own. If you are not to be mine, you will pardon me; but my expectations are greatly encouraged by the words you used when we parted at Gurlyn, that I had better go out free; implying, as I thought, that you would not be unwilling to follow me if I should see it to be the will of God to make the request. I was rejoiced also to see in your letter that you unite your name with mine, when you pray that God would keep us both in the path of duty; from this I infer that you are by no means determined to remain separate from me. You will not suppose, my dear Lydia, that I mention these little things to influence your conduct, or to implicate you in an engagement. — No, I acknowledge that you are perfectly free, and I have no doubt that you will act as the love and wisdom of our God shall direct. Your heart is far less interested in this business than mine, in all probability; and this on one account I do not regret, as you will be able to see more clearly the directions of God's providence. About a fortnight ago I sent you a letter accompanying the duplicate of the one sent overland in August. If these shall have arrived safe, you will perhaps have left England before this reaches it. But if not, let me entreat you not to delay a moment. Yet how will my dear sister Emma be able to part with you and George — but, above all, your mother? I feel very much for you and for them, but I have no doubt at all about your health and happiness in this country.

The Commander-in-Chief has at last appointed me to the station of Dinapore, near Patna, and I shall accordingly take my departure for that place as soon as I can make the necessary preparations. It is not exactly the situation I wished for — though, in a temporal point of view, it is desirable enough. The air is good, the living cheap, the salary £1000 a year, and there is a large body of English troops there. But I should have preferred being near Benares, the heart of Hinduism. We rejoice to hear that two other brethren are arrived at Madras on their way to Bengal, sent, I trust, by the Lord, to co-operate in overturning the kingdom of Satan in these regions. They are Corrie and Parsons, both Bengal chaplains. Their stations will be Benares and Moorshedabad — one on one side of me, and the other on the other. There are also now ten Baptist missionaries at Serampore. Surely good is intended for this country!

Captain Wickes, — the good old Captain Wickes, who has brought out so many missionaries to India, is now here. He reminds me of Uncle S—. I have just been interrupted by the blaze of a funeral pile, within a hundred yards of my pagoda; I ran out, but the wretched woman had consigned herself to the flames before I reached the spot, and I saw only the remains of her and her husband. O Lord, how long shall it be? Oh I shall have no rest in my spirit till my tongue is loosed to testify against the devil, and deliver the message of God to these his unhappy bond-slaves. I stammered out something to the wicked Brahmins about the judgments of God upon them for the murder they had just committed, but they said it was an act of her own free will. Some of the missionaries would have been there, but they are forbidden by the Governor-General to preach to the natives in the British territory. Unless this prohibition is revoked by an order from home, it will amount to a total suppression of the Mission.

I know of nothing else that will give you a further idea of the state of things here. The two ministers continue to oppose my doctrines with unabated virulence, but they think not that they fight against God. My own heart is at present cold and slothful. Oh that my soul did burn with love and zeal! Surely, were you

Letter 5 — Serampore —15 September 1806

here, I should act with more cheerfulness and activity with so bright a pattern before me. If Corrie brings me a letter from you, and the fleet is not sailed, which, however, is not likely, I shall write to you again. Colonel Sandys will receive a letter from me by this fleet. Continue to remember me in your prayers, as a weak brother. I shall always think of you as one to be loved and honoured.

H. MARTYN.

Letter 6 — Dinapore — 24 – 26 October 1807

TO MISS L. GRENFELL.
Dinapore, *Oct. 24.1807.*
MY DEAR LYDIA,

Though my heart is bursting with grief and disappointment, I write not to blame you. The rectitude of all your conduct secures you from censure. Permit me calmly to reply to your letter of March 5, which I have this day received.

You condemn yourself for having given me, though unintentionally, encouragement to believe that my attachment was returned. Perhaps you have. I have read your former letters with feelings less sanguine since the receipt of the last, and I am still not surprised at the interpretation I put upon them. But why accuse yourself for having written in this strain? It has not increased my expectations, nor consequently embittered my disappointment. When I addressed you in my first letter on the subject, I was not induced to it by any appearances of regard you had expressed, neither at any subsequent period have my hopes of your consent been founded on a belief of your attachment to me. I knew that your conduct would be regulated, not by personal feelings, but by a sense of duty. And therefore you have nothing to blame yourself for on this head.

In your last letter you do not assign, among your reasons for refusal, a want of regard to me. In that case I could not in decency give you any further trouble. On the contrary, you say that "present circumstances seem to you to forbid my indulging expectations." As this leaves an opening, I presume to address you again; and till the answer arrives, must undergo another eighteen months of torturing suspense.

Alas! my rebellious heart, what a tempest agitates me! I knew not that I had made so little progress in a spirit of resignation to the divine will. I am in my chastisement like the *bullock unaccustomed to the yoke, like a wild bull in a net, full of the fury of the Lord, the rebuke of my God. The death of my late most beloved sister almost broke my heart; but I hoped it had softened me and made me willing to suffer. But now my heart is as though destitute of the grace of God, full of misanthropic disgust with the world, and sometimes feeling resentment against yourself and Emma, and Mr. Simeon, and in short, all whom I love and honour most. Sometimes in pride and anger resolving to write neither to you nor to any one else again. These are the motions of sin. My love and my better reason draw me to you again * * * **

*But now with respect to **your** mother, I confess that the chief and indeed only difficulty lies here. Considering that she is your mother, as I hoped she would be mine, and that her happiness so much depends on you; considering also that I am God's minister, which amidst, all the tumults of my soul I dare not forget, I falter in beginning to give advice which may prove contrary to the law of God. God forbid therefore that I should say, disobey your parents where the divine law does not command you to disobey them; neither do I positively take upon myself to say that this is a case in which the law of God requires you to act in contradiction to them. I would rather suggest to your mother some considerations which justify me in attempting to deprive her of the company of a beloved child.*

26. A Sabbath having intervened since the above was written, I find myself more tranquillized by the sacred exercises of the day. One passage of Scripture which you quote has been much on my mind, and I find it very appropriate and decisive, — that we are not to "make to ourselves crooked paths, which whoso walketh in shall not know peace." Let me say I must be therefore contented to wait till you feel that the way is clear. But I intended to justify myself to Mrs. Grenfell. Let her not suppose that I would make her, or any other of my fellow-creatures miserable, that I might be happy. If there were no reason for your coming here, and the contest were only between Mrs. Grenfell and me, that is, between her happiness and mine, I would urge nothing further, but resign you to her. But I have considered that there are many things that might reconcile her to a separation from you (if indeed a separation is necessary, for if she would come along with you, I should rejoice the more.) First, she does not depend on you alone for the comfort of her declining years. She is surrounded by friends. She has a greater number of sons and daughters honourably established in the world, than falls to the lot of most parents—all of whom would be happy in having her amongst them. Again, if a person worthy of your hand, and settled in England, were to offer himself, Mrs. G. would not have insuperable objections, though it did deprive her of her daughter. Nay I sometimes think, perhaps arrogantly, that had I myself remained in England, and in possession of a competency, she would not have withheld her consent. Why then should my banishment from my native country in the service of mankind, be a reason with any for inflicting an additional wound, far more painful than a separation from my dearest relatives ?

I have no claim upon Mrs. G. in any way, but let her only conceive a son of her own in my circumstances. If she feels it a sacrifice, let her remember that it is a sacrifice made to duty; — that your presence here would be of essential service to the church of God, it is superfluous to attempt to prove. If you really believe of yourself as you speak, it is because you were never out of England.

Your mother cannot be so misinformed respecting India and the voyage to it, as to be apprehensive on account of the clime or passage, in these days, when multitudes of ladies every year, with constitutions as delicate as yours, go to and fro in perfect safety, and a vastly greater majority enjoy their health here than in England. With respect to my means, I need add nothing to

*what was said in my first letter. But alas! what is my affluence
good for now? It never gave me pleasure, but when I thought you
were to share it with me. Two days ago I was hastening on the
alterations in my house and garden, supposing you were at hand;
but now every object excites disgust. My wish upon the whole is,
that if you perceive it would be your duty to come to India, were it
not for your mother, — and of that you cannot doubt, —
supposing I mean that your inclinations are indifferent, then you
should make her acquainted with your thoughts, and let us leave it
to God how he will determine her mind.*

*In the mean time, since I am forbidden to hope for the
immediate pleasure of seeing you, my next request is for a mutual
engagement. My own heart is engaged, I believe, indissolubly.*

*My reason for making a request which you will account
bold, is that there can then be no possible objection to our
correspondence, especially as I promise not to persuade you to leave
your mother.*

*In the midst of my present sorrow I am constrained to
remember yours. Your compassionate heart is pained from having
been the cause of suffering to me. But care not for me, dearest
Lydia. Next to the bliss of having you with me, my happiness is to
know that you are happy. I shall have to groan long perhaps with a
heavy heart; but if I am not hindered materially by it in the work
of God, it will be for the benefit of my soul. You, sister beloved in
the Lord, know much of the benefit of affliction. O may I have
grace to follow you, though at a humble distance, in the path of
patient suffering, in which you have walked so long. Day and
night I cease not to pray for you, though I fear my prayers are of
little value.*

*But as an encouragement to you to pray, I cannot help
transcribing a few words from my journal, written at the time you*

wrote your letter to me. (7th March.) "On the two last days (you wrote your letter on the 5th), felt no desire for a comfortable settlement in the world, scarcely pleasure at the thought of Lydia's coming, except so far as her being sent might be for the good of my soul, and assistance in my work." How manifestly is there an omnipresent, all-seeing God, and how sure we may be that prayers for spiritual blessings are heard by our God and Father. O let that endearing name quell every murmur! When I am sent for to different parts of the country to officiate at marriages, I sometimes think, amidst the festivity of the company, Why does all go so easily with them, and so hardly with me? They come together without difficulty, and I am balked and disconcerted almost every step I take, and condemned to wear away the time in uncertainty. Then I call to mind that to live without chastening, is allowed to the spurious offspring; while to suffer is the privilege of the children of God.

Dearest Lydia, must I conclude? I could prolong my communion with you through many sheets; how many things have I to say to you, which I hoped to have communicated in person. But the more I write and the more I think of you, the more my affection warms, and I should feel it difficult to keep my pen from expressions that might not be acceptable to you.

Farewell! dearest, most beloved Lydia, remember your faithful and ever affectionate,

H. MARTYN.

Letter 7 — Cawnpore — 30 March 1810

Cawnpore, March 30, 1810.

*Since you kindly bid me, my beloved friend, to consider
you in the place of that dear sister, whom it has pleased God in his
wisdom to take from me, I gratefully accept the offer of a
correspondence, which it has ever been the anxious wish of in my
heart to establish. Your kindness is the more acceptable, because it
is shown in the day of affliction. Though I had heard of my dearest
sister's illness, some months before I received the account of her
death, and though the nature of her disorder was such as left me
not a ray of hope, so that I was mercifully prepared for the event,
still the certainty of it fills me with anguish. It is not that she has
left me, for I never expected to see her more on earth. I have no
doubt of meeting her in heaven, but I cannot bear to think of the
pangs of dissolution she underwent, which have been
unfortunately detailed to me with too much particularity. Would
that I had never heard them, or could efface them from my
remembrance! But, oh, may I learn what the Lord is teaching me
by these repeated strokes. May I learn meekness and resignation.
May the world always appear as vain as it does now, and my own
continuance in it as short and uncertain. How frightful is the
desolation which Death makes, and how appalling his visits when
he enters one's family! I would rather never have been born, than
be born and die, were it not for Jesus, the Prince of Life, the
resurrection and the life. How inexpressibly precious is this
Saviour, when eternity seems near! I hope often to communicate
with you on these subjects, and in return for your kind and
consolatory letters, to send you, from time to time, accounts of
myself and my proceedings. Through you, I can hear of all my
friends in the West. When I first heard of the loss I was likely to
suffer, and began to reflect on my own friendless situation, you
were much in my thoughts, whether you would be silent on this
occasion or no? whether you would persist in your resolution?
Friends indeed I have, and brethren, blessed be God! but two*

Letter 7 — Cawnpore — 30 March 1810

brothers cannot supply the place of one sister. When month after month passed away, and no letter came from you, I almost abandoned the hope of ever hearing from you again. It only remained to wait the result of my last application through Emma. You have kindly anticipated my request, and, I need scarcely add, are more endeared to me than ever.

Of your illness, my dearest Lydia, I had heard nothing, and it was well for me that I did not.

Yours most affectionately,

H. MARTYN.

Letter 8 — Cawnpore — 19 - 26 April 1810

Cawnpore, April 19, 1810.

> *I begin my correspondence with my beloved Lydia, not without a fear of its being soon to end. Shall I venture to tell you, that our family complaint has again made its appearance in me, with more unpleasant symptoms than it has ever yet done? However, God, who two years ago redeemed my life from destruction, may again, for his Church's sake, interpose for my deliverance. Though, alas! what am I, that my place should not instantly be supplied by far more efficient instruments? The symptoms I mentioned are chiefly a pain in the chest, occasioned, I suppose, by over-exertion the two last Sundays, and incapacitating me at present from all public duty and even from conversation. You were mistaken in supposing that my former illness originated from study. Study never makes me ill— scarcely ever fatigues me — but my lungs! death is seated there; it is speaking that kills me. May it give others life! "Death worketh in us, but life in you." Nature intended me, as I should judge from the structure of my frame, for a chamber-counsel, not for a pleader at the bar. But the call of Jesus Christ bids me cry aloud, and spare not. As His minister, I am a debtor both to the Greek and the barbarian. How can I be silent, when I have both ever before me, and my debt not paid? You would suggest that energies more restrained will eventually be more efficient. I am aware of this, and mean to act upon this principle in future, if the resolution is not formed too late. But you know how apt we are to outstep the bounds of prudence, when there is no kind monitor at hand to warn us of the consequences.*

> *Had I been favoured with the one I wanted, I might not now have had occasion to mourn. You smile at my allusion, at least I hope so, for I am hardly in earnest. I have long since ceased to repine at the decree that keeps us as far asunder as the east is from the west, and yet am far from regretting that I ever knew you.*

Letter 8 — Cawnpore — 19 - 26 April 1810

The remembrance of you calls forth the exercise of delightful affections, and has kept me from many a snare. How wise and good is our God in all his dealings with his children! Had I yielded to the suggestions of flesh and blood, and remained in England, as I should have done, without the effectual working of his power, I should without doubt have sunk with my sisters into an early grave; whereas here, to say the least, I may live a few years, so as to accomplish a very important work. His keeping you from me, appears also, at this season of bodily infirmity, to be occasion of thankfulness. Death, I think, would be a less welcome visitor to me, if he came to take me from a wife, and that wife were you. Now if I die, I die unnoticed, involving none in calamity. Oh that I could trust Him for all that is to come, and love Him with that perfect love, which casteth out fear; for to say the truth, my confidence is sometimes shaken. To appear before the Judge of quick and dead is a much more awful thought in sickness than in health. Yet I dare not doubt the all-sufficiency of Jesus Christ; nor can I, with the utmost ingenuity of unbelief, resist the reasonings of St. Paul, all whose reasons seem to be drawn up on purpose to work into the mind the persuasion that God will glorify Himself by the salvation of sinners through Jesus Christ. I wish I could more enter into the meaning of this "chosen vessel." He seems to move in a world by himself, and sometimes to utter the unspeakable words, such as my natural understanding discerneth not; and when I turn to commentators, I find that I have passed out of the spiritual to the material world, and have got amongst men like myself. But soon, as he says, we shall no longer see as in a glass, by reflected rays, but see as we are seen, and know as we are known.

25th.—After another interval, I resume my pen. Through the mercy of God I am again quite well, but my mind is a good deal distressed at Sabat's conduct. I forbear writing what I think, in the hope that my fears may prove groundless; but indeed the children of the East are adepts in deceit. Their duplicity appears to me so disgusting at this moment, that I can only find relief from my growing misanthropy by remembering Him, who is the faithful and true witness; in whom all the promises of God are yea and amen; and by turning to the faithful in Europe — children that will not lie. Where shall we find sincerity in a native of the East? Yesterday I dined in a private way with —. After one year's inspection of me, they begin to lose their dread, and venture to invite me. Our conversation was occasionally religious, but topics of this nature are so new to fashionable people, and those upon which they have thought so much less than on any other, that, often from the shame of having nothing to say, they pass on to other subjects where they can be more at home. I was asked after dinner if I liked music. On my professing to be an admirer of harmony, cantos were performed and songs sung. After a time I inquired if they had no sacred music. It was now recollected, that they had some of Handel's, but it could not be found. A promise however was made, that next time I came, it should be produced. Instead of it, the 145th Psalm-tune was played, but none of the ladies could recollect enough of the tune to sing it. I observed, that all our talents and powers should be consecrated to the service of Him who gave them. To this no reply was made, but the reproof was felt. I asked the lady of the house if she read poetry, and then proceeded to mention Cowper, whose poems, it seems, were in the library; but the lady had never heard of the book. This was produced, and I read some passages. Poor people! here a little, and there a little, is a rule to be observed in speaking to them.

26th. — From speaking to my men last night, and again to-day convening long with some natives, my chest is again in pain, so much so that I can hardly speak. Well! now I am taught, and will take more care in future. My sheet being full, I must bid you adieu. The Lord ever bless and keep you.

Believe me to be with the truest affection,

Yours ever,　　　　　　*H. MARTYN.*

Letter 9 — Cawnpore —14 – 17 August 1810

Cawnpore, August 14, 1810.

> *With what delight do I sit down to begin a letter to my beloved Lydia! Yours of the fifth of February, which I received a few days ago, was written, I perceive, in considerable embarrassment. You thought it possible it might find me married, or about to be so. Let me begin, therefore, with assuring you, with more truth than Gehazi did his master, "Thy servant went no whither;" my heart has not strayed from Marazion, or Gurlyn, or I wherever you are. Five long years have passed, and I am still faithful. Happy would it be if I could say that I had been equally true to my profession of love for Him who is fairer than ten thousand, and altogether lovely. Yet, to the praise of his grace, let me recollect that twice five years have passed away since I began to know Him, and I am still not gone from Him. On the contrary, time and experience have endeared the Lord to me more and more; so that I feel less inclination, and see less reason for leaving Him. What is there, alas! in the world even were it everlasting?*

> *I rejoice at the accounts you give me of your continued good health and labours of love. Though you are not so usefully employed, as you might be in India; yet as that must not be, I contemplate with delight, your exertions at the other end of the world. May you be instrumental in bringing many sons and daughters to glory. What is become of St. Hilary, and its fairy scenes? When I think of Malachy, and the old man, and your sister, and Josepha, &c., how some are dead, and the rest dispersed, and their place occupied by strangers, it seems all like a dream.*

> *15th. — It is only little intervals of time that I can find for writing; my visitors, about whom I shall write presently, taking up much of my leisure, from necessary duty. Here follow some extracts from my journal.*

*   *   *   *

Letter 9 — Cawnpore —14 – 17 August 1810

Here my journal must close. I do not know whether you understand from it how we go on. I must endeavour to give you a clearer idea of it.

We all live here in bungalows, or thatched houses, on a piece of ground inclosed. Next to mine is the church, not yet opened for public worship; but which we make use of at night with the men of the 53rd. Corrie lives with me, and Miss Corrie with the Sherwoods. We usually rise at daybreak, and breakfast at six. immediately after breakfast we pray together, after which I translate into Arabic with Sabat, who lives in a small bungalow on my ground. We dine at twelve, and sit recreating ourselves with talking a little about dear friends in England. In the afternoon, I translate with Mirza Fitrut into Hindostanee, and Corrie employs himself in teaching some native Christian boys whom he is educating with great care, in hopes of their being fit for the office of catechist. I have also a school on my premises, for natives; but it is not well attended. There are not above sixteen Hindoo boys in it at present; half of them read the book of Genesis. At sunset we ride or drive, and then meet at the church, where we often raise the song of praise, with as much joy, through the grace and presence of our Lord, as you do in England. At ten we are all asleep. Thus we go on. To the hardships of missionaries, we are strangers, yet not averse, I trust, to encounter them, when we are called. My work at present is evidently to translate; hereafter I may itinerate. Dear Corrie, I fear, never will, — he always suffers from moving about in the daytime. But I should have said something about my health, as I find my death was reported at Cambridge. I thank God, I am perfectly well, though not very strong in my lungs; they do not seem affected yet, but I cannot speak long without uneasiness. From the nature of my complaint, if it deserves the name, it is evident that England is the last place I should go to. I should go home only to find a grave. How shall I therefore ever see you more on this side of eternity? Well! be it so, since such is the will of God: we shall meet, through grace, in the realms of bliss.

I am truly sorry to see my paper fail. Write as often as possible, every three months at least. Tell me where you go, and whom you see, and what you read.

17th. — I am sorry to conclude with saying, that my yesterday's boasted health proved a mistake; I was seized with violent sickness in the night, but to-day am better. Continue to pray for me, and believe me to be
    Your ever affectionate,
    H. MARTYN.

Letter 10 — Ganges to Calcutta — 6 October – 5 November 1810

From the Ganges, Oct. 6, 1810.

> *MY DEAREST LYDIA,*
>
> *Though I have had no letter from you very lately, nor have anything particular to say, yet having been days on the water without a person to speak to, tired also with reading and thinking, I mean to indulge myself with a little of what is always agreeable to me, and sometimes good for me: for, as my affection for you has something sacred in it, being founded on, or at least cemented by, an union of spirit in the Lord Jesus; so my separation also from you, produces a deadness to the world, at least for a time, which leaves a solemn impression as often as I think of it. Add to this, that as I must not indulge the hope of ever seeing you again in this world, I cannot think of you without thinking also of that world where we shall meet. You mention in one of your letters my coming to England, as that which may eventually prove a duty. You ought to have added, that in case I do come, you will consider it a duty not to let me come away again without you. But I am not likely to put you to the trial. Useless as I am here, I often think I should be still more so at home. Though my voice fails me, I can translate and converse. At home I should be nothing without being able to lift up my voice on high. I have just left my station, Cawnpore, in order to be silent six months. I have no cough, nor any sign of consumption, except that reading prayers, or preaching, or a slight cold, brings on pain in the chest. I am advised, therefore, to recruit my strength by rest. So I am come forth, with my face towards Calcutta, with an ulterior view to the sea. Nothing happened at Cawnpore after I wrote to you in September, but I must look to my journal.*
>
> *I think of having my portrait taken in Calcutta, as I promised Mr. Simeon five years ago. Sabat's picture would also be a curiosity. Yesterday I carried Colonel Wood to dine with me at the Nabob Bahir Ali's. Sabat was there. The Colonel, who had*

been reading by the way the account of his conversion in the Asiatic and East Society Report which I had given him, eyed him with no great complacency, and observed in French, that Sabat might not understand him, "Il a l'air d'un sauvage." Sabat's countenance is indeed terrible; noble when he is pleased, but with the look of an assassin when he is out of humour. I have had more opportunities of knowing Sabat than any man has had, and I cannot regard him with that interest which the "Star in the East" is calculated to excite in most people. Buchanan says I wrote (to whom I do not know) in terms of admiration and affection about him. Affection I do feel for him, but admiration, if I did once feel it, I am not conscious of at present. I tremble for everything our dear friends publish about our doings in India, lest shame come to us and them.

November 5. — Calcutta — A sheet full, like the preceding, I had written, but the moment that it is necessary to send off my letter, I cannot find it. That it does not go on to you is of little consequence, but into whose hands may it have fallen? It is this that grieves me. It was the continuance of my journal to Calcutta, where I arrived the last day in October. Constant conversation with dear friends here has brought on the pain in the chest again, so that I do not attempt to preach. In two or three weeks I shall embark for the Gulf of Persia, where, if I live, I shall solace myself in my hours of solitude with writing to you.

Farewell, beloved friend; pray for me, as you do I am sure, and doubt not of an unceasing interest in the heart and prayers of your ever affectionate,

H. MARTYN.

Letter 11 — At sea Calcutta to Bombay — 4 –18 February 1811

At sea, Coast of Malabar, Feb. 4, 1811.

The last letter I wrote to you, my dearest Lydia, was dated November, 1810. I continued in Calcutta to the end of the year, preaching once a week, and reading the Word in some happy little companies, with whom I enjoyed that sweet communion, which all in this vale of tears have reason to be thankful for, but especially those whose lot is cast in a heathen land. On New Year's-day, at Mr. Brown's urgent request, I preached a sermon for the Bible Society, recommending an immediate attention to the state of the native Christians. At the time I left Calcutta they talked of forming an Auxiliary Society. Leaving Calcutta was so much like leaving England, that I went on board my boat without giving them notice, and so escaped the pain of bidding them farewell. In two days I met my ship at the mouth of the river, and we put to sea immediately. Our ship is commanded by a pupil of Swartz and manned by Arabians, Abyssinians, and others. One of my fellow-passengers is Mr. Elphinstone, who was lately Ambassador at the Court of the King of Cabul, and is now going to be Resident at Poonah, the capital of the Mahratta Empire. So the group is rather interesting, and I am happy to say not averse to religious instruction, — I mean the Europeans. As for the Asiatics, they are in language, customs, and religion, as far removed from us as if they were inhabitants of another planet. I speak a little Arabic sometimes to the sailors, but their contempt of the Gospel, and attachment to their own superstition, make their conversion appear impossible. How stupendous that power which can make these people the followers of the Lamb, when they so nearly resemble Satan in pride and wickedness. The first part of the voyage I was without employment, and almost without thought, suffering as usual so much from sea-sickness, that I had not spirits to do anything but sit upon the poop, surveying the wide waste of waters blue. This continued all down the Bay of Bengal. At length in the neighbourhood of Ceylon we found smooth water, and came to an anchor off Columbo, the principal station in the island. The captain having proposed to his passengers that they should go ashore and refresh themselves with a walk in the Cinnamon-gardens, Mr. E. and myself availed ourselves of the offer, and went off to inhale the cinnamon breeze. The walk was delightful. The huts of the natives, who are (in that neighbourhood at least) most of them Protestants, are built in thick groves of cocoa-nut-tree, with openings here and there, discovering the sea. Everything bore the appearance of contentment. I contemplated them with delight, and was almost glad that I could not speak with them, lest further acquaintance should have dissipated the pleasing ideas their appearance gave birth to. In the gardens I cut off a piece of the bark for you. It will not be so fragrant as that which is properly prepared; but it will not have lost its fine smell, I hope, when it reaches you.

At Captain R.'s, the Chief Secretary to Government, we met a good part of the European society of Columbo. The party was like most mixed parties in England, where much is said that need not be remembered. The next day we stretched across the Gulf of Manaan, and soon came in sight of Cape Comorin, the great promontory of India. At a distance the green waves seemed to wash the foot of the mountain, but on a nearer approach little churches were seen, apparently on the beach, with a row of little huts on each side. Was it these maritime situations that recalled to my mind Perran Church and town in the way to Gurlyn; or that my thoughts wander too often on the beach to the east of Lamorran? You do not tell me whether you ever walk there, and imagine the billows that break at your feet, to have made their way from India. But why should I wish to know? Had I observed silence on that day and thenceforward, I should have spared you much trouble and myself much pain. Yet I am far from regretting that I spoke; since I am persuaded that all things will work together for good. I sometimes try to put such a number of things together as shall produce the greatest happiness possible, and I find that even in imagination I cannot satisfy myself. I set myself to see what is that "good for the sons of men, which they should do under heaven all the days of their life," and I find that Paradise is not here. Many things are delightful, some things are almost all one could wish; but yet in all beauty there is deformity; in the most perfect, something wanting; and there is no hope of its ever being otherwise. "That which is crooked cannot be made straight, and that which is wanting cannot be numbered." So that the expectation of happiness on earth seems chimerical to the last degree. In my schemes of happiness I place myself of course with you, blessed with great success in the ministry, and seeing all India turning to the Lord. Yet it is evident that with these joys there would be mingled many sorrows. The care of all the churches was a burden to the mighty mind of St. Paul. As for what we should be together, I judge of it from our friends. Are they quite beyond the vexations of common life? I think not — still I do not say that it is a question, whether they gained or lost by marrying. Their affections will live when ours (I should rather say mine) are dead.

Perhaps it may not be the effect of celibacy; but I certainly begin to feel a wonderful indifference to all but myself. From so seldom seeing a creature that cares for me, and never one that depends at all upon me, I begin to look round upon men with reciprocal apathy. It sometimes calls itself deadness to the world, but I much fear that it is deadness of heart. I am exempt from worldly cares myself, therefore do not feel for others. Having got out of the stream into still water, I go round and round in my own little circle. This supposed deterioration you will ascribe to my humility; therefore I add, that Mr. Brown could not help remarking the difference between what I am and what I was; and observed on seeing my picture which was taken at Calcutta for Mr. Simeon, and is thought a striking likeness, that it was not Martyn that arrived in India, but Martyn the recluse.

Letter 11 — At sea Calcutta to Bombay — 4 –18 February 1811

10. — To-day my affections seem to have revived a little. I have been often deceived in times past, and erroneously called animal spirits, joy in the Holy Ghost. Yet I trust that I can say with truth, "To them who believe, He is precious!" "Yes, thou art precious to my soul my transport and my trust." No thought now is so sweet as that which those words suggest "In Christ." Our destinies thus inseparably united with those of the Son of God, what is too great to be expected? "All things are yours, for ye are Christ's!" We may ask what we will, and it shall be given to us. Now, why do I ever lose sight of Him or fancy myself without Him, or try to do anything without Him? Break off a branch from a tree, and how long will it be before it withers. To-day, my beloved sister, I rejoice in you before the Lord, I rejoice in you as a member of the mystic body, I pray that your prayers for one who is unworthy of your remembrance may be heard, and bring down tenfold blessings on yourself. How good is the Lord in giving me grace to rejoice with His chosen, all over the earth; even with those who are at this moment going up with the voice of joy and praise, to tread His courts and sing His praise! There is not an object about me but is depressing. Yet my heart expands with delight at the presence of a gracious God, and the assurance that my separation from His people is only temporary. On the 7th we landed at Goa, the capital of the Portuguese possessions in the East. I reckoned much on my visit to Goa; expecting, from its being the residence of the Archbishop and many ecclesiastics, that I should obtain such information about the Christians in India as would render it superfluous to make inquiries elsewhere, but I was much disappointed. Perhaps it was owing to our being accompanied by several officers, English and Portuguese, that the Archbishop and his principal agents would not be seen, but so it was, that I scarcely met with a man who could make himself intelligible. We were shown what strangers are usually shown, the churches and monasteries, but I wanted to contemplate man, the only thing on earth almost that possesses any interest for me. I beheld the stupendous magnificence of their noble churches without emotion, except to regret that the Gospel was not preached in them. In one of the monasteries we saw the tomb of Francis Xavier, the Apostle of India, most richly ornamented, as well as the room in which it stands, with paintings and figures in bronze, done in Italy. The Friar who showed us the tomb, happening to speak of the grace of God in the heart, without which, said he, as he held the sacramental water, the body of Christ profits nothing, I began a conversation with him, which, however, came to nothing. We visited among many other places the convent of Nuns. After a long altercation with the lady-portress, we were admitted to the antechamber, in which was the grate, a window with iron bar, behind which the poor prisoners made their appearance. While my companions were purchasing their trinkets, I was employed in examining their countenances, which I did with great attention. In what possible way, thought I, can you support existence, if you do not find your happiness in God? They all looked ill and discontented, those at least whose countenances expressed anything. One sat by reading, as if nothing were going on. I asked to see the book, and it was handed through the grate. Finding that it was a Latin Prayerbook, I wrote in Latin something about the love of the world, which seclusion from it would not remove. The Inquisition is still existing at Goa. We were not admitted as far as Dr. Buchanan was, to the Hall of Examination; and that because he printed something about the Inquisitors, which came to their knowledge. The priest in waiting acknowledged that they had some prisoners within the walls, and defended the practice of imprisoning and chastising offenders, on the ground of its being conformable to the custom of the Primitive Church. We were told that when the offices of the Inquisition touch an individual, and beckon him away, he dares not resist; if he does not come out again, no one must ask about him; if he does, he must not tell what was done to him.

18.   (Bombay.) — *Thus far I am brought in safety. On this day I complete my 30th year. "Here I raise my Ebenezer; Hither by thy help I'm come." It is sweet to reflect that we shall at last reach our home. I am here amongst men who are indeed aliens to the commonwealth of Israel, and without God in the world. I hear many of those amongst whom I live, bring idle objections against religion, such as I have answered a hundred times. How insensible are men of the world to all, that God is doing! How unconscious of his purposes concerning his Church! How incapable, seemingly, of comprehending the existence of it ! I feel the meaning of St. Paul's words — "Hath abounded toward us in all wisdom and prudence, having made known to us the mystery of his will, that he would gather in one all things in Christ." Well! let us bless the Lord — "All thy children shall be taught of the Lord, and great shall be the peace of thy children." In a few days I expect to sail for the Gulf of Persia in one of the Company's sloops of war.*

Farewell, my beloved Lydia, and believe me to be ever,

Yours most affectionately,

H. MARTYN.

Letter 12 — Muscat — 22 April 1811

Muscat, April 22, 1811.

> *MY DEAREST LYDIA,*

> *I am now in Arabia Felix; to judge from the aspect of the country, it has few pretensions to the name, unless burning barren rocks convey an idea of felicity; but perhaps, as there is a promise in reserve for the sons of Joktan, their land may one day be blest indeed.*

> *We sailed from Bombay on Lady-day; and on the morning of Easter saw the land of Mehran in Persia. After another week's sail across the mouth of the Gulf, we arrived here, and expect to proceed up the Gulf to Bushire, as soon as we have taken in our water. You will be happy to learn that the murderous pirates against whom we were sent, having received notice of our approach, have all got out of the way; so that I am no longer liable to be shot in a battle, or decapitated after it, if it be lawful to judge from appearances. These pestilent Ishmaelites indeed, whose hand is against every man's, will escape, and the community suffer; but that selfish friendship of which you once confessed yourself guilty, will think only of the preservation of a friend. This last marine excursion has been the pleasantest I ever made, as I have been able to pursue my studies with less interruption than when ashore. My little congregation of forty or fifty Europeans does not try my strength on Sundays; and my two companions are men who read their Bible every day. In addition to all these comforts, I have to bless God for having kept me more than usually free from the sorrowful mind. We must not always say with Watts, "the sorrows of the mind be banished from this place;" but if freedom from trouble be offered us, we may choose it rather. I do not know anything more delightful than to meet with a Christian brother, where only strangers and foreigners were expected. This pleasure I enjoyed just before leaving Bombay; a ropemaker who had just come from England understood from my sermon that I was one he*

might speak to; so he came and opened his heart, and we rejoiced together. In this ship I find another of the household of faith. In another ship which accompanies us there are two Armenians who do nothing but read the Testament. One of them will, I hope, accompany me to Shiraz, in Persia, which is his native country.

We are likely to be detained here some days, but the ship that will carry our letters to India sails immediately, so that I can send but one letter to England, and one to Calcutta. When will our correspondence be established? I have been trying to effect it these six years, and it is only yet in train. Why there was no letter from you among those dated June and July, 1810, I cannot conjecture, except that you had not received any of mine, and would write no more. But I am not yet without hope that a letter in the beloved hand will yet overtake me somewhere. My kindest and most affectionate remembrances to all the Western circle. Is it because he is your brother that I love — so much? or because he is the last come into the number? The angels love and wait upon the righteous who need no repentance; but there is joy whenever another heir of salvation is born into the family. Read Eph. i. I cannot wish you all these spiritual blessings, since they are already all yours; but I pray that we may have the spirit of wisdom and knowledge to know that they are ours. It is a chapter I keep in mind every day in prayer. We cannot believe too much or hope too much. Happy our eyes that they see, and our ears that they hear.

As it may be a year or more before I shall be back, you may direct one letter after receiving this, if it be not of a very old date, to Bombay; all after to Bengal, as usual. Believe me to be ever, my dearest Lydia,

Your most affectionate

H. MARTYN

Letter 13 — Shiraz — 23 June - 5 July 1811

Shiraz, June, 23, 1811.

> *MY DEAREST LYDIA,*

> *How continually I think of you, and indeed converse with you, it is impossible to say. But on the Lord's-day in particular, I find you much in my thoughts, because it is on that day that I look abroad, and take a view of the universal church, of which I observe that the saints in England form the most conspicuous part. On that day too, I indulge myself with a view of the past, and look over again those happy days, when, in company with those I loved, I went up to the house of God with a voice of praise. How then shall I fail to remember her who, of all that are dear to me, is the dearest? It is true that I cannot look back upon many days, nor even many hours passed with you; — would they had been more! — but we have insensibly become more acquainted with each other, so that, on my part at least, it may be said that separation has brought us nearer to one another. It was a momentary interview, but the love is lasting, everlasting. Whether we ever meet again or not, I am sure that you will continue to feel an interest in all that befals me.*

> *After the death of my dear sister, you bid me consider that I had one sister left while you remained; and you cannot imagine how consolatory to my mind this assurance is. To know that there is one who is willing to think of me, and has leisure to do so, is soothing to a degree which none can know but those who have, like me, lost all their relations.*

> *I sent you a letter from Muscat in Arabia, which I hope you received; for if not, report will again erase my name from the catalogue of the living, as I sent no other to Europe. Let me here say, with praise to our ever-gracious heavenly Father, that I am in perfect health; of my spirits I cannot say much; I fancy they would be better were 'the beloved Persis' by my side. This name, which I*

once gave you, occurs to me at this moment, I suppose because I am in Persia, intrenched in one of its valleys, separated from Indian friends by chains of mountains and a roaring sea, among a people depraved beyond all belief, in the power of a tyrant guilty of every species of atrocity. Imagine a pale person seated on a Persian carpet, in a room without table or chair, with a pair of formidable mustachios, and habited as a Persian, and you see me.

26.— Here I expect to remain six months. The reason is this: I found on my arrival here, that our attempts at Persian translation in India were good for nothing; at the same time they proposed, with my assistance, to make a new translation. It was an offer I could not refuse, as they speak the purest dialect of the Persian. My host is a man of rank,— his name Jaffier Ali Khan, who tries to make the period of my captivity as agreeable as possible. His wife, for he has but one, never appears; parties of young ladies come to see her, but though they stay days in the house, he dare not go into the room where they are. Without intending a compliment to your sex, I must say that the society here, from the exclusion of females, is as dull as it can well be. Perhaps, however, to a stranger like myself, the most social circles would be insipid. I am visited by all the great and the learned; the former come out of respect to my country, the latter to my profession. The conversation with the latter is always upon religion, and it would be strange indeed, if with the armour of truth on the right hand and on the left, I were not able to combat with success, the upholders of such a system of absurdity and sin. As the Persians are a far more unprejudiced and inquisitive people than the Indians, and do not stand quite so much in awe of an Englishman as the timid natives of Hindostan, I hope they will learn something from me; the hope of this reconciles me to the necessity imposed on me of staying here; about the translation I dare not be sanguine. The prevailing opinion concerning me is, that I have repaired to Shiraz in order to become a Mussulman.

Letter 13 — Shiraz — 23 June - 5 July 1811

Others, more sagacious, say that I shall bring from India some more, under pretence of making them Mussulmans, but in reality to seize the place. They do not seem to have thought of my wish, to have them converted to my religion; they have been so long accustomed to remain without proselytes to their own. I shall probably have very little to write about, for some months to come, and therefore I reserve the extracts of my journal since I last wrote to you, for some other opportunity;— besides that, the ambassador, with whose despatches this will go, is just leaving Shiraz.

July 2. — The Mohammedans now come in such numbers to visit me, that I am obliged, for the sake of my translation-work, to decline seeing them. To-day one of the apostate sons of Israel was brought by a party of them, to prove the Divine mission of Mahomet from the Hebrew Scriptures; but with all his sophistry he proved nothing. I can almost say with St. Paul, I feel continual pity in my heart for them, and love them for their fathers' sake, and find a pleasure in praying for them. While speaking of the return of the Jews to Jerusalem, I observed that the "gospel of the kingdom must first be preached in all the world, and then shall the end come." He replied with a sneer, "And this event, I suppose you mean to say, is beginning to take place by your bringing the Gospel to Persia."

5. — I am so incessantly occupied with visitors and my work, that I have hardly a moment for myself. I have more and more reason to rejoice at my being sent here; there is such an extraordinary stir about religion throughout the city, that some good must come of it. I sometimes sigh for a little Christian communion, yet even from these Mohammedans I hear remarks that do me good; to-day, for instance, my assistant observed, "How he loved those twelve persons? "Yes," said I, "and not those twelve only, but all those who shall believe in him;" as he said, "I pray not for these alone, but for all them who shall believe on me through their word." Even the enemy is constrained to wonder at the love of Christ. Shall not the objects of it say, What manner of love is this?

    I have learned that I may get letters from England much sooner than by way of India. Be so good as to direct to me to the care of Sir Gore Ouseley, Bart., Ambassador at Tehran, care of J. Morier, Esq., Constantinople, care of G. Moon, Esq., Malta. I have seen Europe newspapers of only four months' date, so that I am delightfully near you. May we live near one another in the unity of the Spirit, having one Lord, one hope, one God and Father. In your prayers for me, pray that utterance may be given me, that I may open my mouth boldly, to make known the mysteries of the Gospel. I often envy my Persian hearers the freedom and eloquence with which they speak to me. Were I but possessed of their powers, I sometimes think that I should win them all; but the work is God's, and the faith of his people does not stand in the wisdom of men, but in the power of God. Remember me as usual with the most unfeigned affection to all my dear friends. This is now the seventh letter I send you, without having received an answer.

    Farewell, yours —
    Ever most affectionately,
    H. MARTYN

Letter 14 — Shiraz — 8 September 1811

Shiraz, Sept. 8, 1811.

A courier on his way to the capital, affords me the unexpected pleasure of addressing my most beloved friend. It is now six months since I left India, and in all that time I have not heard from thence. The dear friends there, happy in each other's society, do not enough call to mind my forlorn condition. Here I am still, beset by cavilling infidels, and making very little progress in my translation, and half disposed to give it up, and come away. My kind host, to relieve the tedium of being always within a walled town, pitched a tent for me in a garden a little distance, and there I lived amidst clusters of grapes by the side of a clear stream; but nothing compensates for the loss of the excellent of the earth. It is my business, however, as you will say, and ought to be my effort, to make saints, where I cannot find them. I do use the means in a certain way, but frigid reasoning with men of perverse minds, seldom brings men to Christ. However, as they require it, I reason, and accordingly challenged them to prove the Divine mission of their prophet. In consequence of this, a learned Arabic Treatise was written, by one who was considered as the most able man, and put it into my hands; copies of it were also given to the college and the learned. The writer of it said that if I could give a satisfactory answer to it, he would become a Christian, and at all events, would make my reply as public as I pleased. I did answer it, and after some faint efforts on his part to defend himself, he acknowledged the force of my argument but was afraid to let them be generally known. He then began to inquire about the Gospel, but was not satisfied with my statement. He required me to prove from the very beginning, the Divine mission of Moses, as well as of Christ; the truth of the Scriptures, &c. With very little hope that any good will come of it, I am now employed in drawing out the evidences of the truth; but oh, that I could converse and reason, and plead, with power from on high! How powerless are the best-directed arguments, till the Holy Ghost renders them effectual!

A few days ago I was on the eve of my departure for Ispahan, as I thought, and my translator had consented to accompany me as far as Bagdad; but just as we were setting out, news came that the Persians and Turks were fighting thereabouts, and that the road was in consequence impassable. I do not know what the Lord's purpose may be in keeping me here, but I trust it will be for the furtherance of the Gospel of Christ, and in that belief I abide contentedly.

My last letter to you was dated July. I desired you to direct to me at Tehran. As it is uncertain whether I shall pass anywhere near there, you had better direct to the care of S. Morier, Esq., Constantinople, and I can easily get your letters from thence.

I am happy to say that I am quite well, indeed never better; no returns of pain in the chest since I left India. May I soon receive the welcome news, that you also are well, and prospering even as your soul prospers. I read your letters incessantly, and try to find out something new, as I generally do, but I begin to look with pain at the distant date of the last. I cannot tell what to think, but I cast all my care upon Him who hath already done wonders for me, and am sure that, come what will, it shall be good, it shall be best. How sweet the privilege, that we may lie as little children before Him! I find that my wisdom is folly, and my care useless, so that I try to live on from day to day, happy in His love and care. May that God who hath loved us, and given us everlasting consolation, and good hope through grace, bless, love, and keep my ever-dearest friend; and dwelling in the secret place of the Most High, and abiding under the shadow of the Almighty, may she enjoy that sweet tranquillity which the world cannot disturb. Dearest Lydia! pray for me, and believe me to be, ever most faithfully and affectionately yours,   H. MARTYN

Letter 15 — Shiraz — 21 October 1811

Shiraz, October 21, 1811.

         * * * *It is, I think, about a month since I wrote to you, and so little has occurred since, that I find scarcely anything in my journal, and nothing worth transcribing, This state of inactivity is becoming very irksome to me. I cannot get these Persians to work, and while they are idle, I am sitting here to no purpose. Sabat's laziness used to provoke me excessively, but Persians, I find, are as torpid as Arabs, when their salary does not depend on their exertions, and both very inferior to the feeble Indian, whom they affect to despise. My translator comes about sunrise, corrects a little, and is off, and I see no more of him for the day. Meanwhile I sit fretting, or should do so, as I did at first, were it not for a blessed employment which so beguiles the tediousness of the day, that I hardly perceive how it passes. It is the study of the Psalms in the Hebrew. I have long had it in contemplation, in the assurance, from the number of flat and obscure passages that occur in the translations, that the original has not been hitherto perfectly understood. I am delighted to find that many of the most unmeaning verses in our version turn out, on close examination, to contain a direct reference to the Lord our Saviour. The testimony of Jesus is indeed the spirit of prophecy. He is never lost sight of. Let them touch what subject they will, they must always let fall something about Him. Such should we be, looking always to Him. I have often attempted the eighty-fourth Psalm, endeared to me on many accounts, as you know, but have not yet succeeded. The glorious sixteenth Psalm I hope I have mastered. I write with the ardour of a student, communicating his discoveries, and describing his difficulties to a fellow-student.*

         I think of you incessantly; too much I fear, sometimes: yet the recollection of you is generally attended with an exercise of resignation to His will. In prayer I often feel what you described five years ago as having felt, — a particular pleasure in viewing you as with me before the Lord, and entreating our common

Father to bless both His children. When I sit and muse, my spirit flies away to you, and attends you at Gurlyn, Penzance, Plymouth Dock, and sometimes with your brother in London. If you acknowledge a kindred feeling still, we are not separated, our spirits have met and blended. I still continue without intelligence from India; since last January I have heard nothing of any one person whom I love. My consolation is, that the Lord has you all under his care, and is carrying on His work in the world by your means; and that when I emerge, I shall find that some progress is made in India especially, the country I now regard as my own. Persia is, in many respects, a field ripe for the harvest. Vast numbers secretly hate and despise the superstition imposed on them, and as many of them as have heard the Gospel, approve it; but they dare not hazard their lives for the name of the Lord Jesus. I am sometimes asked whether the external appearance of Mohammedanism might not be retained with Christianity; and whether I could not baptize them without their believing in the divinity of Christ? I tell them, No.

Though I have complained above of the inactivity of my translation, I have reason to bless the Lord that He thus supplies Gibeonites for the help of His true Israel. They are employed in a work, of the importance of which they are unconscious, and are making provision for future Persian saints, whose time is, I suppose, now near. "Roll back, ye crowded years, your thick array!" Let the long, long period of darkness and sin at last give way to the brighter hours of light and liberty, which wait on the wings of the Sun of Righteousness. Perhaps we witness the dawn of the day of glory, and if not, the desire that we feel, that Jesus may be glorified, and the nations acknowledge His sway, is the earnest of the Spirit, that when He shall appear, we shall also appear with Him in glory. Kind love to all the saints who are waiting His coming.

Yours with true affection,

Letter 15 — Shiraz — 21 October 1811

My ever dearest Lydia,

H. MARTYN.

It is now determined that we leave Shiraz in a week; and as the road through Persia is impassable through the commotions which are always disturbing some part or other of this unhappy country, I must go back to Bushire.

Letter 16 — Tabriz — 12 July 1812

Tebriz, July 12, 1812.

 MY DEAREST LYDIA,

 I have only time to say that I have received your letter of February 14. Shall I pain your heart by adding, that I am in such a state of sickness and pain, that I can hardly write to you? Let me rather observe, to obviate the gloomy apprehension my letters to Mr. Grant and Mr. Simeon may excite, that I am likely soon to be delivered from my fever. Whether I shall gain strength enough to go on, rests on our Heavenly Father, in whose hands are all my times. Oh, his precious grace! His eternal, unchanging love in Christ to my soul, never appeared more clear, more sweet, more strong. I ought to inform you that, in consequence of the state to which I am reduced by travelling so far overland, without having accomplished my journey, and the consequent impossibility of returning to India the same way, I have applied for leave to come on furlough to England. Perhaps you will be gratified by this intelligence; but oh, my dear Lydia, I must faithfully tell you, that the probability of my reaching England alive is but small; and this I say, that your expectations of seeing me again may be moderate, as mine are of seeing you. Why have you not written more about yourself! However, I am thankful for knowing that you are alive and well. I scarcely know how to desire you to direct. Perhaps Alexandria in Egypt will be the best place: another may be sent to Constantinople; for, though I shall not go there, I hope Mr. Morier will be kept informed of my movements. Kindest love to all the saints you usually mention.

 Yours, ever most faithfully and affectionately,

 H. MARTYN.

Letter 17 — Tabriz — 28 August 1812

Tebriz, Aug. 28, 1812.

> *I wrote to you last, my dear Lydia, in great disorder. My fever had approached nearly to delirium, and my debility was so great, that it seemed impossible I could withstand the power of disease many days. Yet it has pleased God to restore me to life and health again; not that I have recovered my former strength yet, but consider myself sufficiently restored to prosecute my journey. My daily prayer is, that my late chastisement may have its intended effect, and make me all the rest of my days more humble, and less self-confident. Self-confidence has often let me down fearful lengths, and would, without God's gracious interference, prove my endless perdition. I seem to be made to feel this evil of my heart more than any other at this time. In prayer, or when I write, or converse on the subject, Christ appears to me my life and strength; but at other times, I am as thoughtless and bold, as if I had all life and strength in myself. Such neglect on our part works a diminution of our joys; but the covenant, the covenant! stands fast with Him, for His people evermore. I mentioned my conversing sometimes on Divine subjects, for though it is long enough since I have seen a child of God, I am sometimes led on by the Persians to tell them all I know of the very recesses of the sanctuary, and these are the things that interest them. But to give an account of all my discussions with these mystic philosophers, must be reserved to the time of our meeting. Do I dream? that I venture to think and write of such an event as that! Is it possible that we shall ever meet again below? Though it is possible, I dare not indulge such a pleasing hope yet. I am still at a tremendous distance; and the countries I have to pass through, are many of them dangerous to the traveller, from the hordes of banditti, whom a feeble Government cannot chastise. In consequence of the bad state of the road between this and Aleppo, Sir Gore advises me to go first to Constantinople, and from thence to pass into Syria. In favour of this route, he urges, that by writing to two or three Turkish*

governors on the frontiers, he can secure me a safe passage at least halfway, and the latter half is probably not much infested. In three days, therefore, I intend setting my horse's head towards Constantinople, distant about thirteen hundred miles. Nothing, I think, will occasion any further detention here, if I can procure servants who know both Persian and Turkish; but should I be taken ill on the road, my case would be pitiable indeed. The Ambassador and his suite are still here; his, and Lady Ouseley's attentions to me, during my illness, have been unremitting. The Prince Abbas Mirza, the wisest of the king's sons, and heir to the throne, was here some time after my arrival; I much wished to present a copy of the Persian New Testament to him, but I could not rise from my bed. The book will, however, be given to him by the Ambassador. Public curiosity about the Gospel, now for the first time in the memory of the modern Persians, introduced into the country, is a good deal excited here, at Shiraz, and other places; so that, upon the whole, I am thankful for having been led hither, and detained; though my residence in this country has been attended with many unpleasant circumstances. The way of the kings of the east is preparing. Thus much may be said with safety, but little more. The Persians also will probably take the lead in the march to Zion, as they are ripe for a revolution in religion as well as politics.

Sabat, about whom you inquire so regularly, I have heard nothing of this long time. My friends in India have long since given me up as lost or gone out of reach, and if they wrote, they would probably not mention him, as he is far from being a favourite with any of them. — , who is himself of an impatient temper, cannot tolerate him; indeed I am pronounced to be the only man in Bengal who could have lived with him so long. He is, to be sure, the most tormenting creature I ever yet chanced to deal with — peevish, proud, suspicious, greedy; he used to give daily more and more distressing proofs of his never having received the saving grace of God. But of this you will say nothing; while, his interesting story is yet fresh in the memory of people, his failings had better not be mentioned. The poor Arab wrote me a querulous epistle from Calcutta, complaining that no one took notice of him, now that I was gone; and then he proceeds to abuse his best friends. I have not yet written to reprove him for his unchristian sentiments, and when I do, I know it will be to no purpose, after all the private lectures I have given him. My course from Constantinople is so uncertain that I hardly know where to desire you to direct to me; I believe Malta is the only place, for there I must stop in my way home. Soon we shall have occasion for pen and ink no more; but I trust I shall shortly see thee face to face. Love to all the saints.

Believe me to be yours, ever
Most faithfully and affectionately,

H. MARTYN.

Part Three — Fact turns to Fiction

Frontispiece to *Little Henry and his Bearer*

LITTLE HENRY

AND HIS BEARER.

By MRS. SHERWOOD.

Author of 'The Little Woodman,' etc.

EDINBURGH:
W. P. NIMMO, HAY, & MITCHELL.

Little Henry and his Bearer — India

Lydia's role in Henry's life was rescued from total obscurity and placed centre stage when, in 1871, a hugely successful novel for young girls — *Her Title of Honour* — was published by Harriet Parr under the pseudonym Holme Lee. It was based on Lydia and Henry's love affair and the primary sources were the 17 letters[97] which Henry wrote to Lydia between 1805 and 1812 and his Journals.

Much had changed in India since Henry's death: India had opened up to the missionaries bent on spreading the Christian Gospel; although the warring Marathas had finally been defeated in Western India in the Third Maratha War in 1818, the Indian Mutiny of 1857 with the terrible images of women and children's bodies piled into the well at Cawnpore and other atrocities committed on both sides further defined the necessity of the British to be perceived by the Indians as an elite colonial power. By 1871, when Parr's book was first published, the Raj was well established with the white British rulers sure of their superiority and power over the native. Safe in their European enclaves the memsahibs sought to recreate the familiar world they had left behind; living in bungalows with names borrowed from a familiar British context such as *Windermere,* with carefully tended English gardens; tennis parties, elaborate picnics, amateur dramatics, chintz covers for the furniture and dinner parties where the menu was based round English ingredients, cooked by Indians in conditions of hygiene which shocked many

---

[97] See Part Two.

of the memsahibs on the rare occasion when they ventured into the kitchen. They dressed in European clothes in the stifling heat, trying to follow the latest fashions and spent much of their time suffering from acute boredom. Their husbands toiled in positions of government or maintained the military presence, while the wives escaped to the hill stations in the hottest part of the year.

However, two other books preceded Harriet Parr's book in which Henry's life as an evangelical Christian was also the inspiration. The first was written by his friend from his days in Cawnpore, Mrs. Sherwood, and is a proselytising book for young children. The title is *Little Henry and his Bearer*. Little Henry, the nomenclature by which the real Henry Martyn had been known as a child in Truro, is the saintly hero. The child in the book is based on her first son, called Henry, who died in infancy in India,[98] but his saintly character and piety are based on Henry Martyn whom Mrs. Sherwood had first met in Dinapore and then got to know and admire at Cawnpore. She describes their reason for making contact as follows: *The instant we came to anchor at Dinapore Mr Sherwood set out on foot to carry a letter which he had brought from Mr Parson* (another priest, based at Berhampore, who was described as a Simeonite and who offered much comfort and religious instruction to Mary Sherwood when her infant son died) *to Mr Henry Martyn.*

In a letter written in about 1811[99] from India to her sister, Mrs. Lucy Cameron, her first impressions of Henry are: *In the year 1807 we first became acquainted with the Rev. Henry Martyn. We were at that time going in boats on the river Ganges from Berhampore to Cawnpore & our boats came to anchor about two miles below Dinapore. Mr Martyn came walking down to see us & would insist on our going the next day (as the regiment was to halt a few days near Dinapore) to his quarters in the Cantonments. His first appearance was particularly agreeable to me as I saw in him a strong resemblance to my Father,*

---

[98] Quoted in *The Life and Times of Mrs Sherwood*; ed. F.J. Harvey Darton, London, 1910. (see p. 397). This was the Henry of *"Little Henry and his Bearer,"* not, as has been recently stated, his younger brother who is still living. "Little Henry" died in India (see p. 299). His grave was made a public monument.

[99] MAR 8/3 Fragment of a letter from Mrs. Mary Sherwood, India, ca.1811 with transcipt.: Henry Martyn Centre, Westminster College, Cambridge.

his features were not naturally handsome & he was pale and thin, but his countenance was in general remarkably serene denoting that the peace of God was with him, & at times his whole face was lighted up with a degree of holy fervour such as I seldom if ever witnessed & which shewing the power of mind above matter make a face naturally plain appear really beautiful.

We had been prepossessed in each others favour by common friends therefore we gladly accepted his invitation & spent two days (I think) with him at Dinapore. She describes his living arrangements in her diary and again comments on his appearance:

> *Mr Martyn's quarters at Dinapore were in the smaller square, as far as could be distant from our old quarters, but precisely the same sort of church-like abode, with little furniture, the rooms wide and high, with many vast doorways, having their green jalousie doors, and long verandahs encompassing two sides of the quarters.*

> *Mr Martyn received Mr Sherwood not as a stranger but as a brother, the child of the same father. As the sun was already low he must needs walk back with him to see me. I perfectly remember the figure of that simple-hearted and holy young man as he entered our budgerow. He was dressed in white and looked very pale, which, however, was nothing singular in India; his hair, a light brown, was raised from his forehead, which was a remarkably fine one. His features were not regular, but the expression was so luminous, so intellectual, so affectionate, so beaming with divine charity, that no one could have looked at his features and thought of their shape and form; the outbeaming of his soul would absorb the attention of every observer.*

Mary Sherwood admired Henry greatly for his saintliness and named her second son, born on July 1, 1813, Henry Martyn, to whom Corrie was godfather. He relates how when calling on the Sherwoods some years later in Worcester he heard Hindustani being spoken by a young boy. It was his

323

godson, Henry, addressing Mrs. Sherwood's old servant, Mrs Harrison, from the top of the kitchen-stairs.

Mrs. Sherwood knew Dinapore well as it had been the first cantonment where she and her husband had been located after arriving in India in 1805. In her diaries, which were later published, she describes the horrors of the long sea voyage out all too vividly; arriving at Madras, their journey from Calcutta along the Hooghli, then up the great River Ganges by budgerow and finally their arrival at Dinapore where the heat could be like a burning cauldron during the summer months. For her, this journey was a source of fascination and comment as she watched the ever changing scene and people through fresh European eyes, noting with satisfaction that the tigers are being brought under control with the introduction by the English of a ten rupee reward for every head brought to a collector. By the time the regiment arrived at Dinapore on December 5th she was heavily pregnant with her first son, Henry, who like so many children born in India would fail to thrive. She writes this alarming account of events following her son's birth in India on Christmas day 1805:

> *My room was very large, and there was a bed placed at a distance from mine for the nurse. When she had laid me in bed, with the baby, on the Christmas night, she went to partake of the good things which were going, and Betty Parker took her turn to attend to me till the company left the house. The nurse came back, took the infant, and went to the couch prepared for her. I soon fell asleep, but woke again soon after hearing the child cry. I looked out from my bed and saw the woman sitting up on the couch, having taken up the round pillow of the couch, which she was holding like an infant, rocking backwards and forwards and hushing it, whilst the baby was crying by her side. She was fearfully intoxicated, and I dared not call to her lest I should wake her from her drunken trance, and she should hurt the child. There are no bells to ring in India; there was no one I could call. I was desperate! I looked by the bedside for a pair of shoes or slippers — there was no such thing. Out of my bed I got, with bare feet, went over to the couch,*

took up my baby, the woman being too drunk to be aware of what
I was doing, and got back to bed with my boy, leaving the wretched
creature to sing her lullaby to her pillow. Of course I was never
again left to the tender mercies of this woman.

However, this first son, Henry, like so many babies and young children born in India, died in early infancy in 1807, as did her daughter Lucy in 1808 from dysentery. She records how to her horror she discovers that Henry's ayah has been giving the baby opium to make him sleep, apparently a common practice at the time. She sacks the nurse summarily and finds another to take her place. In June 1806 soon after he was weaned, Henry becomes ill. In her letter to her sister she voices her fears for her children and the dangers of weaning them too soon, having learnt from bitter experience:

Young people must have companions, & to provide for them holy & chearful ones will be a chief care of mine—please God I live to rear my children.

Our children are beginning to suffer, at least in their looks from the heat. They first in the coming on of the heat lose their bloom & then break out in a kind of rash looking something like the Meazles which continues all the hot season. With many persons all kinds of food becomes[sic.] unpleasant in the hot season. I have sometimes myself been a week or fortnight without taking any kind of food whatever & yet not ill nor getting much thinner. Children when weaned too early not uncommonly starve themselves to death not having sense to force their appetites. On this account being unable to carry on the nursing so long as is requisite I am almost forced to get a native nurse for my babes when they are about eight or nine months old.

Yet in spite of her son's precarious health she set up a small school for children. At Dinapore and Berhampore she used the verandah of her bungalow as a classroom. At first about 13 pupils attended lessons between ten and one each day. Mrs. Sherwood was assisted by her husband's clerk, Sergeant Clarke, who fortunately for Mrs. Sherwood, had only a couple of days per month employment on military matters. Soon the school grew to 40 or 50 children, mainly soldiers' children, some of whom Mrs. Sherwood

325

castigates for their wickedness and who were caned by Sergeant Clarke when their language and behaviour needed checking. Her second daughter, Lucy, an outstandingly attractive child, was born on March 25th, 1807 in Dinapore but by this time her infant son, Henry, was ill with whooping cough. In June the 53rd regiment was ordered to Cawnpore but Henry was now critically ill and died that July aged 18 months at the home of Mr. Parson. Her account of Henry's last few days is very moving and enabled her to write the closing scene of her book, *Little Henry and his Bearer,* with such emotional understanding. Although the Henry in the book is eight years and seven months old when he dies, he is able to hold long and erudite conversations with his grieving mama and is evangelical to the last. Mrs. Sherwood's first son, Henry, died at a much younger age and she records his last few hours with moving simplicity:

> *On the Saturday I sat at the door, (or entrance) of the front verandah, with my little boy on a pillow on my lap. After a while he raised himself and looked about him. I took him in my arms and walked with him towards the river; he seemed easier, but towards evening the disease, which had ceased for twenty-four hours, came on again with violence. We sent for the doctor, and two of the women sat up with him. He lay in his nurse's arms, and I saw death in his face.*

> *The native servants were quarrelsome, as they too often are in scenes of trouble. The bearers could not agree who was to air the linen with which the nurse changed the bed of the dying infant. The circumstances made me weep bitterly; for when a cup is full a small thing causes it to overflow.*

> *Dr Penny, the station surgeon, came. He looked at the dying baby, and then, taking my hand, he told me not to grieve if he was taken from me: he was struggling with death. Once again I got my boy in my arms. I walked with him to the further part of the verandah, where I was not under the immediate gaze of any one. There were some lovely golden clouds just above my head ...*

The two surgeons again took me away from my boy. He was still struggling with his last enemy, death, and wanted to be moved from place to place. They brought him into the part of the verandah opposite the door of the room where they detained me. I could remain from him no longer — I hastened to his side. He was changed during the few minutes in which I had been absent from him. Some one said to him "Henry, kiss your mamma." We supposed he had passed all knowledge of present things, but he turned his lovely eyes to me and smiled. A few minutes later the little boy breathed his last. He was buried almost at once. He had lived only a year and a half.

His grave became a public monument just like the fictional little Henry's did.

When Mrs. Sherwood gave birth on August 10th, 1809 to Lucy Elizabeth (baptised by Henry Martyn who gave her the pet name of Serena because of her gentle and loving nature) she is advised to take the baby back to England and leave her in her mother's care but when she and Captain Sherwood arrive in Calcutta in October to find suitable berths he confesses that he cannot bear to be parted from her and they return to Cawnpore. Henry Martyn is delighted at their return. Mrs. Sherwood is fulsome in her praise of Henry's love and affinity with young children:

Among other lovely traits in Mr Martyn's character none appeared more remarkable than his kindness to children. With what earnestness he blessed them — how patiently he endured their attention —how he bore the little ones in his arms. Every parent could not but feel grateful for his Christian tenderness & courtesy towards their children. I remember once seeing him studying Hebrew Etymologies with a large collection of books round him on a couch—My little girl, then very young, climbed upon his couch & placed herself upon his knee, from which station he would on no account allow her to be removed but went on with his labours with the infant in his arms.

It is now that she begins writing *Little Henry and his Bearer* , which was first published in 1814 anonymously and became a hugely successful book with 30 editions having been published by 1840. It was translated into Hindustani, French, German, Chinese and Singhalese. The story is written for children and abounds in overt religious and cultural propaganda which places the white European Christian child, little Henry, at the centre as morally superior to his non-white heathen bearer Boosy, who is devoted to his little master, reflecting the Protestant world view of the time.

Sherwood sets the opening of the story in Dinapore in India, an area which she and Henry Martyn knew well and where they first met. The main character, Henry, is already orphaned at the beginning of the book. His father had served with the East India Company, just as Mary Sherwood's husband had in India: *Henry L — was born at Dinapore in the East Indies. His papa was an officer in the Company's service, and was killed in attacking a mud fort belonging to a zemeendar* while his mother has died *before he was a year old.* The non-fictional Henry Martyn's mother died when he was two. Little Henry is then taken by *a lady who lived in a large puckah house near the river between Patna and Dinapore.* Although she becomes nominally his mama and provides for all his material needs she is portrayed as unable to provide for his emotional or moral needs and leaves him entirely to the care of a native bearer called Boosy, who is the main influence on the infant Henry. Boosy is portrayed as a loving and caring servant, extremely tolerant of the European view of his country and customs, who looks after his small master with great devotion and with whom little Henry is happy:

> *When he was a very little baby, Boosy (for that was the bearer's name) attended to him night and day, warmed his pap, rocked his cot, dressed and undressed and washed him, and did everything as tenderly as if he had been his own child. The first word that little Henry tried to say was 'Boosy;' and when he was only ten months old, he used to put his arms round his neck and kiss him, or stroke his swarthy cheek with his delicate hand.*

In spite of all Boosy's tender and loving care little Henry becomes ill; first when he is two years old and then a *very severe illness* at four. He is described as *never a very healthy child.* Mrs. Sherwood knew only too clearly the dangers posed to European children's health in India, having already lost two children when she wrote the book. This close and loving relationship between Henry and Boosy provides Sherwood with the context for little Henry to take his social and religious references from Hindu society instead of European society with which he has little contact. He speaks fluent Urdu but no English and is dressed like a native child:

> He used to sit on the verandah between his bearer's knees,
> chew paun, and eat bazar sweetmeats. He wore no shoes nor
> stockings, but was dressed in panjammahs and had silver bangles
> on his ankles.

Sherwood sprinkles the text with authentic details drawn from her time in India and provides footnotes to explain the italicised words to her young readers. Henry's European appearance is stressed, he is a blue eyed with light hair and has a *delicate complexion.*

The loving and wise Boosy may be based on Sheikh Saleh, baptised by the Reverend David Brown, Abdul Masih, who Sherwood refers to in her letter to her sister in 1811:

> Amongst these persons was one of a good family from
> Lucknow, a man of fine mind & noble appearance. This man was
> converted by Mr Martyn's preaching, the only one we know of
> these Sunday evening labours in Hindoostani but of this little one
> we hope thousands will come. This man who has since been
> baptized by the name of Abdul Masih having become an active &
> successful preacher of the gospel in the higher Provinces.

Like the Muslim, Masih, Boosy will also convert to Christianity persuaded by the eloquent preaching of his infant teacher to forsake his Hindu gods.

Because he is so neglected by his mama he receives no religious instruction and until he is five he accepts Hinduism and an animistic view of the world. He views the Christian God as one of many Hindu gods and goddesses and accepts unquestioningly that the goddess Gunga, in the form of the Ganges, can cleanse the spirit. But much worse from the evangelical Christian European view he also believes that *the Mussulmans were as good as Christians*

329

which he has been taught by the servants who *being heathens, could not be expected to teach him anything better*. Sherwood lays the blame for these misguided religious ideas on the European lady who has adopted him and failed to instruct him in Christianity. Sherwood herself adopted two girls while in India: Annie and Sally. Henry Martyn knew them well at Cawnpore. Mary Sherwood gave Annie to the Corries to look after when she and her husband set off on their abortive trip to Calcutta to take their new baby, Lucy Elizabeth, back to England. Because the Corries had grown so fond of Annie she remained with them after the Sherwoods returned. Sally, was despatched to Benares but Mrs. Sherwood reclaimed her on their return. Much later Sally moved to England and lived in Worcester, married to a glove-maker. Mrs. Sherwood saw her own salvation in good works which were unending and it was she who after both the Browns died looked after their two daughters.

Little Henry is happily growing up in a heathen world inhabited by the Hindu pantheon when a young English woman arrives from England to stay with his mama. Little Henry is now five years old. She, like Sherwood, is the daughter of a clergyman and is full of evangelical zeal to save the sinner. Sherwood describes how:

> She had brought with her from home a box of Bibles, and some pretty children's books and pictures. When she saw poor little Henry sitting in the verandah, as his custom was, between his bearer's knees, with many other native servants surrounding him, she loved him, and was very sorry for him; for indeed it is a dreadful thing for little children to be left among people who know not God. So she took some of the prettiest coloured pictures she had, and spread them on the floor of the room, the door of which opened onto the verandah near the place where the little boy usually sat.

Gradually little Henry's curiosity gets the better of him and he ventures into the room. It is this young woman who saves Henry by teaching him English and then converts him to Christianity completing the Europeanisation of this innocent little boy. However, Henry does not go meekly and she has to overcome some opposition from him over rejecting his pantheistic beliefs which the lady demonstrates are wrong by smashing a Hindoo clay god and asking the little boy:

> *'Henry, what can this god do for you? It cannot help itself.*
> *Call to it, and ask it to get up. You see it cannot move.' And that*
> *day the little boy was convinced by her arguments.*

Soon she is instructing him in the Holy Trinity before moving on to the nature of sin and salvation. Rapidly she remoulds the young boy as a pious evangelical young Christian who can quote verses from the Bible. She gives him a Bible bound in purple morocco, which he chooses from a box of Bibles she is unpacking, and has a bag of silk made in which to carry it. After a stumbling first attempt in reading Genesis, Sherwood recounts how this little model of Christian zeal soon is able to read any part of the Bible. After spending just 18 months teaching little Henry, she examines him orally on his knowledge of the Bible. He passes with flying colours, quoting chapter and verse with truly amazing fluency and maturity for a child not yet seven. The evangelical lady leaves by budgerow for Berhampore, where she later marries *a very pious young man by the name of Baron* who is based on Mr. Parson, the Sherwoods' chaplain and friend at Berhampore. It is this pious and evangelical young woman who sets little Henry on his missionary path — to convert the faithful Boosy. Boosy, however, is not easily persuaded and argues eloquently against the concept of there being one God:

> *'There are many brooks and rivers of water, but they all*
> *run to the sea at last; so there are many religions, but they all lead*
> *to heaven: there is the Hindoo's way, and the Christian's way; and*
> *one way is as good as another.'*

The fact that Boosy shows exemplary religious tolerance is lost on Mrs. Sherwood.

Little Henry is taken to Calcutta by his mama who wants to visit friends and catch up on the latest European fashions. No doubt Mrs. Sherwood had had plenty of opportunity to observe bored European women who longed to escape to the more socially exciting and fashion-conscious world of Calcutta from the cantonments in Dinapore and Cawnpore when she herself was there. During the long journey by river little Henry, who is far from well, holds long discourses on the nature of religion and India with Boosy when they walk by the Ganges in the evenings, something which both Sherwood, Martyn and the Corries did at Cawnpore where she wrote the book:

> *'Boosy, this is a good country — that is, it would be a very good country if the people were Christians. Then they would not be so idle as they now are; and they would agree together, and clear the jungles, and build churches to worship God in. It will be pleasant to see the people when they are Christians, all going on a Sunday morning to some fair church built among those hills, and to see them in the evening sitting at the door of their houses reading the shaster — I do not mean your shaster, but our shaster, God's book.'*

To a modern reader the tone of the book is breathtakingly Eurocentric with little Henry delivering pious lectures to the generous Boosy on how India could be a much better place if it were Christian and the entire population could be remoulded with European social, religious and moral values which both Sherwood and Martyn shared. Little Henry even wants to change the landscape into a more familiar European one. These views reflect the contemporary view of India of many people who really believed that Europeans had innate superiority to Indians and so naturally occupied the moral and religious high ground.

Once they arrive in Calcutta Mr. Smith, whose wife is the friend of little Henry's mama, one evening observes little Henry sitting on a landing trying to instruct Boosy from the Bible in Urdu. Little Henry is not yet eight. He presents the child with a part translation of the Bible into Urdu and also teaches him the Persian script. Mr. Smith is based on the Reverend David Brown who had helped Henry Martyn so much when he arrived in Calcutta and clearly the references to the Urdu and Persian translations refer to Henry's work at Dinapore and Cawnpore with Mirza and Sabat which Mrs.

Sherwood had observed and recorded in her Diary which was later published by her daughter.

Little Henry remains in Calcutta for a year and is soon fluent in Persian and is teaching Boosy to read the Bible in Urdu. On the return journey to Dinapore little Henry becomes seriously ill. The party stop at Berhampore where Mr. and Mrs. Baron live and little Henry is taken to their home to be nursed. It was of course Mrs. Sherwood who nursed Henry Martyn when he arrived exhausted and very ill on his journey from Dinapore to Cawnpore. However, little Henry is dying and in a highly emotional and moving scene he prays to God to save Boosy who finds himself repeating the prayer in Urdu. Later that evening Boosy appeals to the evangelical little Henry with:

> *'Sahib, I have been thinking all day that I am a sinner,*
> *and have always been one; and I begin to believe that my sins are*
> *such that Gunga cannot wash away.'*

Little Henry is delighted that through him Boosy has been saved. He asks Boosy to cut off a lock of his hair and to take it to Mr. Smith in Calcutta with the request that Mr. Smith take Boosy under his wing so that he can continue the salvation of the soul of the devoted but misguided Boosy. When the dutiful Mrs. Baron is about to cut off a lock of his hair as instructed she breaks down:

> *'O my child! my dear, dear, child! she said, I cannot bear*
> *it! I cannot part with you yet!'*

To which our little hero replies reprovingly by quoting:

> *"If you love me, you will rejoice, because I go to my Father"*
> *(John xiv. 28).*

The death-bed scene which reflects the high mortality among European children in India would have been only too familiar to many European women in India. Little Henry faces death with the same acceptance as Henry Martyn, trusting in God:

*'Ah, Boosy, if I had never read the Bible, and did not
believe in it, what an unhappy creature I should be! for in a very
short time I shall "go down to the grave to come up no more" (Job
vii. 9) that is until my body is raised on the last day. '*

Sherwood continues in this vein for several more pages in which little Henry
calls for his selfish mama to be brought to him:

*He received her affectionately when she went up to his
bedside, and begged that everybody would go out of the room,
saying that he had something very particular to speak about to her.
He talked to her for some time, but nobody knows the particulars
of their conversation, though it is believed that the care of her
immortal soul was the subject of the last discourse which this dear
little boy held with her.*

She takes his Bible and begins to study it and soon is repenting her former
frivolous ways. The following day, a Sunday, little Henry dies. His grieving
mama has a monument built over his grave at Berhampore with his name and
age inscribed on it and two quotations: the first has one word altered *Faithful
is He that called* (you) *me.* (Thess. v.24): and the second: *He which converteth
the sinner from the error of his way shall save a soul from death, and shall hide a
multitude of sins.* (Jas. v.20).

Sherwood ends *Little Henry and his Bearer*, which is only 59 pages in
length, with an update on what happened to the faithful bearer, Boosy. Just
like Sergius, Henry Martyn's Armenian servant, Boosy carries out little
Henry's wishes. Boosy becomes attached to Mr. Smith's family, renounces
caste and is duly baptised John: Sheikh Saleh had renounced Islam after
hearing Henry Martyn preach at Cawnpore and had been baptised by David
Brown in Calcutta.

The book's enormous success — it ran to nearly one hundred editions —
is a reflection of its popular Christian and evangelical message to young
children which places the European child at the centre of the universe with a
clear duty to save the unfortunate heathen in far-off lands. Perhaps Henry
Martyn and Lydia would have approved.

'Reader, I married him' — The Brontë Connection

'Charlotte Brontë will have been aware of the circumstances pertaining to Martyn's life, including the opposition of family and friends to Martyn's career choice and the fact that the choice cost him the love of his life.'[100] The story would surely appeal to any novelist, and — although there is a strong case for the character St. John Rivers, who makes his appearance towards the end of *Jane Eyre* (1847), as being based on Henry Nussey, the brother of Charlotte's school friend, whose proposal of marriage to Charlotte was rejected — Brian Stanley[101] points to Valentine Cunningham's reference to a copy of Sargent's biography of Martyn in Keighley Public Library (not far from Charlotte's home at Haworth in Yorkshire) as 'probably the source of Charlotte Brontë's portrait of St. John Rivers.'[102] Certainly Rivers's life, but not his character, mirrors facts in Martyn's: both attended St. John's College, Cambridge, both were ordained and became clergymen, both lost their patrimony, both went out to India as missionaries and both died relatively young. According to Stanley 'the central motif of that culture is one of Martyn as the ideal embodiment of self-sacrificing missionary ardour. It is a cult which has left its mark on Victorian literature: the forbiddingly pious figure of St. John Rivers in Charlotte Brontë's *Jane Eyre (1847)* is almost certainly modelled on Martyn.'

---

[100] Thormahlen, Marianne: *The Brontës and Religion*; CUP, 1999.

[101] Stanley, Brian: *An Ardour of Devotion, The Spiritual Legacy of Henry Martyn*; HMC.

[102] Cunningham, Valentine: *'God and Nature intended you for a missionary's wife'*: Bowie et al (eds.) *Women and Missions*: Oxford, 1993.

However, there is another intriguing connection made by Cunningham which Graham Kings refers to:[103] Charlotte Brontë's father, Patrick, registered as a student at St. John's College, where he changed his surname from Brunty to Brontë — Greek for thunder — on October 3, 1802 and it was Henry Martyn who, while a curate for Charles Simeon, arranged for Patrick to receive financial aid of £10 per year from each of Henry Thornton and William Wilberforce. Like Henry, Patrick was drawn into Simeon's circle, became an Evangelical and was associated with the Clapham Sect. So there was a direct link to Martyn.

But there is also a Cornish connection: Penzance. Patrick was born in 1777 in Emdale, County Down, the eldest of ten children of a farm labourer. He was largely self-educated yet by the age of 16 had become Master of the village school. He graduated from St. John's College in 1806 and was ordained in 1807. In 1809 he moved from a curacy in Shropshire to Yorkshire where he would fall in love and marry Maria Branwell from Penzance. The Branwells, leading Wesleyan Methodists and a prosperous family owning many properties in Penzance, lived at 25 Chapel Street, in the same street as Samuel John to whom Lydia had once been engaged. At that time the population of Penzance was about 3,000 and the Branwells would have moved in the same very pleasant and active social circle as the Grenfells and Samuel John. Chapel Street, and no doubt much of Penzance, would have gossiped about Lydia's broken engagement to Samuel John and her subsequent involvement with Henry Martyn.

Maria, the Branwells' eighth child, was born into this prosperous family in 1783. Sadly by 1812 both her mother and father had died and at the invitation of her aunt, Jane Fennell, who was married to a Methodist minister, she moved up to Yorkshire leaving behind her friends in Cornwall. Her aunt's husband had recently been made headmaster of a newly opened school, Woodhouse Grove School, in Rawdon. Maria's role was to help her aunt Jane who was the housekeeper at the school. At this time Patrick was curate at Hartshead, 12 miles from Rawdon. He knew John Fennell from their days as curates in Shropshire in 1808. Patrick was asked to Woodhouse

---

[103] Graham Kings: *The Legacy of Henry Martyn*; HMC.

Grove School to inspect the boys in Classics and it was then that he met and fell in love with Maria, marrying her later the same year on December 29th.

Patrick and Maria produced six children of whom Charlotte, born in 1816, was their third daughter (her two older sisters died in 1825 leaving Charlotte as the eldest child) and the first to be born at Thornton near Bradford as were her younger siblings, Patrick Branwell, 1817, Emily Jane, 1818 and Anne, 1820, the same year the family moved to Haworth. Tragically, the following year, Maria developed cancer and it was Elizabeth, Maria's sister, who still lived in Penzance, whom they turned to for help in looking after the six children. Elizabeth Branwell, who was by then a spinster of 45, accustomed to a comfortable life in Penzance, and who enjoyed its society, moved North in the summer of 1821 to the Parsonage at Haworth and the wild moors. Aunt Branwell, like Maria her sister, had an annuity of £50 with which she would later help finance Charlotte's stay in Brussels and also help her launch her literary career. When Maria died in the September Aunt Branwell stayed on organising life in the Parsonage for Patrick and his family. So the Cornish connection continued until she too died in 1842 from a constriction of the bowels.

Aunt Branwell would have been very much part of Penzance society which she missed when she moved North to the parsonage at Haworth. She would have known at first hand the tragic story involving Lydia, who was only a year older than her, Samuel John and Henry Martyn and all the attendant gossip. Both Lydia and the redoubtable Mrs. Grenfell were still alive in 1821 when Aunt Branwell left Cornwall and she corresponded with friends and family there after her departure.

Charlotte Brontë published *Jane Eyre* in 1847, five years after her aunt's death. There is every probability that she drew on Henry and Lydia's story. Did she use her mother and aunt's Cornish connection, Sargent's *The Life and Letters of The Rev. Henry Martyn, B.D* which she could have accessed at Keighley, and her father Patrick's Cambridge connection as the basis for the life of St. John Rivers?

St. John Rivers (an unusual name, but if Brontë was using the Cambridge connection then less so) is a pious clergyman who aspires to become a missionary in India. He is portrayed as being between 28 and 30 years old

339

when we first meet him more than half-way through the book when Jane has fled her beloved master, Mr. Rochester, having discovered that he is married to a deranged wife who inhabits secret quarters in Rochester's house. It is St. John who rescues Jane when he finds her in a state of collapse outside the door of the family home, More House, on a dark and desolate night and gives her sanctuary with his two sisters, Mary and Diana, who are staying there. But Jane and St. John are not kindred spirits as Lydia and Henry were: whereas she is swayed by passion he is coldly cerebral although *zealous in his ministerial labours, blameless in his life and habits.* Henry was clearly far more warm and likeable, not just to Lydia, but also to other people like Mrs. Sherwood and Elphinstone. Yet when Jane hears St. John Rivers preach, *the heart was thrilled, the mind astonished.* St. John Rivers's father had recently died, hence the arrival of his two sisters. Like Henry he has lost his patrimony which, he confesses to Jane, because of his father's debts consists of little more than a crumbling house.

St. John, like Henry, sacrifices the woman he loves for his mission in India. In this conversation with Jane they are discussing the beautiful Rosamond Oliver who clearly lacks the qualities needed in a missionary's life:

"Rosamond a sufferer, a labourer, a female apostle? Rosamond a missionary's wife? No!"

"But you need not be a missionary. You might relinquish that scheme!"

"Relinquish! What! My vocation? My great work? My foundation on earth for a mansion in heaven? My hopes of being numbered in the band who have merged all ambitions in the glorious one of bettering their race – of carrying knowledge into the realms of ignorance – substituting peace for war – freedom for bondage – religion for superstition – the hope of heaven for the fear of hell? Must I relinquish that? It is dearer than the blood of my veins. It is what I have to look forward to, and to live for!"

"After a considerable pause, I said – And Miss Oliver? Are her disappointment and sorrow of no interest to you?"

"Miss Oliver is ever surrounded by suitors and flatterers: in less than a month, my image will be effaced from her heart. She will forget me; and will marry probably, someone who will make her far happier than I should."

Rosamond is much closer to the central character, Eleanour, in the novel *Her Title of Honour* published in 1871, than to Lydia. Henry by contrast saw the requisite qualities in Lydia to make a good missionary's wife in India and it was Lydia who had her own misgivings about such a life but Henry was never 'effaced from her heart.' Nor did she ever marry, whereas Rosamond marries Sir Frederic Granby some 20 pages later.

Having lost the fair Rosamond, St. John decides that Jane will make the perfect wife for him and sets about teaching her 'Hindostanee' but he has misread Jane's character and resolve to marry for love. Henry had no such certainty in 1805 over his feelings about making Lydia his wife. He constantly wrestled with whether celibacy or marriage was the best course to follow and was still vacillating when he wrote his proposal to Lydia in 1806. St. John regards Jane as a commodity which is his by right:

"God and nature intended you for a missionary's wife. It is not personal but mental endowments they have given you: you are formed for labour, not for love. A missionary's wife you must — shall be —. You shall be mine: I claim you — not for my pleasure, but for my sovereign's service!" How much more appealing is Henry's plea to Lydia in his proposal of July 30th, 1806. It is St. John's sister, Diana, who points to the folly of Jane's going out to India: *"You are much too pretty, as well as too good, to be grilled alive in Calcutta"* — thereby recognizing the inherent dangers for a European woman who as a missionary's wife would be exposed to hardships of climate and culture which many missionary families found difficult to sustain.

However, in the novel, Jane finally agrees to go to India not as St. John's wife but as his sister: the same compromise which Lydia offered to Henry when she initiated the resumption of their corresponding once more. St. John rejects this compromise whereas Henry accepted gratefully and gracefully. St. John is about to depart for Cambridge to say goodbye to friends, just as Henry had, when Jane is almost persuaded by the power of his preaching to agree to marriage but realises that the love he could give is not the love she yearns for so passionately: *He is good and great, but severe, and for me, cold as an iceberg.* She returns to Rochester to find true fulfilment with a man who understands her in the best romantic tradition — an outcome denied to Lydia.

Brontë, in the final two paragraphs, gives a rapid update, using the device of letters from St. John to Jane, of what has happened in the intervening ten years since Jane has married. After his last letter Jane accepts that *a stranger's hand will write to me next, to say that the good and faithful servant, has been called at length into the joy of his Lord. And why weep for this?*

Yet many wept when they heard of Henry's death at Tokat: Lydia grieved for the rest of her life.

Her Title of Honour — Cornwall

Her Title of Honour, written by Harriet Parr, which is based on Henry and Lydia's love affair, was published in 1871 under the pseudonym Holme Lee. In the 1875 edition it is listed as *a book for girls* costing five shillings. It is a fascinating mix of fact and fiction which drew this sharp reproof from Henry Martyn Jeffery, Henry Martyn's grand-nephew, in 1883 in the Introduction to *Two Sets of Unpublished Letters of the Rev. Henry Martyn, B.D.: Miss Harriet Parr, who founded her religious novel, entitled "Her title of honor" on the romantic relations of Martyn with Miss Grenfell, ought to have perused this common sense conclusion of the love-tale;* namely that Henry offered friendship but cancelled his attachment to Lydia after she turned down his proposal. He is less than kind when he says: *It should be noticed that Miss Grenfell was senior to Martyn by six years so that in 1805 the disparity of years was striking,* adding *It was unfortunate for Martyn, that he tied himself at the outset of his Indian life.* He conveniently ignores the fact that it was Henry who was so deeply in love with Lydia, whereas she was less sure about the relationship and it was she who ended the romantic relationship, not Henry, and it may well have been her relative maturity which he found so attractive.

Parr sets the novel in both Henry Martyn's and Lydia Grenfell's native county of Cornwall and transforms Lydia into an orphan called Eleanour Trevelyan. Eleanour has been brought up in Croxton, based on Truro, by her Uncle Trevelyan and Aunt Bell. Both Sherwood and Parr make their central character an orphan thereby arousing compassion for the less fortunate in their young and impressionable readers. The novel opens with a prologue in which the narrator is walking in Croxton Close one August. Parr sets a very

English scene in the Cathedral Close. In reality the foundation of Truro Cathedral did not take place until May 1880, and because of financial restraints, the building, which would replace the parish church of St. Mary's close to the grammar school which Henry attended, had to be completed in phases. The opening is couched in somewhat flowery prose:

> *The tall ranks of elms in the outer enclosure were full of leaf, and the reposeful old houses glittered with fiery sunset reflections in the bright diamond-paned lattices of their peaked gables, and the projecting bays and oriels of their lower storeys. About their porches and the quaint nooks and angles of their walks the powdery clematis and fragrant jessamine hung in wreaths and bowers of white and green; and the chamber window-sills had every one a box or balcony of flowers.*

An old lady is walking back to her very attractive cottage in the cloisters:

> *She wore a trailing black silk dress, and her shoulders were draped with a rich Indian shawl. As she went by she glanced at me with large, vivacious blue eyes, and smiled, I thought — a most beautiful old lady, finely and delicately featured, with a fair faded cheek, and silver curls crowning her straight, clear forehead. She was alone, and I wondered who she was.*

She is of course none other than Eleanour Trevelyan. She turns into her gate and disappears. Seven weeks later the narrator returns and there in the cloisters is a new grave near those of two bishops. It is the grave of Eleanour Trevelyan. The sacristan when questioned as to the identity of the lady refers to the Reverend Francis Gwynne and to his Journals:

> *If you have read his Journals, you will remember that there's often mention made in them of a young lady — this Mistress Eleanour Trevelyan was the same. A good lady, a very good lady; but it was her chief title of honour that Francis Gwynne loved her. So people say.*

So Parr defines Eleanour through her relationship with Francis Gwynne, whose character of piety and moral goodness, is based on Henry Martyn. It appears that both Francis and Eleanour have long been held in high regard by the narrator. Eleanour at the opening of the novel is portrayed as the somewhat vain and self-centred but dutiful niece and hostess of Dr. Trevelyan, the vicar at Pengarvon who has a curate by the name of Sargent. Trevelyan later becomes a Canon at Croxton Cathedral. Parr fills in Eleanour's background and introduces Aunt Bell and Uncle Trevelyan:

> *I do not call the vicarage home; Croxton is home to me. I was brought up here till I was twelve years old. I lived with Aunt Bell in the corner house as you come in the Close Gate. Since then she and Uncle Trevelyan share me between them. We shall be more at Croxton than at Pengarvon, now that he is Canon.*

Her Aunt Bell, who is modelled on Mrs. Grenfell, leads a life bounded by gossip and social duty and fills her day with tatting. Parr explains to her young female audience:

> *In the early days of this century, all ladies occupied more or less all their day at needlecraft. Aunt Bell brought out her tatting, a dainty work whose fashion has lately come round again, and at which you may see fingers of all ages busy.*

Parr describes Aunt Bell as:

> *Suffering from ennui, like her niece; but she expected no visitor, and being a lady of spirit, in view of her opportunity she made a hasty toilette and packing up, and came off with her punctilious waiting-woman to spend the rest of the day at the Canon's house, and the night too, if Eleanour asked her, which of course she would.*

It is Aunt Bell who uses moral blackmail later in the novel to persuade the already uncertain Eleanour not to go to India, as it would appear Mrs. Grenfell did from Simeon and Henry's letters on the subject.

Eleanour's social skills are emphasised and she is called upon to preside gracefully at the tea-table in the evenings but Parr makes her politely rebellious:

> *That was Eleanour's favourite time, when she and the*
> *Canon came in from prayers brought a friend home, perhaps two*
> *or three friends, for a talk before they went to dinner.*
>
> *In her parlour at that hour was always to be found the*
> *London Paper, and besides the London Paper, with its*
> *then-a-days very serious annals of the world, were to be found new*
> *books, the newest in the close. They were Eleanour's pet luxury, her*
> *protest against everlasting worsted-work and everlasting chat. The*
> *ladies of her acquaintance called her 'a bit of a blue.' but Eleanour*
> *never minded — she was never dull, and they often were; she had*
> *a spirit and a will of her own, and followed her tastes and caprices*
> *with a lively, gay independence that they wondered at and*
> *condemned.*

Although Eleanour's context is the home just as Lydia's was Parr portrays her as having a much stronger sense of independence and spirit and a love of literature and current affairs than it would appear Lydia possessed from her Diary. Lydia's pious nature is not part of Eleanour's character at all!

In Chapter One Parr introduces the young reader to John Gwynne's household at Pengarvon on the wild Atlantic coast lashed by gales. Pengarvon is based on the real village of Marazion where Lydia grew up but Parr has transposed it as a setting for the young Frank and his family. She has also perhaps transposed St. Hilary Church there: *the church standing on a lofty promontory of the cliffs, a beacon to ships in the Channel for centuries past.* John's wife, Alice, is dying from tuberculosis just as Henry's mother did when he was two years old. There are three children: two older girls, Martha and Mary, and Francis — Frank or *little Gwynne.* Alice is a devout Methodist and is a regular chapel-goer although her husband is not. Francis is depicted as a somewhat saintly child and as his mother's favourite. One of his favourite pastimes is reading from a big picture Bible to his dying mother. Her husband, who is a Cornish miner is described:

> *In hardship and ignorance all his early years, he had*
> *toiled and toiled without knowledge of anything better or more*
> *desirable than the half-savage customs of his own people. But he*
> *had a brain of singular intelligence and power ... was the*
> *beginning of a rise in the world which culminated, before he was*
> *thirty, in his promotion to a post of great trust and responsibility*
> *in Pengarvon mines, and his subsequent marriage to his wife.*

He determines to send his son to the Grammar School where the headmaster is a Dr. Cornelius, clearly based on Dr. Cornelius Cardew, Henry's headmaster. Parr draws on fact to describe Frank's schooldays in which she includes the following description of Frank's academic ability:

> *He was a beautiful, lively child, not more studious than*
> *others of his age, but with an uncommon facility in learning — so*
> *the Doctor said, speaking of him at ten years old as a boy of the*
> *highest promise. The Doctor had a right to know, but so far as*
> *appeared upon the surface, Frank was an idle little dog ... He*
> *seemed to learn by intuition, but the secret really lay in his faculty*
> *of mental concentration; whatever he had to do he could set his*
> *whole attention upon, and thus he contrived to accomplish in a*
> *few minutes what his scattered-brained classmates could hardly*
> *master.*

The young Henry Martyn's scrofulous appearance and the warts covering his hands have been omitted presumably as being unattractive to the female readers. However, the reference to *intuition* echoes the comment made by Dr. Cardew on Henry. At school Francis shines at classics and is bullied just like Henry was:

> *His greater proficiency in the classics did not save him*
> *from oppression in the playground and his fine nervous*
> *irritability, too often roused by the taunts and ridicule of louts*
> *whose strength lay in their fists, made of his earlier school days*
> *days of severe trial.*

James Carden — based on John Kempthorne — becomes his protector and Francis duly follows him to Cambridge, having failed to win a place at Oxford just as Henry did. Parr makes the character of Carden an amalgamation of Kempthorne and Sargent. It is while recovering from his disappointment at failing to get into Oxford that Parr introduces her young readers to the moral theme of humility, a trait which Lydia constantly berated herself for lacking. It is also at this point that Frank and Eleanour meet:

> *It was at this period when all his friends were talking of*
> *Francis Gwynne's disappointment, and how heroically he had*
> *borne it, that he first met the beautiful lady whom afterwards he*
> *loved. The good vicar invited him to breakfast — an honour he*
> *had enjoyed twice before ... and there was Miss Eleanour*
> *Trevelyan, in the rosy radiance of a frosty morning, presiding over*
> *the tea-poy.* [sic.]

However, unlike Lydia, Eleanour is not Cornish but like Lydia comes from a family of much higher social status than Frank does:

> *He had a pretty young lady, his niece with him who has*
> *come to stay the winter at the vicarage. She has never been to*
> *Cornwall before. Both her father and mother are dead: her father*
> *killed at sea, fighting the French.*

Throughout the novel Parr makes contemporary social, religious and political references which also echo those in Henry's Journal and Lydia's Diary.

Francis goes to St. John's College where, like Henry, he excels himself. He duly becomes Senior Wrangler after his initial wrestle with Euclid. When Frank becomes Senior Wrangler, Parr puts the following words into Frank's mouth which are almost taken verbatim from Henry's in his Journal: *I have attained to the highest wish of my ambition, and I feel that I have grasped a shadow.*

While at Cambridge Frank meets the Reverend Barrington at St. Mary's, the former based on Simeon, the latter on Holy Trinity Church, Cambridge, and abandons his plan to study law. Instead with Barrington's encouragement he decides to be ordained. During the two-year wait until he is old enough to do so he decides to become a missionary. Parr makes reference to Frank's being inspired by Vanderkemp's and Brainerd's accounts of their missions.

Stylistically Parr borrows the device of a journal which is kept by Mary, Frank's sister, who is an amalgamation of Sally and Emma, to keep the narrative link between Cornwall and Cambridge. Mary describes Eleanour in glowing terms to her brother:

> *'Oh Frank, but she is a most lovely lady, the brightest, serenest spirit that ever blessed a house I think.'*

Obviously a role model for the intended readership of young girls who would aspire to being sweet, gentle, good hostesses and dutiful wives. However, Eleanour is portrayed as wanting more than life at Pengarvon or Croxton can offer. When asked by Frank if she likes life in town her response is:

> *I like to be within easy access to books, news, and agreeable company. We have not much at Pengarvon, and it is dull and formal besides. My visit to London will be my first plunge into the world of great society. We are to stay with my Aunt Hardwicke, you know that Sir George Hardwicke is in the Ministry, a friend of Mr Pitt's. It will be delightful, there are so many things I wish to see and hear — the new opera and the play! And I want to meet some of the famous men of the time and to go to court at least once.*

Lydia's eldest brother, Pascoe, was a well-known M.P. and successful businessman but Lydia did not share his commercial view of life nor seek the bright lights of London and wrote this about him on August 6th, 1807:

351

> *My eldest and best brother arrived on Monday from London. Much as I love him, still O how impossible I find it to enjoy his society. This wretched world and its concerns cannot now interest me, its vanities weary and disgust me. O that he felt the vanity of the things he now pursues.*

Although Eleanour is depicted as morally good Parr does not depict her as overtly pious or ardently evangelical. No doubt these qualities would not appeal so much to the young, impressionable female reader whereas going to the opera or seeing a play would hold much more appeal and so be easier to identify with.

Eleanour wants to be part of the social scene in London and Parr stresses her good social connections which later in the novel cause a gulf between the aspirations that Sir George and Lady Hardwicke have for their attractive niece and Frank's apparent rejection of an assured successful life in England for his evangelical calling and life in India. Sir George and Lady Hardwicke represent the material world and high society where social ambition is not allied to a spiritual vocation; a world that Lydia's brother, Pascoe Grenfell, inhabited. Sir George is well placed to act as benefactor to the young Frank for *You know that Sir George Hardwicke is in the Ministry, a friend of Mr Pitt's.* However, Frank's evangelical calling does not impress Sir George Hardwicke who had taken a liking to him and is able and willing to offer preferment to him *and, if he would, his fortune at home was made. So he was told. Possibly he did not realise all that was meant to be conveyed in the intimation; for he paid it little heed.*

Clearly he is being groomed for high office and as husband for Eleanour. The exchange continues with Sir George asking him about his future:

> *'What is this I hear of you, Mr Gwynne — that you are training to be a missionary?' the man of the world enquired with incredulous amazement. Frank coloured with something of shamefacedness as he replied that what Sir George had heard was true: it was his intention to be a missionary. Sir George turned off on his heel, as much to say:*

*'Then what do you come to Hardwicke for?' Thus Frank
interpreted his gesture of contempt.*

It is while Frank and Eleanour, who have fallen in love, are staying at the
Hardwickes' Norfolk Estate one Easter that Parr depicts Lady Hardwicke's
misgivings about their growing attachment:

> *Not a word she spake save in admiration of his projected
> sacrifice, though she privately deplored it as a cruel waste; ... she
> had besides entire confidence in Eleanour's discretion, and felt
> assured that unless Eleanour could convert Mr Gwynne from his
> doctrine of self-renunciation, his hopes of her must be his first
> practical steps in that hard and narrow way.* She also observes:
> *Personal insignificance was what her pride could not tolerate in
> the man she would accept as her lover and master.*

Clearly she disapproves of Frank's very different values and perhaps shares
some of Mrs. Grenfell's feelings about Henry Martyn's evangelical mission in
life. Poor Frank! His holiday at Hardwicke is not a happy one. Even his
beloved Eleanour is having her doubts:

> *Eleanour was complacent too, with just a dash of
> melancholy. Eleanour quite believed in Frank, and let him see it;
> but when he talked to her of the matters nearest and dearest to his
> conscience, there was a sad, half-wondering pity in her eyes, much
> like other people's. Hardwicke was not the place where he could
> hope to bring her mind into true accord with his; but then, what
> right had he to wish so to bring it? He asked himself this question
> again and again; he knew it was unwise, he knew it was unsafe,
> but the fact remained: he did wish it ardently.*

Conversely in real life it was their belief in God which was the lasting bond
between Lydia and Henry.

Frank is presented as a very attractive character indeed with an innate
goodness who would appeal to the young female readership. At yet another

encounter over tea, at which Eleanour presides, Frank is described in glowing prose:

> *He had a beautiful animated countenance ... He wore no beard, and his hair curled over his head in close crisp curls, his eyes were dark grey, very clear, with a certain melancholy which was almost gloom when his mouth was in repose. He was not above the middle height, but his figure, his gait, his air were elegant, distinguished.*

This description reflects the image in the portrait painted in India by Hickey of Henry in which he gazes out with a look of meditative melancholy. Parr makes the point of Frank's moral goodness when his sister Mary, says to Eleanour who is sharing one of his letters with her:

> *'We love him dearly; he is all the world to us ... but we would rather have him good than great.'*

> *'He is good;' said Eleanour, 'He is very good; I wish I were a tithe as good! But it is not in me.'*

> *'It is none of us by nature; it is a gift of God ...'*

> *Eleanour gazed down on the gentle preacher, and cried, 'You are a household of saints! But don't make Frank a methodist!'*

> *'His mother was one,' replied Mary; 'but holiness, but christian perfection, do not depend upon a name.'*

Eleanour is portrayed as very pretty but self-centred and vain; the latter a characteristic which Lydia constantly berated herself for. However, Eleanour lacks Frank's evangelical calling and piety which Lydia did understand and admire. Lydia also possessed an intelligent articulacy which Eleanor is sadly lacking. In a conversation between Frank and Martha, his elder sister, she comments to Frank:

> *'I am afraid she will be no partner for you, Frank. To speak five words and even to imagine five things is not evidence of the power or will to do them. Miss Trevelyan is beautiful to look at and listen to, but hers is not a great soul.'*

> *'You don't know her, Mattie; her enthusiasm is pure light!'*

> *'She may reach after noble deeds, and so she does, but she will not attain to them any more than I, with my hard nature, shall attain to the devout spiritual mind of our Mary. It is not in her nature to love any creature absolutely better than herself.'*

The fictionalised Lydia, filled with self-love and pride does not receive a sympathetic portrayal from Parr! Parr introduces the theme of social disparity between the two lovers right from their first meeting at the tea-table where they are both described as physically beautiful — a necessary attribute for the hero and heroine of a romantic novel:

> *He was as beautiful as she was, but far more modestly reserved — and when their eyes met, she looked kindly, to encourage him to be at ease. She was a sweet little lady, with a perfect sense of the degrees in society, and no inclination to trespass upon them; she imagined Frank must of course, feel shy among his betters and shamefaced about his defeat at Oxford, her goodness taught her to be sweeter to the humble and discouraged.*

Henry does not appear to have experienced any humiliation at not getting into Oxford. In fact quite the reverse as he writes that he fears he would have led a dissolute life if he had gone there instead of Cambridge. Nor does he ever appear to have been ill at ease even when meeting William Wilberforce and Charles Grant. Parr paints Eleanour as very aware of her own superior position in society to Frank:

> *Miss Eleanour said in her own mind that he might have been a gentleman's son for anything that appeared to the contrary in his figure and behaviour. She wore a scarlet ribbon among her soft brown curls, and some sort of dark dress with white ruffles at her throat and wrists, and was quite the gentlewoman in her place at table.*

There is no evidence that Lydia herself felt any sense of social disparity between herself and Henry though she would have been fully aware of her family's opinion about Henry, especially her mother's.

However, Frank persists in his plan to go to India and offers himself to the Missionary Society. Disaster strikes with the loss of his small patrimony, just as Henry lost his in 1804, and it is the East India Company which offers him the opportunity to fulfil his dream. He travels down to Cornwall to say his farewells and preaches at the church in Pengarvon. Parr makes a direct reference to Frank's disappointment at not seeing Eleanour in the morning when he is preaching at Witherspin Church near the mines. But he does see her in the evening. Parr writes a scene which takes place in the garden in which Eleanour expresses her doubts about life with Frank and India:

> *'Ah Frank;' she said, 'but I am not good enough! I am not self-denying; and life is terrible in India.'*

The unknown India is represented consistently as an unattractive alternative to her safe and comfortable life with her aunt and uncle. A theme which, post Indian Mutiny, would have struck a chord in the gentle female readership who were all dutiful and god-fearing daughters of Albion fixed in their belief in European Christian superiority over the infidel. Parr describes Frank wrestling with his love for Eleanour and his missionary calling and then rather unkindly describes Eleanour:

And Eleanour? Eleanour was much less distressed. She knew herself beloved, and that is always something to a woman. She was sanguine by temperament, and prone to exaggerate difficulties.

And Eleanour later confides:

'No. I should be afraid of India ... He knows I could not go to India. I have told him so.'

This vacillation between Eleanour's love for Frank and her fear and anxiety about committing herself to life in India is very close to entries in Lydia's Diary in which she expresses her remorse for apparently having encouraged Henry unwittingly; and Mrs. Grenfell's view of India which Henry Martyn refers to as *misinformed* in one of his letters.

Parr describes Frank's tumult as he is torn between her and his mission in life.

These arguments, and others like them, Francis Gwynne had heard and also answered until he was sick of hearing and answering. That he might have Eleanour by forsaking his call to the East, he regarded in the light of a temptation, and in no other light. He certainly would not forsake it — for rather would he give up his fond hopes of her.

Just like Henry, Frank struggles to find a solution to his dilemma:

Every thought of Eleanour is accompanied by a sort of vague pain which I know will increase when she is beyond my reach. I struggle faintly to forget her and delight in the vocation to which God has called me, but my struggles are ineffectual. My mind is so taken up with her that I can think of nothing else. I am weary of the world. I almost long for death, that I may be free from the troubles of this life.

Again it all reads very closely to Henry Martyn's Journal for 1805 when he is agonising over whether or not to commit himself to marriage or to remain celibate. Parr also describes Frank's having long discussions with old India hands on the pros and cons of marrying. A Colonel Harley, based on Colonel Sandys at Lanarth, a retired Indian officer settled at Pengarvon, gives his opinion that the climate in India will be good for Frank's health *and expressed a hope that he meant to provide himself with a wife before he started.*

Meanwhile, Frank is preparing for India and attends India House where he is appointed chaplain on the Bengal Establishment with a salary of £1,200. Parr certainly imbues the character of Frank with the same missionary zeal as Henry.

Eleanour continues with her round of good works for the needy and sick and as Frank observes her he realises that:

> *Eleanour Trevelyan was kind, pure and true to the heart's core, though she had not the strong devotion of Ruth, though she could not be brave to follow him whithersoever he might think himself called to go. She must be dealt gentlier with, her lines must be laid for her in pleasant places. He felt, as he watched her performing her sweet offices of charity, that no heavier burden than these ought to be put upon her. And a certain tender sympathy, as for one softer and weaker than himself filled his mind. After all there was a positive consolation in this — his love was worthy, that he might cherish her memory, and hope to walk with her in the realms of glory, if here they must live and die apart.*

Again echoes of both Henry and Lydia's expressions of their trust that they will be united in death.

Frank returns to Cambridge and resumes his study of *Hindostanee in anticipation when it would need to be a familiar foreign tongue to him.* Carden also breaks the news that he is to be married and commiserates with Frank who tells him about Eleanor: *It is as bad as decided. She will not go. I dared not urge it, and I try not to regret it.* Henry never ceased regretting it. Meanwhile Eleanour is still struggling to make a decision about her future life:

> *of two things which was the easier? To give up*
> *home-comfort, or to give up heart's love? Of two things which was*
> *the nobler? To abide in secure ease and dulness of life, or to rush*
> *upon hazard and change with him who adored her? For her*
> *ultimate satisfaction, finally, what was best to be done?*

> *In a few days Francis Gwynne would be gone from*
> *Cornwall not to return again. She knew his wishes perfectly, and*
> *she discerned that he was too generous to press them gainst her*
> *indecision.*

Parr captures the fictional heroine's heart-searchings reflecting those Lydia must have experienced in 1805 while Henry was in Falmouth. Eleanour's friends observe:

> *A general idea existed amongst Miss Trevelyan's friends*
> *that she had a predilection in favour of Mr Gwynne, but nobody*
> *believed that she would have the generous courage to give up her*
> *easy, graceful part in the world at home, to cast in her lot with his*
> *elsewhere: In the first place, her own people would be against it; in*
> *the next she has too many daintinesses and caprices. It is a rough*
> *life at the best in India.*

It seems that they know that the love affair is doomed and that Eleanour will opt for her known and comfortable world because of pressure or moral blackmail from her family just as Lydia did. It is interesting that Parr does not go into greater detail on the negative aspects of life in India which is here described as *rough* and earlier as *terrible*. Just as the real life Lydia vacillated so does our heroine and it is at this point that Parr introduces her central theme of familial duty for young women. Her uncle, the Canon, who has observed this indecision tells her very firmly:

> *'There is no room for perplexity. You are not going to India.'*

To which Eleanour responds:

> *'If my relatives set their faces against it, I do not expect that I shall go to India,' replied Eleanour, and honestly supposed herself to be yielding to family pressure. It is much, however, to be doubted whether her surrender would have been so prompt if the garrison had not been faint-hearted.*

Parr makes Eleanour's family the one insurmountable obstacle to her joining Frank in India yet implies that she would not have defied her Aunt and Uncle even if she had been really determined to marry Frank. Whether Lydia took refuge in her mother's refusal to let her join Henry remains debatable but it seems quite possible when she appears perfectly able to defy her mother over religion and as Henry clearly points out in his letter dated October 24th, 1807 Mrs. Grenfell did not depend on Lydia alone for the comfort of her declining years.

Parr uses the device of letters to add a dramatic twist to the story and to build up the tension as to whether or not Eleanour will agree to go with him to India. Frank decides to write to Eleanour but addresses the letter, out of propriety, to the Canon who unfortunately puts it on one side. Eleanour does not discover it until three months later when Frank has already been ordained a priest at St. James Chapel in London, just as Henry was. Having received no reply and with only one day left before embarking for India from Portsmouth Frank decides to go down to Croxton to see Eleanour and plead his case. Parr writes a highly charged scene in which Eleanour uses her family as the reason for not joining him:

> *'I could not leave them all — they would not let me leave them.' To which Frank pragmatically replies: 'In the course of nature they must leave you. Then will you come to me?'*

360

Eleanour's tears fell like rain. 'I dare not promise. But, O Frank! believe that I love you.'

'You will let me write to you? You will write to me again?'

'Oh, yes, yes — it will be all that we shall have!'

'God for ever bless you!'

They kiss for the *first and last time* and Eleanour is left subsiding into torrents of tears. Like Lydia, Eleanour is still torn by doubts and a growing realisation that she has lost her chance of true happiness in the romantic world which she inhabits in the novel. Although she is the Canon's niece and acting as his housekeeper there is no suggestion on Parr's part that she is overtly religious in any way. Parr suggests that there will be a later opportunity for her to change her mind:

Was it yet too late? When her test time came again,
would her courage have grown up to the occasion? Would she be
ready to go to him in India, when other ties were broken, other ties
withdrawn?

Frank departs for Portsmouth where James Carden, Doctor Cornelius and Mr. Barrington arrive to say their farewells. Frank is presented with a silver compass by his university friends just as Henry was. Frank experiences the same emotions as Henry as he sails down the Channel. There is no delay at Falmouth.

The following morning they sighted The Mount and The
Lizard, and the coast of Cornwall continued visible after sunset.

Frank stayed on deck half through the sweet summer
night. He almost fancied that he could see Pengarvon Church and
Beacon ...

On the morrow the shores of England were lost to sight, and it was "Goodbye" to them for ever!

"Miss Eleanour ... entreated Mary to let her read the letter"

Her Title of Honour — India and Persia

The novel now moves to India with a chapter entitled *The Voyage to India Sixty-five Years Ago*. Parr draws on historical detail from Henry Martyn's Journal to set the scene for her young female readers:

> *People make excursions to India now-a-days by way of a holiday tour; but when Francis Gwynne went out at the beginning of the century, there was no overland route, no rail or steam to bring remote parts of the world together, and the wearisome voyage round the Cape was prolonged for several months — in his instance, by reason of the war that was going on, for nearly ten months.*

In this latter part of the novel Parr describes the voyage out and Frank's mission in India and later descriptions of his journey through Persia and Turkey. She describes the *Union* — retaining the name — being delayed at Cork while the rest of the fleet assembled and then it calling at Madeira and then anchoring off the Cape of Good Hope with descriptions of the aftermath of the Battle of Blaauberg where Frank offers comfort to the dying soldiers. He even meets Vanderkemp just as Henry did. She describes his feelings of isolation and self-doubt as he tries to preach to the unreceptive 59th Regiment. She however, omits the drama of the Falmouth delay entirely having dealt with that scenario in Frank's flying visit to Croxton one day before he left from Portsmouth.

Frank arrives at Madras and then moves to Calcutta where he receives a letter from Eleanour as well as receiving the news of his sister Martha's death. Here Parr has changed the sequence of real events. Eleanour's letter re-awakens all his passion for her and on the advice of a chaplain:

> *this gentleman strongly recommended him to try and*
> *bring the young lady out to India, assuring him that his future*
> *position and usefulness in the country would depend on his being*
> *married.*

This reflects the advice that Brown and other ministers gave Henry which was based on the view that it was advisable for missionaries in India to be married rather than remaining celibate.

Frank writes a letter in which he proposes to Eleanour and at the same time writes to a friend in London asking him to send out things *necessary to the formation of a household* including a reference to a *Queens Ware* dinner service which the optimistic Frank has ordered for the new marital home because, like Henry, he is supremely confident that the woman he loves will come out to India and share his mission. He goes to Dinapore and is advised to study Sanskrit as a foundation for Oriental languages. At Dinapore Parr describes *the evident scorn and hatred with which the native population regarded him as he passed to and fro amongst them, merely because he was English,* echoing Henry's real feelings of isolation, anomie and of xenophobia.

Meanwhile Eleanour is leading a dull, domestic life at Croxton with both her Aunt Bell and her uncle, who has by now retired in poor health, when she receives the following letter of proposal from Frank:

> *She kissed the seal with a sad, lingering tenderness, then*
> *cut carefully round it, lest by any means she should lose a word.*
> *She knew beforehand the pith of what was in it; and if the writer*
> *could have seen that wistful, regretful gesture, he would not have*
> *augured sanguinely for his suit. Eleanour fancied for several weeks*
> *after that she was doubting, hesitating, making up her mind; but*
> *from the very first moment there was no real doubt or hesitation,*
> *in her thoughts. She never would of her choice go to India; she*

*would never of her choice leave home and home treasures. Love
was very sweet, very dear, but, weighed in the balance against all
her other possessions, it did not outweigh them. She was not one of
the passionate, self-devoted souls who will give the world for it. So
she read Frank's long letter with tears, sadly; sorry for him, more
sorry for herself, but not insuperably pained.*

*And yet he wrote persuasively, wrote to prevail. He told
her how entirely his earthly happiness was bound up in hers, and
with what delight he should welcome her as the greatest aid that
could be vouchsafed to him in his ministry. He told her what joy
and courage her letter had infused into his heart, and how blessed
he should be to have such a counsellor always near him. The
impression of the voyage had worn off a little from his own mind,
and he assured her that it was agreeable, and that the climate and
people of India would please her much. The natives were mild and
inoffensive, the land was a land of peace and plenty. She would
never be left in solitude, because no chaplain was stationed where
there was not a large English society. His house, servants, and
salary were sufficient for their needs, and even their luxuries, and
he was thankful to be able to tell her that his health was stronger
than it had ever been in England. From these details, with a slight
apology for assuming her consent, he went on to give her directions
for coming out to Calcutta: suggested that a ship with the wife of a
man of high rank in the service on board would be the best, and
bade her bring Gilchrist's 'Indian Strangers' Guide' to study on
the voyage, which, he said, it would be desirable for her to make
with the February fleet.*

*When Eleanour had read thus far she paused, meditated,
gazed ruefully into the fire. She was figuring, to herself poor
Frank's disappointment. It was some minutes before she could
continue her perusal of his letter, which waxed warmer, more
urgent, towards the close, as if he could hardly lay aside his*

pleading pen. 'My heart is drawn to you with a tenderness that I cannot describe. Dearest Eleanour, in the sweet and fond expectation of your being given to me by God, and of the happiness which I hope you might yourself enjoy here, I find a pleasure in breathing out the assurance of my ardent love. I have now long loved you most affectionately, and my attachment is more strong, more pure, more heavenly, because I see in you the perfection of Christian, womanliness. I unwillingly conclude by bidding my beloved Eleanour adieu.'

The loud cathedral chimes to usher in the Christmas morning had ceased at half-past nine, and now began the slow old ding-dong call to prayers. Eleanour wiped her eyes, put Frank's letter into her pocket, carried the others to her uncle to read in his room, and then wrapped herself up warmly to go to church. She was moved, she was disturbed, she was glad, and she was troubled. She thought much of Frank, alone, as he described himself and her heart melted with sweet compassion — ah, how happy she would be to comfort him, to keep him company, the sacrifice of herself was not so dreadful. 'He will come home again,' she whispered, and nestled in the kind delusion. 'He will come home again — why should he not?'

Much of this fictional letter is based closely on Henry's eloquent letter dated July 30th, 1806 from Serampore in which he proposed to Lydia. Parr includes factual references to the voyage and life in India, Gilchrist's invaluable book and the suggestion that Eleanour should leave in February. In fact Lydia did not receive Henry's proposal until March 1807 due to the vicissitudes of the postal service available at that time. Bearing in mind that Jeffery's edited extracts from Lydia's Diary would not be published until 1890 the arrival of the proposal on Christmas morning is pure fiction based on Parr only having access to the letters and journal entries from Henry and not having access to Lydia's Diary entries for that period.

Parr interprets Lydia's refusal by consistently emphasising that Eleanour is not willing to sacrifice her home comforts for the unknown in India which to many of the readers of the time would be fully justifiable and they would agree with Eleanour's self-centred conviction that Frank would return to claim her. To the Victorian reader and certainly to the young female audience at which this novel was targeted Britain was the centre of the universe whilst India was a far off sub-continent which held untold dangers and sacrifices for any woman brave or foolish enough to leave the safe shores of England for the unknown.

Parr creates a superb cliff-hanging few pages as Eleanour receives conflicting advice as to what she should do. She meets strong opposition from her family, this time in the form of the implacable Aunt Bell in the following exchange:

> *'Kill him! it would kill us both! I wonder you have*
> *broached it to **me** — it will prevent my sleeping tonight, and then*
> *I shall have a miserable day — I always have a miserable day*
> *when I lose my rest at night.'*

> *'It is necessary that I should take time to consider before*
> *answering so serious a proposal.'*

> *'Consider! it ought not to take much considering! It ought*
> *to be peremptorily declined!'*

> *'You forget that we love one another'*

> *'I forget nothing! I know that you have both thrown the*
> *world away — **he**, for the sake of a fanatical vagary, and **you**, for*
> *his sake.'*

She continues with moral blackmail about neglect and old age and then:

> *The old lady rallied, however, almost as suddenly as she*
> *had broken down. 'But you will not go, Nelly; promise me you will*

*not go. You like your comforts, and he could give you none out
there. Perhaps, if you are firm, he may come back.'*

Whether Mrs. Grenfell believed this to be the case is highly doubtful
although Lydia does cling to the hope that Henry will return one day.

It is a Mrs. Temple, the wife of a former suitor of Eleanour, who offers
much more sensible advice:

> *... Mrs. Temple knew the beginning of the story long
> before.*
>
> *'What is the good to either of you of your incomplete
> sacrifice?' said she, with frankness. 'An incomplete sacrifice is of all
> things the most unsatisfactory. You have given Mr. Gwynne your
> heart and word — why not be generous, and carry out your
> pledge? What does a little suffering matter? If you have it not in
> one form, you will have it in another. I see no lawful impediment
> as regards the Canon and Mrs. Bell — they have been father and
> mother to you, but they have friends — they have faithful
> servants. I very much doubt, half a dozen years hence, having
> stayed at home on their account will quite satisfy your conscience, if
> you have lost your lover.'*
>
> *'I don't know what to say. I think he might have
> remained in England.'*
>
> *'Somehow, one does not expect the man to forego his
> vocation for a woman ... You should remember his honour — he
> could not love you so well, loved he not honour more.'*

Mrs. Temple encapsulates both Simeon's and Henry's arguments to Lydia.
She sensibly points out that Eleanour will wait in vain for Frank to return to
her and *thought Miss Trevelyan but half-hearted in her love; and she had heard
enough of Francis Gwynne to believe that he deserved more of her than that.*
Perhaps Parr merges fiction with fact when she writes:

370

> *Her acquaintances said one to another quietly, that the*
> *secret of her indecision was, that in point of fact she did not wish to*
> *go to India. And that was about the truth — if the truth may be*
> *ascertained from results.*

Barrington and James Carden also do their best to persuade her but like Lydia she refuses:

> *But her answer to her lover, when at length she wrote it,*
> *was a distinct refusal — on the plea that she could not be satisfied*
> *with herself, or hope to be happy with him, if in their old age and*
> *infirmity she left to themselves those two who had stood to her in*
> *the light of her parents.*

Like Lydia her sense of filial duty forces her to pass up the opportunity for real happiness with the man she loves. She settles instead for the reality of spinsterhood in spite of all its constricts and the dull provincial domestic and social round. Frank accepts the rejection but asks to continue to correspond with her at which Eleanour *rejoiced and was exceedingly glad: it confirmed her belief that his affections were too inalienably fixed upon herself for him to enjoy any dream of happiness apart; it raised her expectation that he would return to her, and that his return would not be long deferred.* Of course just like Henry, Frank does not return.

In the closing stages of the novel Parr describes Frank translating The New Testament with the help of two assistants who caused many problems, based on Sabat and Mirza, and the detrimental effects on his health of his journey to Cawnpore. He continues to write to Eleanour and finally after *seven successive letters* which received no reply he gets a letter from her, just as in real life, in which *She had reminded him that it might be his duty, for his health's sake, to go home to England, and to this he rejoined, that if it were so, it would be her duty not to let him return to India alone; and he told her plainly that he thought it would have gone better with him from first to last if he had had her by his side.* Here, Parr has used the letter Henry wrote to Lydia on October 6th, 1810 regretting that he had not insisted on extracting a promise from her to join him when he said farewell in Marazion.

371

By now Eleanour is free at last to act independently as both the Canon and Aunt Bell have died and she is living in Aunt Bell's cottage in Croxton cloisters:

> *Eleanour Trevelyan was free of all ties in the world. It was just five years since she and Francis Gwynne had parted. Three years ago she had laid her poor Aunt Bell in the solemn repose of the cloisters, and within twelve months after she had buried the good old Canon. She was residing now in the pretty little house near the Close Gate, which Mrs Bell had bequeathed to her.*

A very different position from Lydia whose mother did not die until 1826, 14 years after Henry's death.

Frank has set off on his final tragic journey. Eleanour receives a letter from Calcutta and is full of renewed hope that he will come back for her:

> *'He will come home from Calcutta; he will certainly come home now,' she said to herself, poring tenderly over the tender words, and she let her fancy flow into beautiful dreams of reunion ... Her friends, her servants, remarked that from that time Miss Trevelyan recovered much of the gay sprightliness of her girlhood. She was regarded as a pattern of constancy, for all her world knew of her long engagement to Francis Gwynne, and of the temptation she had had to break it. But after her manner, she loved him with her whole heart.*

In reality of course there had been no engagement and by 1810 Lydia was filled with pessimism about the state of Henry's health and the unlikelihood of his surviving a return journey. Their relationship by then is platonic and based on deep religious commitment and trust in God — something which the fictional Eleanour does not share.

Parr incorporates factual details when describing the voyage to Bombay, along the Malabar coast and rounding Cape Comorin using Henry's letter to Lydia on February 4th, 1811:

> *... the waves washed a narrow margin of the beach, with
> green hills rising behind, and little churches and dwellings on the
> slopes, that reminded him of Cornwall; and he asked did she ever
> revisit Pengarvon now, did she ever walk the white sands and
> imagine that the billows breaking on them had rolled all the way
> from India?*

Compared with the original:

> *At a distance the green waves seemed to wash the foot of
> the mountain, but on a nearer approach little churches were seen,
> apparently on the beach, with a row of little huts on each side.
> Was it the maritime situations that recalled to my mind Perran
> church and town on the way to Gurlyn; or that my thoughts
> wander too often on the beach east of Lamorran? You do not tell
> me whether you ever walk there, and imagine the billows that
> break at your feet, to have made their way from India.*

The next letter Frank writes is from Muscat and the following one from Shiraz just as the originals were in April and June 1811 and the content is close to the original letters. Parr also refers to letters getting lost in transit and the delays between sending and receiving letters. In his penultimate letter to Eleanour Frank is racked with fever. This is based on the first Tabriz letter dated July 12th, 1812 when Henry is recovering from his journey from Shiraz to Tabriz. In his final letter, based on Henry's final one to Lydia dated August 28th 1812, Frank is more cheerful and setting out for Constantinople. Fact and fiction are fused when he ends the letter with the same hope as Henry does:

> *... soon they would have no more need of pen and ink, but
> would see each other face to face.* Henry writes: *Soon we shall have
> occasion for pen and ink no more; but I trust I shall shortly see thee
> face to face.*

Eleanour is full of optimism and excitement:

> *She counted the months, weeks, days, hours, that must
> elapse before her faithful lover could arrive. No doubt for a
> moment obscured his coming.*

She is confidently expecting Frank home for Christmas or at the latest New Year whereas Lydia was far more pessimistic about the chances of Henry surviving the long and arduous journey home.

Frank's final journey from Tabriz describes his setting out on September 1st with two Armenian servants and carrying letters to the local Governors of towns plus a letter to the English Ambassador at Constantinople. Parr describes the journey briefly but mentions the heat and the plague at Tokat. She describes his death simply: *after thirteen hours of one day, urged forward by his servants from sunrise to sunset, did the home-bound traveller persevere on his road, and then, at last, he sank by the wayside exhausted, with the cry on his lips: "Lord thy will be done! living or dying, remember me!"* — words which appear in Henry's entry in his Journal on October 1st, 1812.

Parr describes his papers and other *matters of minor importance* being delivered to Constantinople by one of the Armenians and it is James Carden who receives the journals in London and takes them to Eleanour in Croxton:

> *She rose with eager, beautiful animation to welcome him,
> he had but to lift his hand, pointing to heaven, and his tale was
> told.*

Parr ends the novel with an epilogue in which Eleanour and James Carden are looking at the journals:

> *'I have read his journals again and again; I know them by
> heart; they have been my study for twenty years; but I cannot, no, I
> cannot see what profit there was in his life...'*

The speaker was Miss Trevelyan, her hearer, James Carden.

> *'... He held disputations with several learned Eastern
> doctors — did he convince any? He preached to five hundred*

374

beggars at one time — did he convert any? With the help of native
scholars he made translations from Holy Writ. I believe he
baptised one poor old Hindoo woman. I know he bore with much
ridicule, scoffing, mockery; I know he suffered a martyrdom of
sorrows; I know he died alone in a strange land — alone. If God
accepted his sacrifice where is his witness?'

Lydia had no such misgivings and regards Henry as a saint whom she loves
even more in death than in life and trusts that one day she too will enjoy the
blessing of heaven when she joins Henry before God's throne.

Parr uses James Carden, partially based on the real life John Sargent,
Henry's close friend at Cambridge, to deliver a eulogy to Eleanour on Francis
Gwynne's life and surely expresses many of Lydia's thoughts on Henry
Martyn:

> *'It is not true that success makes the hero. Some day you*
> *will be satisfied that what Francis Gwynne did was well done; you*
> *will not call his journals only a pathetic record of a disappointed*
> *life. He was happier than you or I, for he fulfilled more perfectly*
> *the will of his heavenly Father.'*

> *'The sweet peace in his Saviour that he felt when dying,*
> *worn out in His service, is, I suppose, the moral of his story.'*

> *'It is a beautiful story, a noble story, look at it as you will.*
> *Yes — take that for the moral of it. So God giveth His beloved*
> *sleep.'*

On the last page of the novel Parr has Eleanour entrusting Frank's papers
some 20 years later to Carden to edit and publish — a task which in reality
fell to Samuel Wilberforce. Parr also makes reference to a memoir *but Miss
Trevelyan called it too glowing.* This is a reference to John Sargent's *Memoir*
published in 1816 while Lydia Grenfell was still alive and which she refers to
in her Diary in 1815 on December 26th:

> *Wrote this day to Mr Simeon. I have reason to search into*
> *my heart and watch the risings of pride there, both respecting the*
> *notice of this blessed saint, and the avowal to be expected of my*
> *being the object of so much regard from another still more eminent*
> *in the Church of Christ. I have ever stood amazed at this, and*
> *now that in the providence of God it seems certain that my being*
> *so favoured is likely to be made known, vanity besets me. O how*
> *poor a creature am I! Lord, I pray, let me be enabled to trace some*
> *evidence of Thine eternal love to me, let this greater wonder call off*
> *my thoughts from every other distinction. But how do I learn that*
> *in the whole of this notice my thoughts have not indeed been*
> *Thine, O Lord, nor my ways Thy ways? How much above all, I*
> *could have conceived of, have been the designs of God? I sought*
> *concealment, and lo! all is made known to many, and much will*
> *be even known to the world. It is strange for me to credit this, and*
> *strange that with my natural reserve and the peculiar reasons that*
> *exist for my wishing to have this buried in silence, I am*
> *nevertheless composed about it. But, Lord, I would resign myself,*
> *and all things that concern me, to Thy sovereign will and pleasure.*
> *Preserve me blameless to Thy eternal kingdom, and grant me an*
> *everlasting union with Thy servant above.*

We shall never know what *the peculiar reasons were*. One interpretation would be that Lydia felt she had acted less than honourably in the relationship and therefore, quite understandably, did not wish her role to become public information. Certainly Parr's character, Eleanour, is portrayed in a less favourable light than Frank, based on the saintly Henry Martyn. Lydia's comfort lay not in the earthly realms of romantic fiction but in her conviction that she and Henry would be united in Heaven.

The novel is a fascinating mixture of romantic fiction and fact with strong moral overtones for the young readership. The message is transparent: that indecision on the part of a beautiful, vain, self-centred, well-connected woman, caused by a desire for material comfort and governed by over-riding filial duty when it comes to following a lover to a far off land, is rewarded by a wasted life of self-doubt and bitterness; whereas a life dedicated to saving others from hell and damnation in a far-off heathen land, in spite of being offered material success in one's homeland, while still remaining faithful to one's true love after years of separation, is held up as a model of true humility for others to emulate.

The fictionalised Lydia is not treated kindly by Parr although it is interesting that she is portrayed throughout the novel as being far less mature than Frank whereas in real life Lydia was six years older than Henry. Eleanour is far more worldly than Lydia appears from her Diary and Eleanour is not obsessed by pious thoughts and mental torment as Lydia was. Perhaps because the letters which Lydia wrote to Henry have been lost, and the profile and requested miniature have never been found, any image of her is drawn from her Diary. Because it was primarily a religious diary the lasting impression of Lydia is of a woman who is struggling to live a life of true piety while beset with self-doubt and anxieties but who has an intelligence and independence of thought which deeply attracted Henry Martyn who regarded her as his soul-mate. Parr fails to do justice to or to understand Lydia by her characterisation of Eleanour, who remains vain and self-centred throughout the novel. Perhaps Parr is nearer to fact than fiction when she attributes Eleanour's refusal to risk all for love and marry Frank by bowing to filial duty because, like Lydia, she was flattered by being wooed by a highly intelligent, deeply sensitive and articulate young man whose evangelical mission in life led him to India. Like Lydia, she could not or would not give her commitment to share his vocation by agreeing to marry and follow him out to what she and her family perceived as a dangerous unknown world.

Parr compromises with a final reference to the papers: *Half the world who read them took her view of them; the other half took his friend Carden's.* She ends her novel with Eleanour's true legacy:

> *But all the world was of one mind to consider it Eleanour Trevelyan's title of honour that Francis Gwynne loved her.*

With that there can be no argument. A simple truth both in fiction and fact.

"He sank by the wayside exhausted"

Appendix 1 — Maps

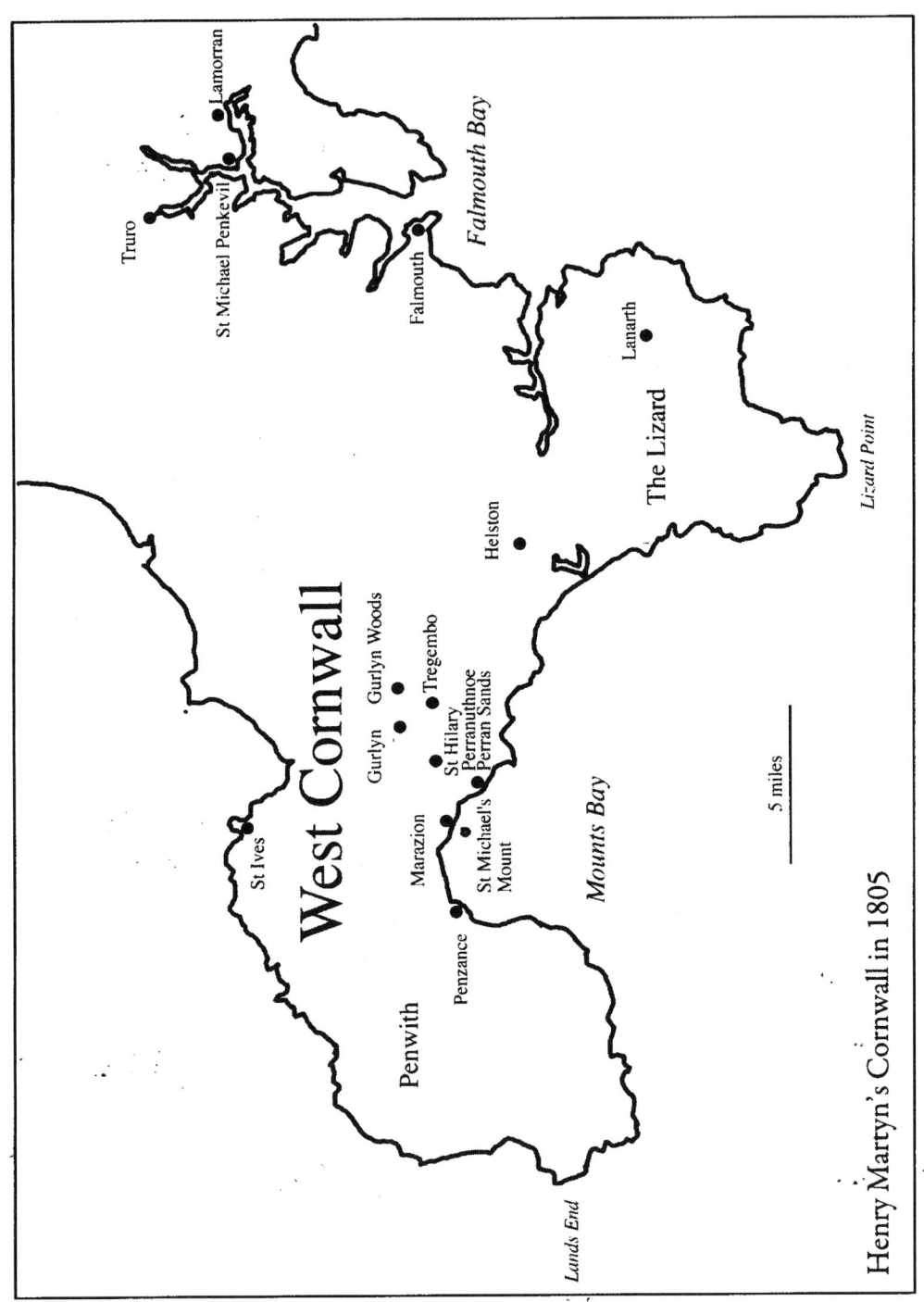

West Cornwall

Lamorran

Truro

St Michael Penkevil

Falmouth

Falmouth Bay

Lanarth

The Lizard

Lizard Point

Helston

Gurlyn Woods

Gurlyn

Tregembo

St Ives

Penwith

Marazion

St Hilary
Perranuthnoe
Perran Sands

St Michael's
Mount

Penzance

Mounts Bay

Lands End

5 miles

Henry Martyn's Cornwall in 1805

382

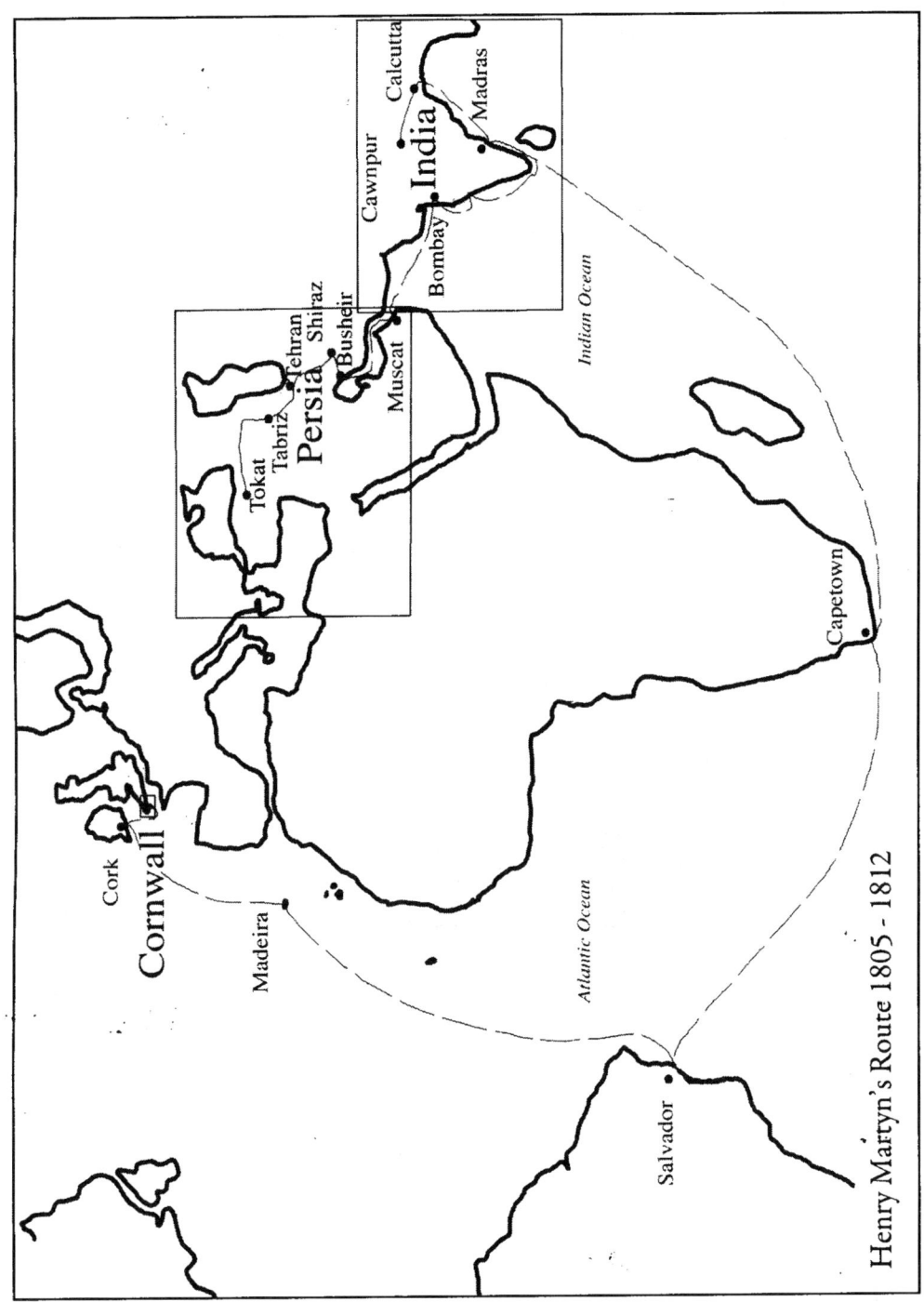

Henry Martyn's Route 1805 - 1812

383

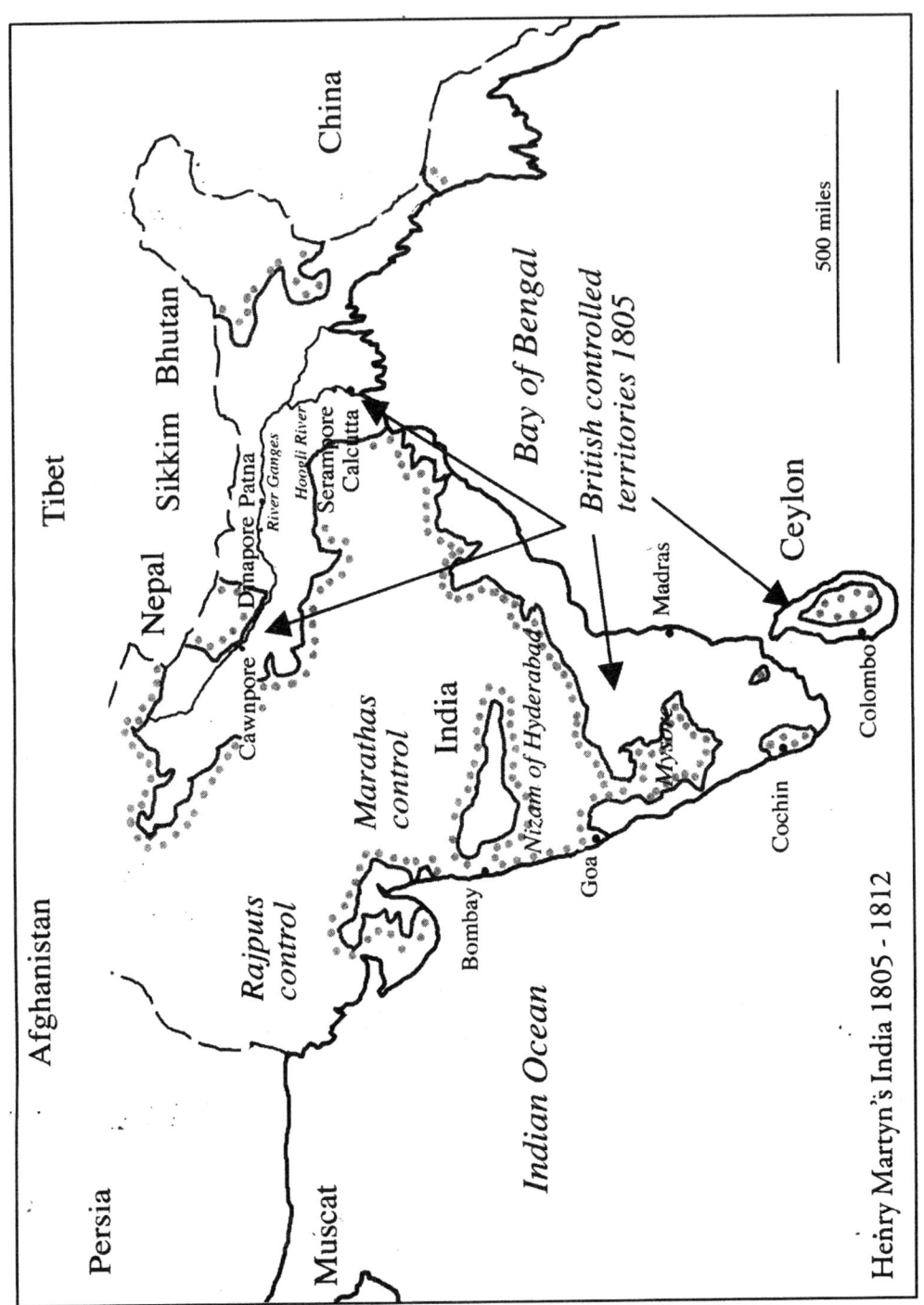

Henry Martyn's India 1805 - 1812

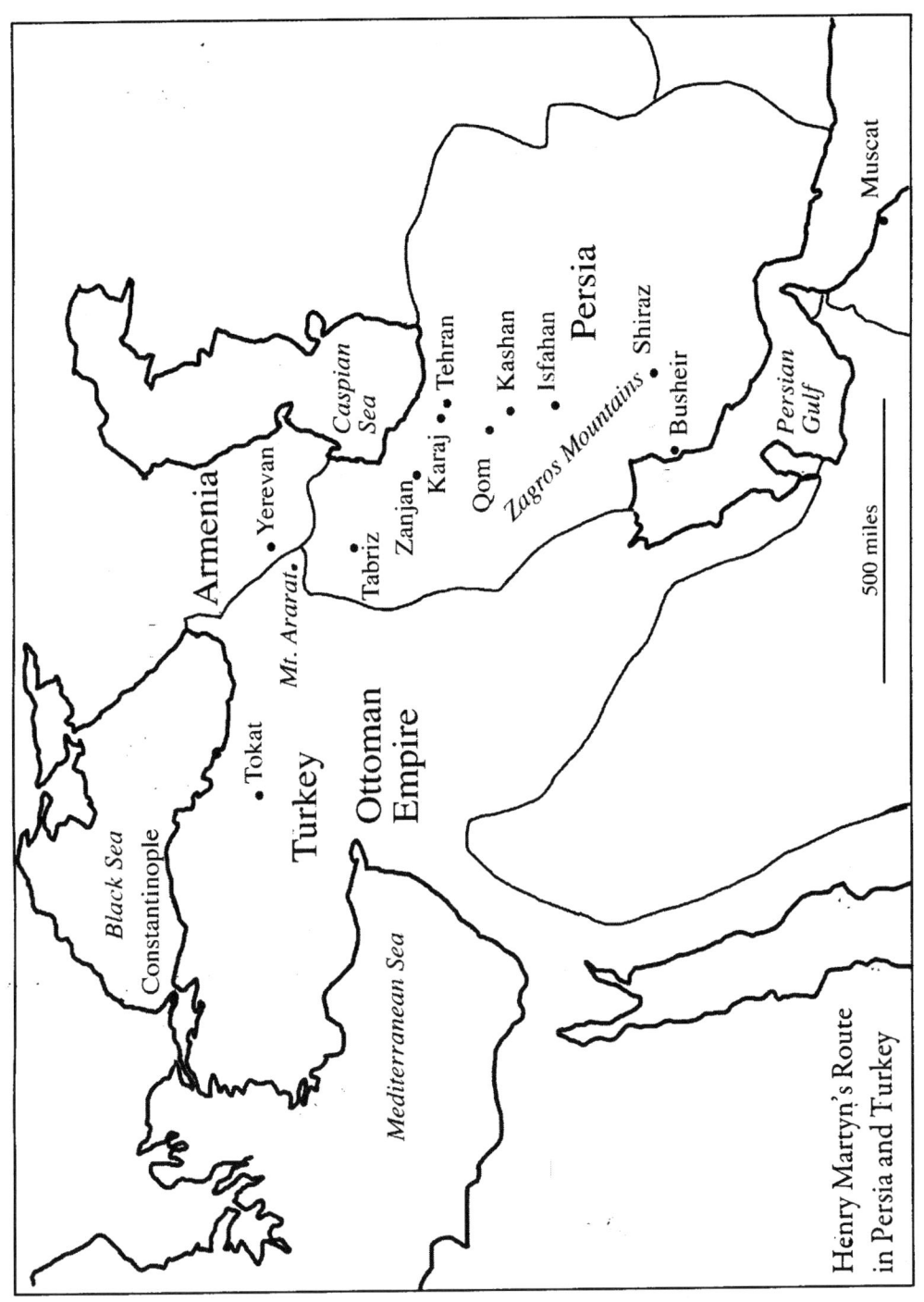

Muscat

Persia

Caspian Sea

Tehran

Kashan

Isfahan

Shiraz

Qom

Zagros Mountains

Karaj

Zanjan

Busheir

Persian Gulf

Yerevan

Armenia

Tabriz

Mt. Ararat

Turkey

Tokat

Ottoman Empire

Black Sea

Constantinople

Mediterranean Sea

500 miles

Henry Martyn's Route
in Persia and Turkey

Appendix 2 — Family Trees

Dates prior to the adoption of the Gregorian calendar in 1752 have not been cross checked.
They could appear to be 1 year out.

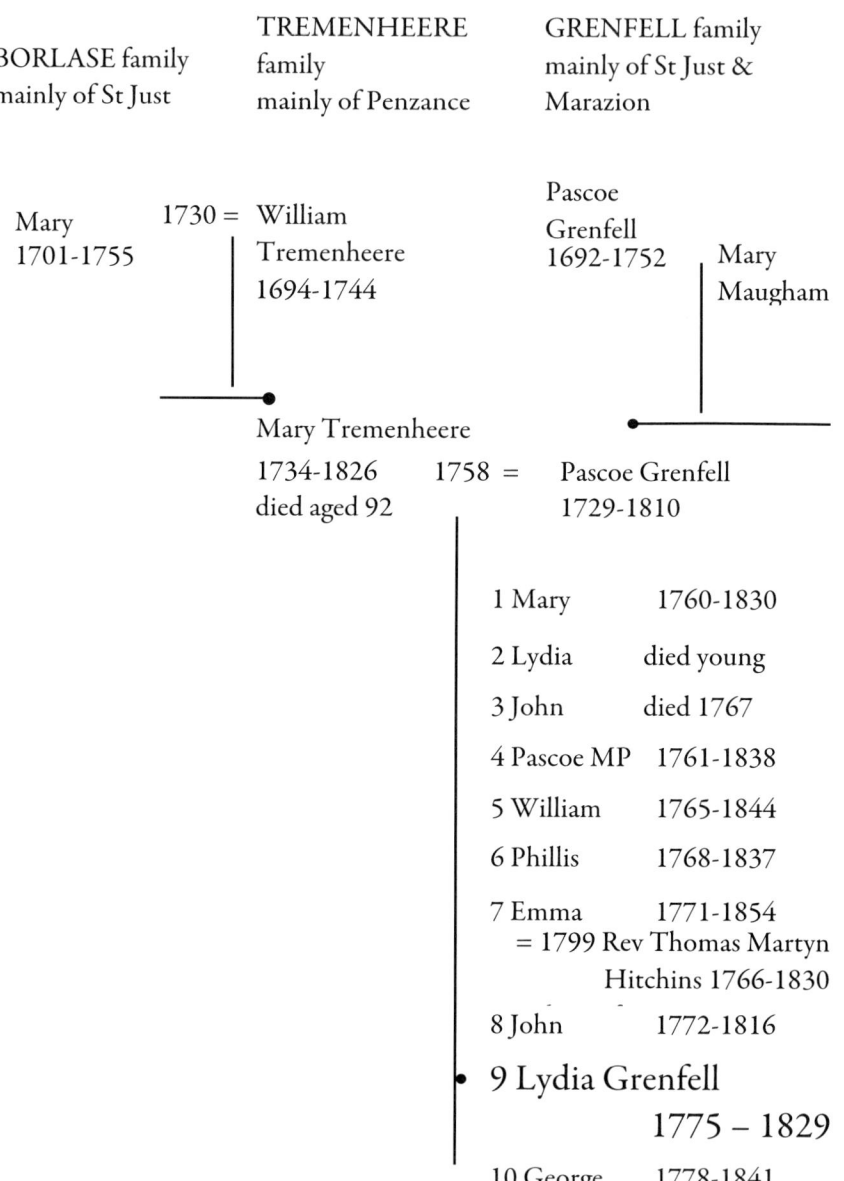

BORLASE family
mainly of St Just

TREMENHEERE
family
mainly of Penzance

GRENFELL family
mainly of St Just &
Marazion

Mary
1701-1755

1730 =

William
Tremenheere
1694-1744

Pascoe
Grenfell
1692-1752

Mary
Maugham

Mary Tremenheere
1734-1826
died aged 92

1758 =

Pascoe Grenfell
1729-1810

	1 Mary	1760-1830
	2 Lydia	died young
	3 John	died 1767
	4 Pascoe MP	1761-1838
	5 William	1765-1844
	6 Phillis	1768-1837
	7 Emma	1771-1854
	= 1799 Rev Thomas Martyn Hitchins 1766-1830	
	8 John	1772-1816

9 Lydia Grenfell
1775 – 1829

10 George   1778-1841

MARTYN family
mainly of Gwennap & Truro,
Mining engineers & administrators

HITCHINS family
mainly of Marazion
clergy & solicitors

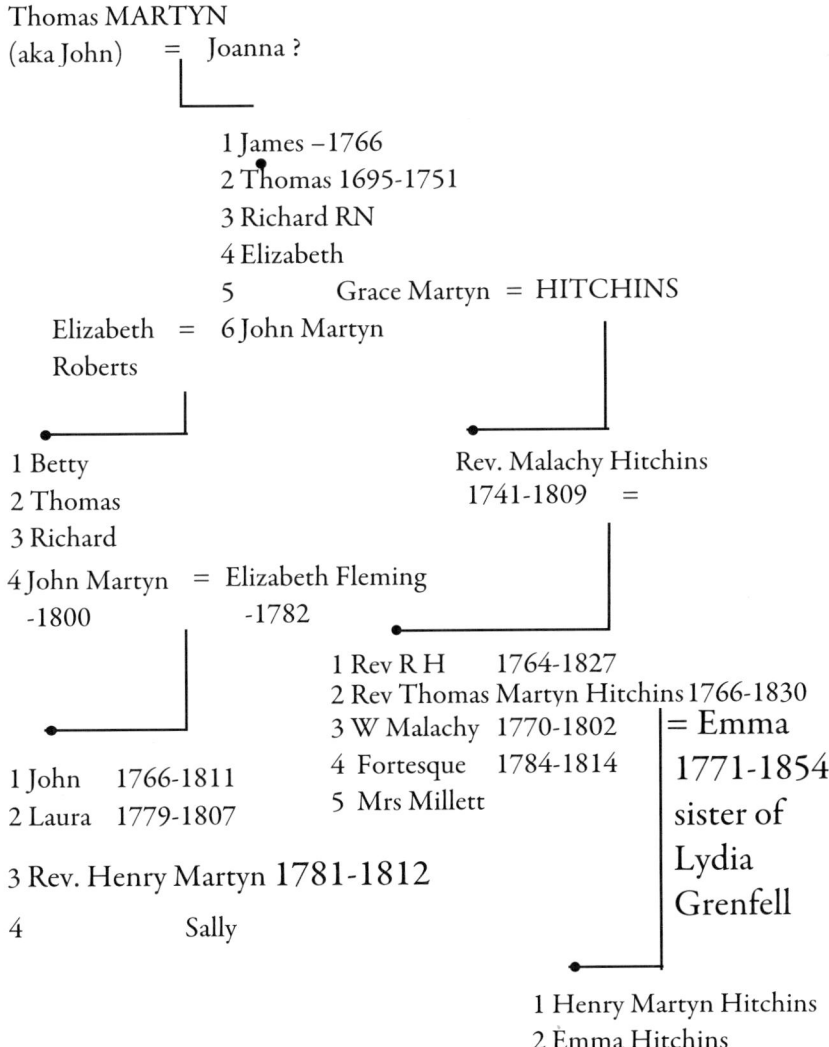

Thomas MARTYN
(aka John)   =   Joanna ?

1 James –1766
2 Thomas 1695-1751
3 Richard RN
4 Elizabeth
5   Grace Martyn = HITCHINS
Elizabeth = 6 John Martyn
Roberts

1 Betty
2 Thomas
3 Richard
4 John Martyn = Elizabeth Fleming
  -1800   -1782

Rev. Malachy Hitchins
1741-1809   =

1 Rev R H   1764-1827
2 Rev Thomas Martyn Hitchins 1766-1830
3 W Malachy   1770-1802
4 Fortesque   1784-1814
5 Mrs Millett

= Emma
1771-1854
sister of
Lydia
Grenfell

1 John   1766-1811
2 Laura   1779-1807

3 Rev. Henry Martyn 1781-1812
4   Sally

1 Henry Martyn Hitchins
2 Emma Hitchins

389

Appendix 3 Chart of Letters between Lydia Grenfell and Henry Martyn 1805 – 1813

Lydia Grenfell's Correspondence with Henry Martyn

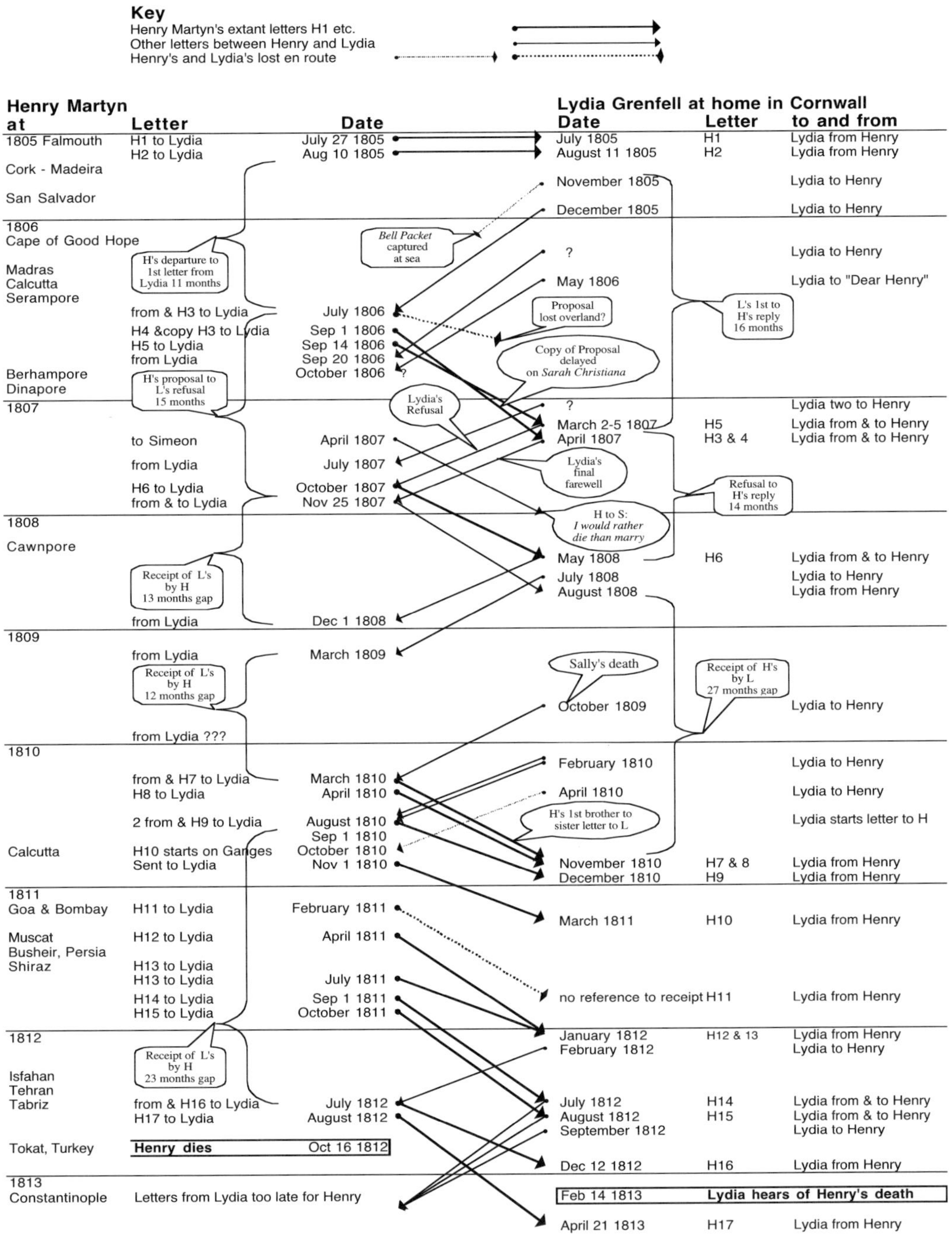

Henry Martyn at	Letter	Date	Date	Letter	Lydia Grenfell at home in Cornwall to and from
1805 Falmouth	H1 to Lydia	July 27 1805	July 1805	H1	Lydia from Henry
	H2 to Lydia	Aug 10 1805	August 11 1805	H2	Lydia from Henry
Cork - Madeira			November 1805		Lydia to Henry
San Salvador			December 1805		Lydia to Henry
1806 Cape of Good Hope		*Bell Packet captured at sea*	?		Lydia to Henry
Madras	H's departure to 1st letter from Lydia 11 months		May 1806		Lydia to "Dear Henry"
Calcutta Serampore	from & H3 to Lydia	July 1806			L's 1st to H's reply 16 months
	H4 &copy H3 to Lydia	Sep 1 1806	*Proposal lost overland?*		
	H5 to Lydia	Sep 14 1806			
	from Lydia	Sep 20 1806	*Copy of Proposal delayed on Sarah Christiana*		
Berhampore		October 1806			
Dinapore	H's proposal to L's refusal 15 months		?		Lydia two to Henry
1807			March 2-5 1807	H5	Lydia from & to Henry
	to Simeon	April 1807	April 1807	H3 & 4	Lydia from & to Henry
	from Lydia	July 1807	*Lydia's final farewell*		
	H6 to Lydia	October 1807			Refusal to H's reply 14 months
	from & to Lydia	Nov 25 1807	*Lydia's Refusal*		
1808 Cawnpore			*H to S: I would rather die than marry*		
	Receipt of L's by H 13 months gap		May 1808	H6	Lydia from & to Henry
			July 1808		Lydia to Henry
			August 1808		Lydia from Henry
	from Lydia	Dec 1 1808			
1809	from Lydia	March 1809	*Sally's death*		
	Receipt of L's by H 12 months gap		October 1809		Receipt of H's by L 27 months gap
	from Lydia ???				Lydia to Henry
1810			February 1810		Lydia to Henry
	from & H7 to Lydia	March 1810	April 1810		Lydia to Henry
	H8 to Lydia	April 1810	*H's 1st brother to sister letter to L*		
	2 from & H9 to Lydia	August 1810			Lydia starts letter to H
Calcutta	H10 starts on Ganges	Sep 1 1810			
		October 1810			
	Sent to Lydia	Nov 1 1810	November 1810	H7 & 8	Lydia from Henry
			December 1810	H9	Lydia from Henry
1811 Goa & Bombay	H11 to Lydia	February 1811	March 1811	H10	Lydia from Henry
Muscat	H12 to Lydia	April 1811			
Busheir, Persia	H13 to Lydia				
Shiraz	H13 to Lydia	July 1811	no reference to receipt H11		Lydia from Henry
	H14 to Lydia	Sep 1 1811			
	H15 to Lydia	October 1811			
1812			January 1812	H12 & 13	Lydia from Henry
	Receipt of L's by H 23 months gap		February 1812		Lydia to Henry
Isfahan Tehran					
Tabriz	from & H16 to Lydia	July 1812	July 1812	H14	Lydia from & to Henry
	H17 to Lydia	August 1812	August 1812	H15	Lydia from & to Henry
			September 1812		Lydia to Henry
Tokat, Turkey	**Henry dies**	Oct 16 1812			
			Dec 12 1812	H16	Lydia from Henry
1813 Constantinople	Letters from Lydia too late for Henry		**Feb 14 1813**		**Lydia hears of Henry's death**
			April 21 1813	H17	Lydia from Henry

Sources

Barclay, John: Original and bound MS transcript of *Lydia Grenfell's Religious Diary 1801 – 1826* (about 1922) in Courtney Library

Bentley-Taylor, David: *My love must wait: The story of Henry Martyn* (Inter-Varsity Press, 1975)

Bowie et al (eds): *Women and Missions* (Oxford 1993)

British and Foreign Bible Society: *Eleventh Report* (1815)

Brontë, Charlotte: *Jane Eyre* (1847)

Brown, H. Miles: *Truro Cathedral* (Tor Mark Press, Redruth. 1997)

Canning, William: original letter held by Henry Martyn Centre, Westminster College, Cambridge

Carus, William (ed): *Memoirs of the Life of the Rev. Charles Simeon, M.A., with a selection from his writings and correspondence* (Hatchard and Son, London 1847)

Church Quarterly Review: *Henry Martyn* (October 1881)

Clarke: *Tour through South England* (1791)

Cunningham, Valentine: *God and Nature intended you for a missionary's wife*: in Bowie et al (eds): *Women and Missions* (Oxford 1993)

Dalrymple, William: *White Mughals* (HarperCollins, London 2002)

Darton, F.J. Harvey (ed): *The Life and Times of Mrs Sherwood (1775 – 1851)* (London 1910)

Davies, Norman: *Europe a History* (OUP, Oxford 1996)

Dyson, K.K.: *A Various Universe: A Study of Journals and Memoirs of British men and women in the Indian sub-continent 1765 – 1856* (OUP, Delhi 1978)

Elphinstone, Hon. Mountstuart: *History of India* (1839)

Finnie, Kelsye M: Beyond the Minarets: *A Biography of Henry Martyn* (STL Books, Kent, England 1988)

Garlick, Kenneth and Macintyre, Angus (eds): *The Diary of Joseph Farington* (New Haven, London 1978)

Giddy, Davies: *Davies Giddy's Diary* (DG/14) November 21st/22nd 1789 Cornwall County Records Office, Truro

Gilchrist, John B.: *The Strangers' East Indian Guide to the Hindoostanee*: (Calcutta 1802)

Grenfell, Lydia: MS Diary 1801 – 1826 (original and transcript held by Courtney Library, Royal Institution of Cornwall, Truro)

Hafez: *Divân* (1325? – 1389, Persian poet)

Hill, Bridget: *Women Alone. Spinsters in England, 1660 – 1850* (Yale University Press 2001)

Hunt, Giles (ed): *Mehitabel Canning – A Redoubtable Woman* (Royston 2001)

James, Lawrence: *RAJ The Making and Unmaking of British India* (Little, Brown and Company, London 1997)

Jeffery, Henry Martyn (ed): *Extracts from the Religious Diary of Miss L. Grenfell of Marazion Cornwall* (Falmouth 1890)

Jeffery, Henry Martyn (ed): *Two sets of Unpublished Letters of the Rev. Henry Martyn, BD, of Truro*; (Truro 1883) Reprinted from Supplement XXVI Journal of Royal Institution of Cornwall; (the originals of letters referenced 12 & 13 are held at the Courtney Library, Royal Institution of Cornwall, Truro which also holds an original letter from Henry Martyn at St. John's College, Cambridge to D. Giddy dated February 4th, 1805)

Keay, John: *India a History* (HarperCollins, London 2000)

Kings, Graham: *Foundations for Mission and the Study of World Christianity: The Legacy of Henry Martyn*; (the Henry Martyn Centre, Westminster College, Cambridge)

Laird, M.A.: *Missionaries and Education in Bengal 1793– 1837* (1972)

Lee, Holme: pseudonym, see Parr, Harriett

Lyte, Henry Francis: quoting W. Maxwell-Lyte in *Brixham's Poet and Priest* (B. G. Skinner 1974)

MacMillan, Margaret: *Women of the Raj* (Thames and Hudson, London 1988)

Marazion History Group, The: *The Charter Town of Marazion* (Marazion Town Council, 1995)

Marshall: *The British Discovery of Hinduism* (quoted by Dalrymple in *White Mughals*)

Martyn, Henry: various documents and artefacts (held by Henry Martyn Centre, Westminster College, Cambridge)

Martyn, Henry: various documents (held by the Oriental and India Office Library, British Library, London)

Martyn, Henry: various documents (originals held by the Courtney Library, Royal Institution of Cornwall, Truro)

Martyn, John R.C.: *Henry Martyn (1781 – 1812) Scholar and Missionary to India and Persia. A Biography*; (The Edwin Mellen Press, USA 1999)

Maton, W. G.: *Observations on the Western Counties of England* (1794 – 6)

Padwick, Constance E.: *Henry Martyn: Confessor of the Faith* (London 1953)

Page, Jesse: *Henry Martyn of India and Persia* (Pickering & Inglis, London 1930)

Parr, Harriet: *Her Title of Honour* (published under pseudonym of Holme Lee) (London 1871)

Pearce, John: *The Wesleys in Cornwall* (1964)

Price: *Mineralogia Cornubiensis* (1778)

Robinson, Jane: *Angels of Albion* (Viking, London 1996)

Sa'di: *Bustân, Golestân* (1189 – 1290, Persian poet and traveller)

Sargent, John: *Memoir of the Rev. Henry Martyn B.D.* (London 1819)

Sargent, John: *Life and Letters of The Rev. Henry Martyn, B.D. & Appendix of 17 Letters* (London 1862)

Scott, Robert Forsyth (ed): *Admissions to the College of St John the Evangelist in the University of Cambridge, Part IV, July 1767 –July 1802*; (CUP for the College, Cambridge 1931)

Sherwood, Mrs. Mary Martha: *The History of Little Henry and his bearer* (first published anonymously, Edinburgh 1814)

Sherwood, Mrs. Mary Martha: letter, original and transcript (held by Henry Martyn Centre, Westminster College, Cambridge)

Simeon, Rev. Charles: letters to Charles Grant (held by Henry Martyn Centre, Westminster College, Cambridge)

Skinner, B.G.: *Henry Francis Lyte: Brixham's Poet and Priest* (University of Exeter 1974)

Smith, George: *Henry Martyn, Saint and Scholar* (The Religious Tract Society, London 1892)

Stacey, Vivienne: Life of Henry Martyn; (Henry Martyn Institute, Hyderabad 1980)

Stanley, Brian, *An Ardour of Devotion: The Spiritual Legacy of Henry Martyn* (the Henry Martyn Centre, Westminster College, Cambridge)

Starr, Stephen Z: *The Life of a Soldier of Fortune. Colonel Grenfell's Wars* (1995)

Thormahlen, Marian: *The Brontës and Religion* (CUP 1999)

Tremenheere Papers: (held by Morrab Library, Penzance)

Tremenheere, S.G.: *The Tremenheeres* (reprinted for private circulation, London 1925)

Watts-Russell, Penny: *Henry Martyn's Dulcinea* (*The Cornish Banner*, November 2002)

Wilberforce, Samuel (ed): *Journals and Letters of the Rev. Henry Martyn, B.D.* (2 Vols, London 1839)

Wild, Antony: *The East India Company — Trade and Conquest from 1600* (HarperCollins *Illustrated*, London and HarperCollins *Publishers,* Delhi 1999)

Yule, Col. Sir Henry and Burnell, A. C.: *Hobson-Jobson — A Glossary of Colloquial Anglo-Indian Words and Phrases* (1886): Second Edition, Crooke, William (ed) (Linguasia, Sittingbourne 1994)

Acknowledgements

Cornish Studies Library, Redruth
The Courtney Library, Royal Institution of Cornwall, Truro
Divinity Faculty Library, Cambridge
Henry Martin Institute of Islamic Studies, Hyderabad, India
Henry Martyn Centre, Westminster College, Cambridge
Hypatia Trust, Penzance
Royal Cornwall Museum, Truro
St. John's College Library, Cambridge

I am indebted to the following people: Melissa Hardie of Hypatia Trust for her belief and enthusiasm to publish the book; Penny Watts-Russell for all her generous advice and detailed knowledge of the Grenfell family; Tess Barlow for getting me started and proof reading early drafts; Anne Bye for all the laughter and language we shared; Sheilagh Burlton of Penzance; Andrew Symons of Hypatia Trust for his invaluable help and advice on the Cornish background; Dr. Sue Sutton at the Henry Martyn Centre; B V Henry with whom I exchanged research; Dr. John Hutchison in accessing special favourite haunts of Henry in St. John's College, Cambridge; Anne Dinsdale, Librarian at the Brontë Parsonage Museum, Haworth; above all to Tim, my husband. Thank you all!

Their help has been invaluable: any remaining errors are my own.

Picture Credits:

Coloured images for the Cover:
> British Library for:
>> A view of Calcutta from a Point Opposite Kidderpore: James B Fraser, 1826.
>
> Penlee Gallery, Penzance, for:
>> Regatta at St. Michael's Mount: anon.

Black and white images in the book:
> British Library for:
>> Necessaries for a Writer to India,
>> Landing on the North Beach at Madras,
>> Missionary Influence,
>
> National Maritime Museum for:
>> A Fleet of EastIndiamen at Sea,
>> Near Gangwaugh Colly on the River Hoogly.
>
> Henry Martyn Centre, Cambridge for:
>> Miniature of Henry Martyn and a lock of hair. (TE)
>
> St. John's College, Cambridge for:
>> Copy Portrait of Henry Martyn. (TE)
>
> Courtney Library, Royal Cornwall Museum, Truro for:
>> A page from Lydia Grenfell's Diary. (TE)
>> Letter from Henry Martyn to Emma Hitchens. (TE)
>
> Royal Cornwall Museum, Truro for:
>> Tea Caddy. (TE)
>
> Morrab Library, Penzance for:
>> The Old Chapel at Marazion.
>
> Royal Borough of Windsor and Maidenhead for:
>> Portrait of Pascoe Grenfell. (internet photo Penny Watts-Russell)
>
> Images scanned from books (see Sources) (TE):

William Carus:	Portrait of Rev. Charles Simeon,
J Harvey Darton:	Portrait of Mrs M M Sherwood,
Harriett Parr:	'He sank by the wayside' and 'Miss Eleanor entreated',
Mrs M M Sherwood:	Little Henry with Children,
	A History of Little Henry and His Bearer, title page,
George Smith:	He was known as a man of God,
S G Tremenheere:	Portrait of Mrs Grenfell.

Tim Eaton (TE above) for design and layout of the book, maps, family trees and letter chart:

and for photographs of:
> Mullahs at Isfahan,
> The Shah's Garden at Kashan.

Index

References to HM refer to Henry Martyn and LG to Lydia Grenfell.